The American City and
the Evangelical Church

The American City and the Evangelical Church
A Historical Overview

Harvie M. Conn

Baker Books

A Division of Baker Book House Co
Grand Rapids, Michigan 49516

©1994 by Harvie M. Conn

Published by Baker Books
a division of Baker Book House Company
P.O. Box 6287, Grand Rapids, MI 49516-6287

Printed in the United States of America

Library of Congress Cataloging-in-Publication Data

Conn, Harvie M.
    The American city and the evangelical church : a historical overview / Harvie M. Conn.
      p.   cm.
    Includes bibliographical references and index.
    ISBN 0-8010-2590-7
    1. Evangelicalism—United States—History. 2. City churches—United States—History. 3. City missions—United States—History. 4. Church growth—United States—History. 5. United States—Religion—1901–1945. 6. United States—Religions—1945– I. Title.
BR1642.U5C65   1994
277.3′009173′2—dc20   94-26121

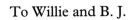
To Willie and B. J.

Contents

List of Tables

List of Figures

Preface

Criticism of the city is as old as Juvenal. Writing in the second century A.D., he denounced Rome as a hotbed of corruption. "What can I do in Rome?" he asked. "I have never learnt to lie."

While Juvenal was writing, a different approach to the city was taking shape. All over the cities of the Empire, in tiny upper rooms and private homes, an urban revolution had been brewing. More than 100,000 troops were already involved. The instruments of the revolution were not Uzis or terrorist kidnapings. They were prayers, songs, and the breaking of bread.

"No church colleges, no mountain top retreat centers, and certainly no coinage saying, 'In God we trust.' The isolated group of Christians, first in houses and then in house churches, began their inevitable march toward the City of God. Their faith was warm and contagious; they were terribly confident and as Hans Küng has said, they took dead aim on the Roman Empire; its slavery, its idolatry, its imperial arrogance, its awesome power. And they won."[1]

The principal target of the church in its first three hundred years was the city. In fact, the Latin word *paganus*, appropriated by that early church to describe the unbeliever, originally meant rural dweller.

Perspectives have changed somewhat since those days. Two caricatures approaching mythologies have distorted our understanding of the city and the church in the city. One continues the anti-urban

---

1. George Gallup Jr. and David Poling, *The Search for America's Faith* (Nashville: Abingdon, 1980), 126–27.

bias of Juvenal and sees the city as "a precinct of sin and impiety . . . wicked and secular."[2] The other celebrates the success of the church in the rural and village world. Piety is proclaimed as more easily achieved in the countryside. One writer in 1880 put it this way: "In the city neither the rich nor the poor can realize the infinite charm of the Christian ideal. The heart is troubled there, and God is not in the whirlwind of human passion."[3]

The purpose of this history, with particular attention to 1920 until the present, is to examine the accuracy of these assumptions in terms of the American city. How did the church, particularly the evangelical church, see the city? How did it understand its mission to the city? And what do we mean by evangelical? Perhaps the simplest and most useful definition is supplied by sociologist James D. Hunter: "At the doctrinal core, contemporary Evangelicals can be identified by their adherence to (1) the belief that the Bible is the inerrant Word of God, (2) the belief in the divinity of Christ, and (3) the belief in the efficacy of Christ's life, death, and physical resurrection for the salvation of the human soul."[4]

This survey is, in some respects, a pioneering one and therefore more "rough and ready" than most. The reader may miss more careful attention to some topics that he or she feels should be here. Not enough attention, I admit with regret, is paid to the interaction of the church and the rich contribution of the Jewish community to the city. The role of women in the city is left grossly undeveloped. Particularly in the earlier pages, I make wide use of secondary sources.

At the same time, I can only defend these omissions in view of my focused interest in these pages on the ethnosociological makeup of the city. My purpose is simpler—to link together the isolated histories of city and church usually traced separately.

The paths have not always been easy ones to merge. The social scientists who have focused on the history of American cities have paid very little attention to the impact of the church in the city. In far too much of this research referred to even in this volume you will find little or nothing about the church.

2. Roger Finke and Rodney Stark, *The Churching of America, 1776–1990* (New Brunswick: Rutgers University Press, 1992), 203.

3. John L. Spalding, "The Country" and "the City, 1880," in *The Church and the City, 1865–1910*, ed. Robert D. Cross (New York: Bobbs-Merrill, 1967), 8.

4. James D. Hunter, *American Evangelicalism: Conservative Religion and the Quandary of Modernity* (New Brunswick: Rutgers University Press, 1983), 7.

And when some have pointed to the church, they have followed the lead of earlier decades and viewed city life as muzzling the world of faith. The church for them exists on the urban periphery, silenced by the power of the city. Pastors like A. J. Gordon (1836–1895), whose Boston ministry spanned twenty-five years, slip into the background from the central place he and his Clarendon Street Church occupied in urban history. Misplaced also are the Dwight L. Moody revivals that stirred Gordon's heart and sparked his church's ministry to the alcoholic, the homeless, and the unemployed. The Boston Industrial Temporary Home, "a fixture of Boston's social service in the late nineteenth century"[5] and a Gordon creation, loses its "spiritual" place in urban historiography.

Church histories too frequently have not done much better. Their pictures of the church are drawn with a large sweeping brush in which the city is relegated to the distant background. Churches appear to be in the city but not really of it. City and not church occupies the periphery.

And, in common with the social scientists, some of such church histories are too quick to assume that the city is unfriendly to the church and its evangelical tradition. A classic work made use of in this study affirms that one of the "particularly devastating consequences" of urbanization was that "large elements of the new urban population had no contact with any Protestant churches."[6] Another notes that "there is wide agreement that Protestant churches have historically tended to be more at home in rural and town America than in the America of great cities."[7]

The message of this book offers another response: it isn't that easy. The story of evangelical church and American city is more complicated, more ambiguous than these generalizations allow.

Consider, for example, A. B. Simpson (1843–1919), the founding father of the Christian and Missionary Alliance (1887). Looking back at the brief history of the Alliance in 1899, he noted its first converts among the urban poor and the "neglected classes" here and abroad.[8]

5. Dana L. Robert, "The Legacy of Adoniram Judson Gordon," *International Bulletin of Missionary Research* 11, no. 4 (October 1987): 176.

6. Sydney Ahlstrom, *A Religious History of the American People* (Garden City, N.Y.: Image Books, 1975), 194.

7. Kendig Brubaker Cully and F. Nile Harper, eds., *Will the Church Lose the City?* (New York: World, 1969), 90.

8. A. B. Simpson, "An Ideal Church," *Alliance Weekly*, 7 October 1899, 292.

The priority he gave to "consecrated evangelism" left wide space also for "Christian philanthropies," providing "real help for human suffering as well as human sin."[9]

Simpson's Gospel Tabernacle, planted in New York and eventually finding its way to Eighth Avenue and West 44th Street, mothered a network of agencies with that same commitment—seven rescue missions, three for homeless men and four for prostitutes; an orphanage for homeless boys; a soup kitchen and a health clinic; language ministries to German and Italian immigrants.[10]

Yet, though he drew repeated attention to "the oppression of the poor," Simpson seems to have thought that restructuring society was not to be encouraged. In 1893 he wrote, "If we had a hundred million dollars, we would not spend one cent of it in establishing another school at home, or an institute abroad, unless it were simply for the purpose of training persons directly to preach the gospel."[11]

How do we explain this apparent disparity? Why, in 1908, did the Alliance turn away from social action, a turn that Simpson apparently accepted, if he did not inspire it? "Was it because of his expectation of the imminent return of Christ? Was it because he believed that such effort would encourage people to fix their hopes on this world rather than on the world to come? Was it because of the laissez-faire spirit of the times? Was it because he shared the widespread optimism of the day concerning the American 'way of life'?"[12] To these complications and ambiguities we now turn.

Some final words of appreciation are appropriate before we do. Many of the earlier draft pages of this manuscript were written at the Overseas Ministries Study Center in New Haven where I spent a delightful time in the early months of 1992 as senior mission scholar in residence. Here preliminary ideas were tried out before a discerning group of the Lord's people gathered in residence from all over the world.

I am grateful also for the invaluable help offered me by the library

9. John V. Dahms, "The Social Interest and Concern of A. B. Simpson," *The Birth of a Vision*, ed. David Hartzfeld and Charles Nienkirchen (Regina: *His Dominion* Supplement No. 1, 1986), 51.

10. George Reitz, "A. B. Simpson, Urban Evangelist," *Urban Mission* 8, no. 3 (January 1991): 23.

11. *The Christian Alliance and Missionary Weekly*, 20 October 1893, 243.

12. Dahms, "The Social Interest and Concern of A. B. Simpson," 63.

staffs and resources of Westminster Theological Seminary and the Yale Divinity School.

And before these concepts touched the page, my Westminster colleague, Manny Ortiz, advised, shared, and listened to me with patience as we talked them over inside of class and outside. Before they reached the final form in which you read them, Clair Davis, professor of church history at Westminster, surveyed the first seven chapters and offered much encouragement to complete the task. I am grateful for so much wise help. Needless to say, the end product is my responsibility, not theirs.

1

The Early American City
The Beginnings of Context

Scholars and pioneers have given America's colonial cities rich titles: "pearls on the coast and lights in the forest."[1] William Bradford, in a more disillusioned time, could still celebrate Boston as a blessing from God, a great tree whose roots spread throughout New England as "all trade and commerce fell in her way."[2] William Penn designed Philadelphia as "a green garden town" where every household would have "room enough for House, Garden, and small Orchard." Charles Town reminded many of a miniature London.

The cities of the Northwest and mid-Atlantic were small compared to their urban neighbors to the south. Mexico City had a population of some 70,000 by 1750, Lima around 60,000. And their history was shorter.

Spanish colonization in North America had begun almost a century before with the founding of St. Augustine (in Florida) in 1565. From this first European city the Spanish had pushed westward toward Georgia and Alabama and into the Southwest.[3] But these

1. Raymond Mohl, ed., *The Making of Urban America* (Wilmington, Del.: SR Books, 1988), 12.
2. Sylvia Doughty Fries, *The Urban Idea in Colonial America* (Philadelphia: Temple University Press, 1977), 56–57.
3. Harold J. Recinos, *Jesus Weeps: Global Encounters on Our Doorstep* (Nashville: Abingdon, 1992), 61.

15

Spanish cities, isolated from the regions around them, were symbols of Old World power and domination. They were administrative centers for colonial control. By contrast, cities like Boston, New York, and Philadelphia saw the New World as their setting and their hope.

Several generations later, population statistics for the colonies, though not awesome, were impressive. By "1850 only six American cities had over 100,000 inhabitants. . . . In 1850 only 5 percent of the American population lived in urban places of more than 100,000 inhabitants."[4] The tide had begun to turn.

New, gloomier perspectives on the city also preceded and followed these demographic changes. By 1698, Cotton Mather was already preaching that the Boston Ebenezer was in danger of becoming a Sodom. Mortality had carried away "the old Race of our First Planters" and "the Power of Godliness is grievously decay'd among us."[5] In 1834, Ralph Waldo Emerson moved from Boston to Concord, claiming that "whilst we want cities as the centers where the best things are to be found, cities degrade us by magnifying trifles."[6] Nathaniel Hawthorne advised, "All towns should be made capable of purification by fire, or of decay, within each half-century."[7] The visions of Winthrop and Penn were becoming bad dreams for some.

Urban pathologists underlined these kinds of concerns and began to use terms like "decay," "sprawling," "centerless" to describe this urban movement. Theodore Dreiser looked at Chicago's streetcar network and saw a "parasite Gold Thread" linking the neighborhoods and draining the pockets of its citizens. Lewis Mumford, a later historian of cities, idealized the walled city of the medieval world and spoke of America's metropolitan areas as stretching "over the countryside in an amorphous blob."

What happened to create this changing mentality toward the city? Will we find in this early history roots whose path we must follow as they touch later periods as well? This chapter examines these questions.

---

4. Jon C. Teaford, *The Twentieth-Century American City* (Baltimore: Johns Hopkins University Press, 1986), 1.

5. Cotton Mather, *The Boston Ebenezer* (Boston, 1698), 1– 11, 29–42.

6. Quoted in Morton White and Lucia White, *The Intellectual Versus the City* (New York: Oxford University Press, 1977), 27.

7. Ibid., 53.

Colonial Beginnings

The first colonists to arrive in Massachusetts Bay carried from their homelands in Europe a special vision of urban life. It centered around the township as a rural unit with a small village center. "It was not designed to accommodate a nonfarming population nor was it designed for a population which could not gather in a single assembly to discuss town affairs."[8] That was unique enough. By the seventeenth century, "fewer than one person in twenty had ever experienced urban life."[9]

The city, these colonists decided, would offer them security, commerce, and human society. Massachusetts Bay, according to John Winthrop, was to be "as a City upon a Hill." William Bradford in 1620 spoke with nostalgia of the urban world they had left behind: "They had now no friends to welcome them nor inns to entertaine or refresh their weatherbeaten bodys, no houses or much less townes to repaire too, to seeke for succoure . . . Besids, what could they see but a hidious and desolate wilderness, full of wild beasts and wild men? and what multituds ther might be of them they knew not."[10]

Table 1
Population Growth in the Major Colonial Cities, 1690–1775

	1690	1720	1742	1760	1775
Boston	7,000	12,000	16,382	15,631	16,000
Charleston	1,100	3,500	6,800	8,000	12,000
New York	3,900	7,000	11,000	18,000	25,000
Newport	2,600	3,800	6,200	7,500	11,000
Philadelphia	4,000	10,000	13,000	23,750	40,000

From David Goldfield and Blaine Brownell, *Urban America: A History*, 2d ed. (Boston: Houghton Mifflin, 1990), 36. Reprinted by permission.

Five communities soon spearheaded and changed these utopian expectations of urbanization—Boston, Newport, New Amsterdam (New York), Philadelphia, and Charles Town (Charleston). All five

8. Fries, *The Urban Idea in Colonial America*, 49.

9. Eric H. Monkkonen, *America Becomes Urban* (Berkeley: University of California Press, 1988), 35.

10. William T. Davis, ed., *Bradford's History of Plymouth Plantation* (New York: Scribners, 1908), 96.

were either seaports or cities located on a navigable river, market cities pointing to the homeland as the recipient of their trade and commerce. But commerce, not Christianity, built them.

Boston, the "Center Towne and Metropolis of this Wildernesse," had barely 300 residents in the 1630s. But by 1742, its population had reached 16,000. Six-year-old Philadelphia had 4,000 inhabitants. But by 1720 it rose to 10,000. Unique among the five, Charleston had only 1,100 people two decades after its founding; and by the 1740s over half of its inhabitants were slaves.

The legacy of colonial walking cities had its supporters and its critics. Benjamin Franklin the city-builder fought no battles over the virtues of urban versus rural life. J. Hector St. John Crevecoeur saw the cities of Europe as "the confined theatre of cupidity" but lavished praise on American urbanization.

Thomas Jefferson was of another mind. With a love for the soil and a horror of Europe's growing industrial revolution, his *Notes on Virginia* spoke with vehemence of the growing American city of the 1780s. "The mobs of great cities," he judged, "add just so much to the support of pure government, as sores do to the strength of the human body."[11] By 1823, the War of 1812 had mellowed his antagonism. But he could still compare New York to London and classify it as "a Cloacina of all the depravities of human nature." Philadelphia came out better by comparison.

Individualism and the Private City

What was the legacy that the colonial city left to our day? If Eric Monkkonen is right, the legal and political heritage was slight.[12] But in at least one significant area, that of ideology, a pattern was being formed that would make a permanent mark on the American psyche.

The "habit of the heart" was individualism, the proverbial independence of the Connecticut Yankee characteristic of more regions than merely New England.

The twenty-five-year-old Frenchman, Alexis de Tocqueville, saw it in his ten-month visit to the new land in 1830. For him, the Americans "owe nothing to any man, they expect nothing from any man; they acquire the habit of always considering themselves as standing alone, and they are apt to imagine that their whole destiny is in their own

11. White and White, *The Intellectual Versus the City*, 6–14.
12. Monkkonen, *America Becomes Urban*, 53–54.

hands . . . it throws him back for ever upon himself alone, and threatens in the end to confine him entirely within the solitude of his own heart."[13] Tocqueville focused on its connections to the new world's fledgling democracy. But it could be seen in other areas as well.

The image of the colonial city in many ways epitomized a spirit dubbed "privatism" by Sam Bass Warner. Cities were founded on individuals and interest groups pursuing their own private goals.[14] Even the geography of the cities spoke of it—open, leaving the individual uncontained. The tiny and fragile settlements that became the colonial city quickly abandoned the walls that marked Europe's urban centers. Never more than palisades or ditches to begin with, even the constraining wall of New Amsterdam that guarded what is now lower Manhattan, the Bowery, and Battery Park area disappeared quickly. Only its name remained to mark, appropriately enough, its financial center—Wall Street.

The same individualism created conflict with Native Americans. Urban life was not new to them; they had already constructed cities hundreds of years before European contact.[15] The conflict arose not over cities but how two cultures perceived the land. Named "Indians" by the migrant Europeans, they saw the land as common property, belonging to no one; they lived on it as community tenants, rather than its private masters. The individualism of the colonist could not live with this mobile view of life and land.

Two worldviews quickly clashed. And when a growing number of Native Americans embraced the Christian faith in the seventeenth century, Christian colonials turned to the "private city" to nurture the converts and draw them into proper Christian civilization. The Massachusetts Bay authorities set up "praying towns" to turn the Indians from their wandering view of the land to a merger of Christianity and "proper" civilizing.[16]

Individualism shaped even the business world of the eighteenth-century colonial city. Towering above the other heroes of this urban

13. Alexis de Tocqueville, *Democracy in America, Vol. 2* (New Rochelle, N.Y.: Arlington House, n.d.), 106.

14. Sam Bass Warner, *The Urban Wilderness: A History of the American City* (New York: Harper and Row, 1972).

15. Recinos, *Jesus Weeps*, 59.

16. William R. Hutchison, *Errand to the World* (Chicago: University of Chicago Press, 1987), 28; Gary Nash, *Red, White, and Black* (Englewood Cliffs, N.J.: Prentice-Hall, 1974), 122–27.

environment was the business entrepreneur. The acquisition of wealth began to erode the heritage of urban Europe's social stratification by birth or lineage. The American city was to be a place of opportunity for the industrious and bold. And Benjamin Franklin was the city's model of the plucky and shrewd person who might advance from apprentice to owner.

Poor Richards in the cities, a role popularized by Franklin, could rise rapidly from the bottom of the social ladder to modest wealth through hard work and frugality. At the top of America's social classes one looked for the professionals of Boston, the more successful merchants of Philadelphia, the planters of Charles Town.

The growing ideology of individualism could be seen in the world of politics as well. Individual liberties and individual rights became the natural rights of John Locke. And when these were seen as threatened, there were urban groups like the Sons of Liberty to defend them. The Boston Tea Party reflected that same urban ideology, concerned about parliamentary control of a free, that is, privatized economy. The Revolution had its roots in the city. But the roots were more than geographical. They were also ideological. Many colonists saw the need for war, not in the name of revolution but in the name of the natural rights of every individual for independence.[17]

"Outsiders" in the Private City

The bright prospects of individualism, however, were not always available to all. Urban poverty created a floating population called the "strolling poor," the colonial version of the homeless. By the early 1750s Boston officials were describing "Numbers of Wretches hungry and naked shivering with Cold, and, perhaps languishing with Disease."[18] On the eve of the Revolution in Providence and Newport, Rhode Island, between 30 and 45 percent of all adult males were too poor to be included on the assessor's lists. In Philadelphia the figure reached a fifth of the population, the richest 5 percent of the city controlling as much wealth as the rest of the population combined. In Charles Town the top 10 percent accounted for about 62 percent of the city's wealth. Class lines based on wealth were hardening.

17. Mark A. Noll, *Christians in the American Revolution* (Washington, D.C.: Christian University Press, 1977), 15–27.

18. Quoted in Gary Nash, "The Social Evolution of Preindustrial American Cities, 1700–1820: Reflections and New Directions," *Journal of Urban History* 13, no. 2 (February 1987): 124.

By the 1760s the newest and most impressive structures in the growing seaport cities were the workhouses, the almshouses, and the prisons. And New England theologians like Cotton Mather in 1712 were warning, not the wealthy, but the poor to see their plight as a providential call to repentance from pride and submission: "Let your Experience of the Provision which you find a Gracious God thus marketing to you, be the Encouragement of your Expectation to be still provided for."[19]

Another colonial community, like the Native Americans, found the promise of individualism often out of reach to them. The only involuntary immigrants to colonial shores, Africans soon swelled not only Southern working plantations but the cities of the Northeast as well. In 1684, 150 slaves arrived to face a white Philadelphia population of 1,000.[20] From the 1720s to the 1760s, 150,000 new African slaves arrived. And by the mid-eighteenth century, the populations of New York City and Albany were 20 percent slave, with 30 to 40 percent of the white householders owning human property. By 1790, the time of the first national census, between 250,000 and 300,000 slaves had been imported into the thirteen colonies and made up 19 percent of the population.

Among the slave populations were a much smaller number of indentured blacks who served their indentureship and then were free to take up land and fend for themselves. By 1790, "free persons of color" numbered about 60,000. "Many northern states abolished slavery, and many individuals (and the whole Quaker community) manumitted their slaves in the ideological aftermath of the American Revolution."[21]

This community had a large head start in urbanization and formed a black elite. Philadelphia was home to one of the largest concentrations of free blacks. And after 1830, they asserted leadership of their community at the national level. They played an active role in promoting abolition.[22]

19. Cotton Mather, *Some Seasonable Advice unto the Poor: to be Annexed unto the Kindnesses of God, that are Dispensed unto Them* (Boston, 1712), 5.

20. Gary B. Nash, *Forging Freedom: The Formation of Philadelphia's Black Community, 1720–1840* (Cambridge: Harvard University Press, 1988), 8.

21. Thomas Sowell, *Ethnic America* (New York: Basic, 1981), 195.

22. Julie Winch, *Philadelphia's Black Elite* (Philadelphia: Temple University Press, 1988), 1–4.

But whether slave or free, blacks knew little of the rewards or blessings that accompanied the growing ideology of individualism. When the British stormed Bunker Hill, black patriots were in the ranks. By the end of the war, some 5,000 blacks, slaves and freemen, had shouldered arms. More than 100,000 slaves received their freedom as a direct result of that participation.

But laws on the books into the early nineteenth century restricted even free blacks from free migration. And for slaves, valued only as economic property, the picture was worse. Slaves could not enter into contracts and could not bequeath or inherit property. Their marriages were not legally binding, and families could be broken up at the discretion of the slaveholder. As property, they could be sold, traded, or given away.[23]

Into the Industrial Era: 1790–1870

By 1790, only 5 percent of the new nation's 4 million people lived in places of 2,500 or more. The country boasted only nineteen cities with a population in the 1,500–10,000 range. And only five exceeded the 10,000 figure. Except for New York with 33,000 inhabitants, the city was barely visible.

Eight decades later, in 1870, the demographic picture was changing dramatically. More than one out of four Americans lived in cities. Every decade between 1820 and 1870 saw urban population grow three times as fast as national population. There were eight cities with more than 100,000 inhabitants. And the nation's commercial flow moved toward the emerging world metropolis of New York, by 1870 a city of more than 942,000 people.

Geographical Growth

The conquest of the wilderness west of the Allegheny Mountains to the shores of California was a dramatic part of the new changes. The opening of the Western frontier meant a new urban frontier. Following in the path of the pioneer came new settlements, towns that quickly became cities.

Along the shores of Lake Michigan, Fort Dearborn was built in 1804. By the War of 1812 a dozen cabins and forty or fifty people oc-

23. Howard Bahr, Bruce Chadwick, and Joseph Strauss, *American Ethnicity* (Lexington, Mass.: D.C. Heath, 1979), 17–18, 23.

Figure 1
Urban versus Rural Population, 1790–1870
(in millions)

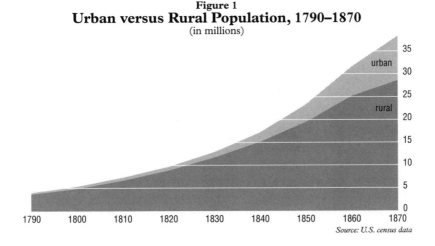

Source: *U.S. census data*

cupied the settlement. By 1870, its population had reached nearly 300,000 and the settlement had a new name—Chicago.[24]

At the other end of the frontier, whalers and hide-and-tallow ships were harboring in the protected bay of Yerba Buena Cove. By 1841, the settlement had a Hudson's Bay Company building, a store, a grog shop with a billiard table, a blacksmith shop—perhaps twenty buildings in all. Within ten years, gold had been discovered in the surrounding areas and San Francisco was born. By 1850, its population had swelled to 35,000, by 1870 to nearly 150,000.

This urban history repeated itself in the land spread between these two cities. Instant cities sprang up along the river fronts—Cincinnati, Louisville, St. Louis, and New Orleans. Cities like Denver, founded in 1858 and strictly a gold-rush community, grew in spite of their geography.

Urban expansion in the South was a different story. Like a "wall-flower at the ball,"[25] its cities fared poorly in comparison with those in the North and the West. With a long history of dependency on the urban Northeast, Southern cities, unlike those in the North, did little trading with each other or Europe. Their economy was heavily oriented to agriculture, specifically to tobacco and, increasingly so after

24. Richard A. Bartlett, *The New Country: A Social History of the American Frontier, 1776–1890* (London: Oxford University Press, 1974), 407–10.
25. David Goldfield and Blaine Brownell, *Urban America: A History*, 2d ed. (Boston: Houghton-Mifflin, 1990), 104.

1793 with the invention of the gin, to cotton. Railway building was limited and more local than in the North.

Added to all was the devastating impact of the Civil War. The urban South died on November 15, 1864, as General William T. Sherman watched his troops burn Atlanta.[26] And as late as 1880 it had not recovered. "Between 1870 and 1880 cities with more than 10,000 inhabitants increased nationally from 165 to 228, but only from 26 to 30 in the South. . . . Of 99 communities over 20,000, only 17 were in the South. Of 20 metropolises over 100,000, only 4 were in the South."[27]

Railway links were rebuilt. But such reconstruction efforts were limited in comparison to the North and the West. Only 4,000 of the 35,000 miles of railroads built in the decade following the Civil War were in the South; more than half of this was in only three states. Commercial relationships were restored but only with Southern cities.

Transportation Breakthroughs

In the 1820s, new life was pumped into the cities through new transportation technologies. Canals linked emerging Western towns to the Great Lakes of the North. The 1830s became boom times for Cleveland, Toledo, and Chicago. The Erie Canal was completed in 1825, joining the Great Lakes and the Atlantic Ocean at New York City. On one end of the canal, Buffalo became the fastest-growing city in the state. And on the other end, New York City's already strong commercial position became stronger.

Steamboats appeared on the Mississippi in the 1820s, creating new cities and making old ones grow. Waterways linked New Orleans and Natchez, Memphis, St. Louis, and Louisville.

But preeminently it was the railroad that accelerated urban growth. Baltimore, appearing almost from nowhere to become the third largest city in the nation, opened the railroad era in 1827 as its merchants chartered the Baltimore and Ohio Railroad. No city would be the same again.

Intraregional trade expanded as rail systems grew out of centers like Boston and communities embraced the railroad as the Iron Messiah. One Presbyterian minister from New York hailed the railroads

26. Lawrence Larsen, *The Rise of the Urban South* (Lexington: University Press of Kentucky, 1985), 18.
27. Ibid., 21.

as "the evolution of divine purposes, infinite, eternal—connecting social revolutions with the progress of Christianity and the coming reign of Christ."[28]

Chicago was perhaps the sterling example of what the railroads could mean for urban expansion. Its business leaders saw the railroad's potential while Chicago's rival city, St. Louis, pinned its hopes for growth on the Mississippi. Chicago, a major rail terminus, won the competition. During the 1860s, its population tripled while St. Louis's multiplied less than twofold.

Even the shape of the city itself began to change. Prior to 1825, no city anywhere possessed a mass transit system. By 1832, the horse-drawn streetcar was following rail lines through the streets of New York City, and steam railroads were offering commuter travel to 125th Street. By 1843, rails stretched to New Haven, Connecticut.

Commuter lines were springing up throughout the Northeast. "During the 1850s, the rail route between Newark and Jersey City was one of the busiest in the world. By 1859 in Philadelphia, more than forty trains were making commuter stops in the northwestern suburb of Germantown, while in Chicago the northern town of Evanston was growing rapidly because of the frequent service of the Chicago and Milwaukee railroad."[29] The walking city of the colonial era was slowly disappearing.

Marketplace Expansion and Urban Spread

The spirit of individualism that broke open the frontier, drove the trains, and created the cities of this era had its final destination in the marketplace. Commerce was at the center of the expanding, unregulated urban economy. "GAIN! GAIN! GAIN! is the beginning, the middle and the end, the alpha and omega of the founders of American towns."[30]

From the waterfront edges of the colonial city commerce moved to create a new place for business called the downtown. By the 1850s, businessmen like Lord and Taylor of New York, Marshall Field of Chicago, and John Wanamaker of Philadelphia were bringing retail

---

28. Blaine Brownell and David Goldfield, eds., *The City in Southern History: The Growth of Urban Civilization in the South* (Port Washington, N.Y.: Kennikat, 1977), 53–54.

29. Kenneth Jackson, *Crabgrass Frontier* (New York: Oxford University Press, 1985), 37.

30. Quoted in John Reps, *The Making of Urban America: A History of City Planning in the United States* (Princeton: Princeton University Press, 1965), 349.

activities under one roof. The emporium and department store fast
became the American city's substitute for the cathedrals of medieval
Europe.

Increasingly crowding the downtown also were the growing number of factories (actually glorified workshops) and manufacturers, the
first vanguard of the flood still to come. By 1860, the United States
was still an agricultural nation. But already it was also the second-
ranking industrial power in the world. And the city held it all. Commercial, industrial, and financial users of space were crowding out the
single-family homeowner for downtown locations.

Rail and horse-drawn streetcars offered escape from downtown
and a new evolution in urban life: the residential neighborhood. What
might be called the first suburban movement in American city life
had begun.

The first to go were the well-to-do. Highly exclusive zoning re-
quirements attracted them to large suburban estates on the edges of
cities like Philadelphia and Boston. The genteel retreated from urban
life to New York's Scarsdale or the North Shore of Chicago. By
1850, New York's Association for the Improvement of the Condition
of the Poor (AICP) had begun complaining that "many of the rich
and prosperous are removing from the city, while the poor are pressing in."[31]

A new complexion to the city was forming. During the decade
from 1850 to 1860, New York's city population expanded by 57.8
percent, her suburbs by 88.5 percent. In St. Louis, the gap between
city and suburban expansion rates was even more spectacular. There
was a 20 percent growth in the city and 100.7 percent in the suburban
residential areas.

"Outsiders" in the Marketplace Cities

This push to the suburbs was accelerated as two realities merged
into one in the minds of anxious Anglo-Saxons: the expanding presence of the city's immigrant and minority populations and their identification as the "unworthy" poor.

The Eastern cities exemplified the trend. Blacks became a separate
urban nation, their residential areas isolated and confined, and their
right to vote after the Civil War maintained only in New England. In
Boston they were found in two areas: "New Guinea" along the

31. Jackson, *Crabgrass Frontier*, 29.

wharves and the infamous "Nigger Hill" near downtown. In Philadelphia both Irish and German immigrants were scattered throughout the city; blacks were concentrated near the downtown area.

Exclusion touched also the growing wave of German and Irish people who made up the bulk of immigrants in the early nineteenth century. Over 250,000 migrated in 1857 alone. Pushed to the new land by crop failures in Ireland, the British Isles, and the lower Rhine valley, they came impoverished and desperate. The Irish especially had higher numbers who were poor and unskilled.

Would this rising tide of foreign immigration reproduce feared conditions in Europe? Could poverty drive immigrants to inevitable depravities? to a failure of self-discipline? Stereotypical images of the Irish poor became harsher and more explicit. And soon these generalizations were expanded to the poor and the slums in general. As early as the end of the 1820s, the poor were being categorized as worthy or unworthy. "Most poverty was being attributed to moral defects of character and failures of individual self-discipline."[32]

By 1852, the AICP was verbalizing this growing distaste:

> The worst part of the refuse class which is thus thrown upon our shores, here clan together and remain in the city, nor can they be persuaded to leave it. These mostly consist of imbecile and thriftless parish paupers and dependents, the former inmates of poor-houses and even of prisons, who being unwilling or unable to gain an honest subsistence anywhere, have been sent here, in order to rid the country from which they come of their support . . . Many of them are afflicted with pestilential diseases, more or less developed, which, as they wander about in search of shelter, are disseminated through the city to the manifest detriment of public health and to the destruction of life.[33]

Across the nation in San Francisco, another new urban immigrant community were victims of the same stereotypes. The Chinese, pushed by poverty in their homeland and pulled by American demands for cheap labor, began to arrive before the Civil War. There were 25,000 in California by 1851.

Come to work in the mines and on railroads, the Asian newcomers were pushed off to their own Little Chinas or Chinatowns. Their

---

32. David Ward, *Poverty, Ethnicity, and the American City, 1840–1925* (Cambridge and New York: Cambridge University Press, 1989), 21.

33. Ibid., 26.

reception was harsh and violent. "After nineteen Chinese arrivals were killed in a Los Angeles riot in 1871, the governor started speaking of 'an irrepressible conflict' between the civilizations of China and America."[34] The Chinese presence had become "the Chinese problem."[35]

The City's Emerging Self-Understanding

Out of all this history the American city was shaping its vision of itself. And the vision in turn was shaping the city.

It began as a vision of boundless optimism, of an urban millennium in the wilderness, of individual progress. Then and now, that picture has controlled. "Most Americans feel that through their efforts a better future can be brought about which will not compromise the welfare and progress of others. There is enough for everyone—a belief which is valid for people living in a country with an expanding economy and rich resources."[36]

For the colonial Puritan, that hope had a theological twist. New England would one day become the New Jerusalem. Quickly, however, Providence gave way to Reason and Natural Right. The church in the town square stepped back for the department store in the downtown. And a dark side to individualism had become easier to see.

In the name of progress the Native American was sacrificed. In the name of progress the African became a slave. The poor, formerly worthy objects of charity, became unworthy objects of scorn. The people that had come to build cities began to turn from the city and ride the rails of technology toward the "new" wilderness in the suburbs just beyond the edge of the city.

Some, like Henry David Thoreau, saw the city and urban optimism turned into a romantic anti-urban return to nature. From Walden Pond he looked with suspicious eyes on Boston and New York. Herman Melville and Nathaniel Hawthorne looked deeper.

34. Martin E. Marty, *Pilgrims in Their Own Land: 500 Years of Religion in America* (Boston: Little, Brown and Company, 1984), 262.

35. Christian G. Fritz, "Due Process, Treaty Rights, and Chinese Exclusion, 1882–1891," in *Entry Denied: Exclusion and the Chinese Community in America, 1882–1941*, ed. Sucheng Chan (Philadelphia: Temple University Press, 1991), 25–56.

36. Edward C. Stewart, *American Cultural Patterns: A Cross-Cultural Perspective* (Washington, D.C.: Society for Intercultural Education, Training, and Research, 1972), 66.

They "were disturbed and offended by the American city's effect on the human spirit in the period before the Civil War. And so for them the city scene was a backdrop for frightening experiences, personal defeat, icy intellectualism, heartless commercialism, miserable poverty, crime and sin, smoke and noise, dusk and loneliness."[37]

What was the city becoming?

37. White and White, *The Intellectual Versus the City*, 37.

2

The Church in the City
The Beginning of Mission in Context

Early in American life, anti-urban sentiment was to appear. With his eye on what he saw as the depraved morals and corruption of the European city, Thomas Jefferson could reflect on an outbreak of yellow fever in the colonies in 1800: "the yellow fever will discourage the growth of great cities in our nation and I view great cities as pestilential to the morals, the health, and the liberties of men."[1]

The Church and the Colonial City

Jefferson's comments, however, were not typical. Other Old World immigrants to the American shores had come with different images. En route to the New World in 1630, John Winthrop had a dream for the cities he predicted would emerge in the Massachusetts colony. "We shall find that the God of Israel is among us . . . For we must consider that we shall be as a city upon a hill, the eyes of all people are upon us."

Winthrop's Puritan ideal was to shape even the very laying out of the early New England city. The church became not only the spiritual center of the town, but its geographical and social focus as well.

---

1. Quoted in Morton White and Lucia White, *The Intellectual Versus the City* (New York: Oxford University Press, 1977), 17.

Town meetings were at first both civil and ecclesiastical. The city was to be a commonwealth "under God."[2] Here in the New World would be built "towns of order in which religious and civil authority was officially redistributed from the situation that had existed in *old* England, but knit together under the federal theology of a God whose providence ordered all things. Here old Boston in Lincolnshire was reconstituted, and so were many other old cities of England. It became a New Haven for many."[3]

The Puritan vision began to fade quickly. From Maine to Long Island it flourished before the colonies had a town large enough to call a city. And it was nourished by only a small minority of the population. In the colonial period no more than 10 to 20 percent of the population actually belonged to a church, about 17 percent on the eve of the Revolution.[4]

The Puritan post-Reformation dream of a God-centered community where order and stability would enable people to live according to a biblical ethic of love and virtue had new worldview competitors that became far more popular as time wore on. The Enlightenment and its commitment not to revelation but to reason was in the beginning stages of an immense impact on the colonial mentality. Wealth from a thriving West Indian trade was providing new temptations in the name of progress. "God became less respected as man became more respectable."[5]

By 1702, Cotton Mather had published his *Magnalia Christi Americana* to mourn the lost American Jerusalem in the wilderness. "The golden age" had gone, lost in the falling-away from the covenant, desertion of the churches, and half-heartedness among the people."[6] By 1720 the Puritan hope of a corporate, organic ideal of social order under God was eroding under American individualism into a contractual, atomistic social structure of natural rights and obligations.

2. Sydney Ahlstrom, *A Religious History of the American People* (New Haven: Yale University Press, 1972), 147–48.

3. Robert W. Spike, "The Metropolis: Crucible for Theological Reconstruction," in *The Church and the Exploding Metropolis*, ed. Robert Lee (Richmond: John Knox, 1965), 28.

4. Roger Finke and Rodney Stark, *The Churching of America, 1776–1990* (New Brunswick: Rutgers University Press, 1992), 15–30.

5. Edwin S. Gaustad, *The Great Awakening in New England* (New York: Harper and Brothers, 1957), 15.

6. Martin E. Marty, *Pilgrims in Their Own Land* (Boston: Little, Brown and Company, 1984), 109–11.

The Great Awakening and the City

In the 1730s, a divine interruption in this downward slide began in the village of Northampton, Massachusetts. Under the preaching of Jonathan Edwards, revival broke out in the churches and followed a path along the Connecticut River valley as far as Long Island Sound.

Before it ran its course in 1760, this revival had touched the major urban centers of the colonies—New York, Philadelphia, Charles Town, even Boston, where resistance was most vocal. One hundred and fifty New England towns were touched by the movement that later observers would call "the Great Awakening" as it crossed the restricting boundaries of denominations. Its Grand Itinerants, George Whitefield, the Tennent family, and others, would carry its power through the Middle Colonies and the South. Maryland, the Carolinas, Virginia, and Georgia felt its effect.

The impact on the growing cities and their problems was large. The Great Awakening came at an opportune time of remarkable population growth in the colonies, from an estimated 360,000 in 1713 to 1,600,000 in 1760. "The defenders of the old way knew well enough what was going on. The Harvard faculty, for example, sharply criticized the most eloquent awakener of them all, Whitefield, saying that the awakening preachers 'thrust themselves into Towns and Parishes, to the Destruction of all Peace and Order, whereby they have to the great impoverishment of the Community, taken the People from their Work and Business, to attend their Lectures and Exhortations, always fraught with Enthusiasm, and other pernicious Errors.'"[7]

"Thrust into towns and parishes," most assuredly they did. But one could hardly describe that thrust as a "great impoverishment of the community." The Puritan vision of God's bringing at last his millennial kingdom into full visibility was welded by Edwards to the Awakening call for the new birth and the restoration of all things in Christ. A renewed piety and a growing church were seen as only part of the divine design.

Out of the Great Awakening came Christian support for the welfare of the poor. Edwards argued "that we cannot deny help to the undeserving, since this would clash with God's gift of grace to us and our consequent obligation to love even our enemies. Nor can we fail

7. Robert T. Handy, *A Christian America: Protestant Hopes and Historical Realities* (New York: Oxford University Press, 1984), 18.

to help the man whose indigence is due to his own financial improvidence; this is not necessarily sin but may be due to a want of economic sense which is as real a handicap as blindness."[8]

In that spirit, Whitefield founded an orphanage in Georgia. And, on a much larger scale, a new social consciousness came into being, renouncing the rationalist ethic of self-interest for "public service." A new concept of government and public good emerged. Under the older Puritan ideal, the duty of government was seen as the restraint of the selfishness of the individual for the sake of the commonwealth. Now the civil authority began to be seen also as the public's agent and not merely its disciplinarian.[9]

From the revival quickening came the impetus for founding new American universities, modeled after the Log Cabin training school of the Tennents. In rapid succession appeared the College of New Jersey at Princeton, Dartmouth in New Hampshire, Bethesda in Georgia, Brown University in Rhode Island, among others.

The "Outsiders" and the Awakening

The "outsiders," and sympathy for them, began to be stirred. When Whitefield came to Philadelphia on his second American tour in 1739, many of the city's approximately 1,000 slaves heard him and responded to the similarities of Awakening practices and African style. In the years that followed, Philadelphia's slaves and a few free blacks found new meaning in Christ through the evangelists of the Awakening.[10] "During the eighteenth century there were more blacks and whites worshiping in the same congregation, proportionate to their numbers as baptized Christians, than there are today."[11]

Characteristic of whites of this time, Whitefield did not attack the institution of slavery. But, stirred by the wrongs done to the poor, he spoke against its abuse. And his response was heard. Under his inspiration, a Philadelphia dancing master, Robert Bolton, renounced the "devilish diversions" of his dancing school and closed it down to open a school for "Black scholars." At the Forks of the Delaware in north-

---

8. Richard Lovelace, *Dynamics of Spiritual Life* (Downers Grove: InterVarsity, 1979), 366–67.

9. William G. McLoughlin, *Revivals, Awakening, and Reform* (Chicago: University of Chicago Press, 1978), 79–80.

10. Gary B. Nash, *Forging Freedom: The Formation of Philadelphia's Black Community, 1720–1840* (Cambridge: Harvard University Press, 1988), 18–20.

11. Gayraud Wilmore, *Black Religion and Black Radicalism* (Maryknoll: Orbis, 1983), 74.

east Pennsylvania, near Easton, Whitefield bought five thousand acres on which to establish a charity school for blacks and a refuge for oppressed English Methodists. Entrusted eventually to the Moravians, the school he established gave its name to the city that grew there, Nazareth.[12]

But the seeds of the Awakening would produce even more fruit in the years to come. As the nation approached 1776, pamphleteering opponents of slavery began to write. And among the Quakers who led the struggle was a Presbyterian doctor, Benjamin Rush. Touched by the Awakening at Princeton (then the College of New Jersey) and its evangelical president, Samuel Davies, Rush attacked not only the slave trade but slavery itself. He became the most important liaison between the black community and its white supporters. The grandchild of the Awakening was stirring more than charity; he was calling for justice.

By the end of the century the liberating theology of the revivalists was producing more among blacks than simply a sense of personal release in conversion. Black preachers were appearing in growing numbers in the years after 1740. And by the 1750s, the first known black churches were organized near the Bluestone River in Mecklenberg, Virginia, and on the South Carolina bank of the Savannah River, not far from Augusta, Georgia.[13] In 1787 in Philadelphia, Richard Allen, Absalom Jones, and other black worshipers were pulled from their knees during worship in a gallery they did not know was closed to blacks. They withdrew to form the African Methodist Episcopal (AME) Church. The Awakening was still alive.

Another "outsider" community was touched by the Awakening. The missionary calling of the church to the long-neglected Native American stirred again. Fresh efforts began in western New England and the Middle Colonies. The Society for the Propagation of the Gospel in Foreign Parts (SPG), founded in 1701, had a total of 309 missionaries working up and down the coast by the end of the century.

But earlier patterns of civilizing and Christianizing continued to dominate. None of the SPG missionaries lived among the Indians; some accepted native children in schools, where they were taught En-

12. Charles C. Maxson, *The Great Awakening in the Middle Colonies* (Gloucester, Mass.: Peter Smith, 1958), 57–58.
13. C. Eric Lincoln and Lawrence Mamiya, *The Black Church in the African American Experience* (Durham: Duke University Press, 1990), 23.

glish habits of dress, speech, and worship. Forced acculturation was the center of missionary strategy. Cotton Mather's attitude was typical: "the best thing we can do for our Indians," he argued, "is to Anglicize them in all agreeable Instances; and in that of Language as well as others."[14]

Jonathan Edwards, for example, worked among the Housatonic people in Stockbridge, Massachusetts, for seven years in the 1750s. But he always spoke through an interpreter and spent most of his time writing theological treatises for whites, not for Native Americans.

Ultimately, even among vigorous evangelists like David Brainerd, fruit was small. In New Jersey, said by some to be the scene of his most productive labors, converts totaled no more than fifty. The resurrected mission as a whole was not to last. Nor were its effects.

The Church at the End of the Colonial City

The Awakening prepared the way for the Revolutionary War. Those denominations that had been built up by the revival, like the Presbyterian and the Baptist, almost unanimously took up the side of the colonies in the struggle. Their meeting houses were burned as nests of rebellion, their pastors sought as instigators of treason.

By 1800, a visitor could see the church's presence in the cities. "In Philadelphia, for example, such a visitor would have witnessed people crowding into thirty-five churches representing fourteen denominations and eight ethnic groups, whereas a century before worshipers had attended only the churches of four English denominations and one Swedish chapel. Even in Boston, less than half the size of Philadelphia, nineteen churches of eight denominations existed at the end of the eighteenth century."[15]

But something was missing. Even the Great Awakening could not alter one important fact: most colonists remained unaffiliated with any church. Church membership continued its decline in New England by the last half of the century. And in the Middle Colonies and the South many people were untouched by the revivals.

"The church remained a prominent, even essential, social institution, but it was not the only one. And for many urban colonists, cer-

---

14. Quoted in Henry W. Bowden, *American Indians and Christian Missions* (Chicago: University of Chicago Press, 1981), 136.
15. Raymond Mohl, ed., *The Making of Urban America* (Wilmington, Del.: SR Books, 1988), 27.

Figure 2
Rates of Religious Adherence, 1776–1980

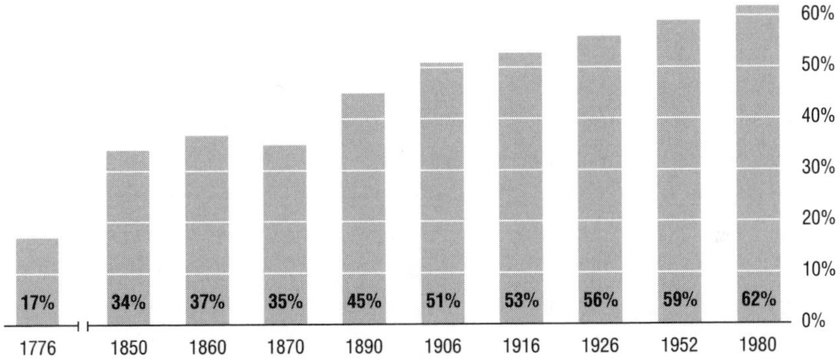

From Roger Finke and Rodney Stark, *The Churching of America, 1776–1990* (New Brunswick: Rutgers University Press, 1992), 30. Reprinted by permission.

tainly as the colonial era unfolded, the tavern became a much more central part of their lives than any organized church."[16]

Even the Revolution, though commended by the supporters of the Awakening, transformed the millennial expectations of the Puritan hope into a secularized republican ideology. The dream of a "Christian commonwealth" dedicated to the glory of God became the assertion of the glory of America. At no time in the country's religious history was vitality lower.

The Church Meets the Emerging Industrial City

The first half of the nineteenth century offered a new challenge to the church—the emergence of the industrial city. "From 1790 to 1840, every decade but one saw a rate of urban growth nearly double that for the population as a whole, and greater than any post-Civil War decade!"[17]

The compact and relatively stable urban scene of pre-revolutionary days began to change. The problems that were part of that older world began to intensify as the city welcomed commerce, marketing, and immigrant newcomers. Congestion, poverty, and social disorder multiplied. The reputation of the city began to wane and the image of the city as a threat began to grow.

16. David Goldfield and Blaine Brownell, *Urban America: A History,* 2d ed. (Boston: Houghton Mifflin, 1990), 55.
17. Paul Boyer, *Urban Masses and Moral Order in America, 1820–1920* (Cambridge: Harvard University Press, 1978), 3.

In 1817, one Christian pastor was already describing New York's poor wards as "a great mass of people beyond the restraints of religion, . . . thousands who are grossly vicious."[18] By the 1830s, John Todd, a Philadelphia pastor, was warning, "Let no man who values his soul, or his body, ever go into a great city to become a pastor . . . You cast the salt into the water, and soon see that you are trying to salt a river; it all runs away at once."[19]

By the middle decades of the nineteenth century, this image of the "wicked city" had become a stereotype already deep in the national consciousness. In 1852, some saw a growing disinterest of the church in the city because of it. Stephen Colwell, a welfare economist and Old School Presbyterian, was complaining, "The Gospel is sent to the heathen of far distant lands, but the heathen at home are neglected."[20]

There were other signs of flight as well. The same year the General Conference of the Methodist Church voted to sanction the practice of pew rental, a practice that at least one church paper denounced as part of "a gospel to the rich." The practice, now officially sanctioned, was already prevalent in Boston and New York where churches were moving to the well-to-do uptown areas and competing for attention with impressive edifices. Worship, critics accused, had become "conditioned on a good pew rent," and Wesley's metropolitan followers were said to be forsaking his advice against costly buildings. "Pewsyism," they warned, would leave the free-church field open to the Episcopalians and the New York Tabernacle of Charles Finney.[21]

The Second Great Awakening, 1800–1830

But with those who were turning from the city, there were those who reached out to the city in compassion and on behalf of justice. And once again revivalism made the difference.

From 1800 to 1830, a new outpouring of the Holy Spirit swept through the churches, but not uniformly.[22] The old channels of the Northeast felt the waves with new power. Between 1790 and 1830

---

18. Ibid., 9.

19. John Todd, *The Sabbath School Teacher* (Northampton, Mass. 1837), 83, 91, 113.

20. Quoted in Aaron I. Abell, *The Urban Impact on American Protestantism, 1865–1900* (Hamden, Conn.: Archon, 1962), 6.

21. Timothy Smith, *Revivalism and Social Reform* (Nashville: Abingdon, 1967), 164.

22. Terry D. Bilhartz, *Urban Religion and the Second Great Awakening* (Cranbury, N.J.: Associated Universities Presses, 1986), 137.

Baltimore Methodism grew at the astonishing rate of 1,550 percent. By 1820, an estimated 6,000 Methodist converts from the revival had become regular church-goers in New York. Wealthy merchants like William Dodge and the brothers Arthur and Lewis Tappan, touched by the new Awakening, were establishing a string of missions in rented storefronts and facilities throughout the city. By 1832, these "free churches" (no pew rent was required) were adding about 4,000 members. In the same year, Charles Finney (1792–1875), a prominent leader of the Second Awakening, opened a permanent revival center in a rented theater near Five Points, the heart of New York's worst slum area.

The South also felt deeply the Awakening.[23] But since urbanization was much later in coming than in the North, its impact was on a more rural and frontier mindset. Thus its preeminent symbol in the South was the camp meeting under the trees. And because of this, argues William McLoughlin, "its religious institutions came to play a much larger role than in the North as a civilizing and acculturating force."[24]

Also unlike the North, Southern revivalism had little impact on social reform. The Southern general endorsement of slavery restricted morality to those personal areas of moral reform that brought order to the community by self-restraint, self-discipline, and the encouragement of familial and neighborly responsibilities. Christianizing the urban social order in the South meant converting every individual to the basic moral pattern or rural middle-class virtue of private self-control. "In a land with little real poverty, no urban slums or factory towns, minimal cultural conflict with Roman Catholic immigrants, with the Indians removed to the West and the blacks considered childlike beneficiaries of civilization, the white southerner felt that his region of the nation was already closer to millennial perfection than any other part of the country."[25]

This time also the Awakening stirred the West, moving now through the "old West" of Pittsburgh, St. Louis, and Cincinnati and

---

23. Differences exist on exactly when the Second Awakening should be dated in the South. John Boles dates it from 1787 to 1807 in *The Great Revival, 1787–1895* (Lexington: University of Kentucky Press, 1972). Charles Johnson, in his study, *Frontier Camp Meeting* (Dallas: Southern Methodist University Press, 1955), traces it to the camp meetings that began in the 1790s and continued through the nineteenth century.

24. McLoughlin, *Revivals, Awakenings, and Reform*, 131.

25. Ibid., 137.

following the expanding frontier. The colonial image of the wilderness gave way to that of the promised land and to the church as the Israelites who were called to conquer it.

None did it better than the Methodists. Though the growth rate of Methodism lagged far behind New York's population increases after 1820, it exploded through the West. By 1830, instead of one regional conference west of the Alleghenies, there were eight. Membership had grown from 30,000 to more than 175,000. And among these were nearly 2,000 Native Americans and more than 15,000 blacks.[26] By 1844, it was America's largest Protestant community, with 1,068,525 members.

The Church as Conscience of the Emerging City

As the century moved toward its mid-mark, the contrasts of urban life were becoming too great for the church to ignore: opulent town houses and crowded tenements; luxurious wealth and crushing poverty; 10,000 prostitutes said to be in New York by 1824, along with thousands of children, the "ragged outcasts" of the streets of Baltimore and Chicago, St. Louis, Cleveland, and San Francisco.

The Great Awakening had left its deep imprint on the cities; now the Second Great Awakening provided the same initiating spiritual power as the church turned toward the city again. Piety responded with methods both old and new to the church.

Some patterns were more church-oriented than others. The formation of the American Bible Society was one. Tirelessly the society insisted that America's greatest challenges were her unchurched frontier and her cities. Its most active branches were located in the principal cities of the nation, with special attention to the growing immigrant population. The American Tract Society, formed by a coalition of such local societies in 1825, inundated the urban streets with literary missiles aimed for the poor.[27] House-to-house campaigns were launched. Bulk shipments went to poorhouses, prisons, orphanages, and immigration depots. Through the tract, its supporters argued, millions could be reached in the West and in cities who were

---

26. William W. Sweet, *Religion in the Development of American Culture, 1765–1840* (New York: Charles Scribner's Sons, 1952), 119.

27. Malcolm V. Mussina, "The Background and Origin of the American Religious Tract Movement," unpublished Ph.D. dissertation, Drew University, 1936.

"destitute of that influence which is so essential to the preservation of all our social, civil, and religious blessings."[28]

Like the tract movement, the Sunday school also achieved prominence in the early nineteenth century as a response to urban social dislocation. "Vice is pouring into the city like a torrent, the population is wonderfully increasing," said the *American Sunday School Magazine* in 1827, "and the best shield against immorality is the sabbath school institution."[29] Young men, migrating into the cities from America's farms and small towns, were said to need the moral shelter of the Sunday school; it was to be a "co-labourer" with the family in the child's upbringing. Painted against a strong anti-urban backdrop and a growing perception of lower-class life as perverted and degrading, uniform lessons from the American Sunday School Union promoted an apologetic of each person's economic, social, and civic obligations. The message had a class dimension of middle-class behavior, decorum, and restraint.[30]

Throughout the 1820s, in fact, a host of volunteer agencies were set up by evangelicals to respond to the growing list of urban needs. After all, it is not a far step from individualism to voluntarism. "A sample includes: the American Female Moral Reform Society; the Association for the Relief of Respectable Aged, Indigent Females; the Connecticut Society for the Suppression of Vice and the Promotion of Good Morals; the Philadelphia Society for the Encouragement of Faithful Domestics; the Penitent Females Society—and even an American branch of a British society to aid the Ruptured Poor."[31]

By the mid-century, interest and support for the tract and Sunday school movements as reform instruments were fading. But the problems of urban poverty, accelerating immigration, and its impact on "street urchins" were being more narrowly targeted by the churches. Voluntarist energy concentrated now exclusively on the "wicked cities." With it came an increasing sense that the poor in a prosperous urban society were responsible for their own predicament. It would appear as well that the evangelical flavor of the models were becoming less and less apparent.

28. Quoted in Boyer, *Urban Masses and Moral Order*, 25.
29. *American Sunday School Magazine*, January 1827, 11.
30. Boyer, *Urban Masses and Moral Order*, 43–53.
31. Martin E. Marty, *Righteous Empire* (New York: Dial, 1970), 93.

Several new projects underlined the heightened concern and the more liberal, secularized direction. The founding in 1843 of New York's Association for Improving the Condition of the Poor (AICP) was one.

The AICP provided a prototype for similar experiments in Brooklyn, Albany, Boston, Baltimore, and elsewhere. Leadership came from the city's business and professional ranks. And the central aim of such organizations was to "make the poor a party to their own improvement," "not merely to alleviate wretchedness, but to reform character."[32] Echoing the growing impact of environmental heredity themes by men like Unitarian William Ellery Channing, the centers argued the causes of poverty were "chiefly moral." "Physical evils produce moral evils," argued Robert Hartley, founder of the AICP. "Degrade men to the condition of brutes, and they will have brutal propensities and passions."[33]

In the years following the Civil War, the AICP's dynamic faded. But there were other institutions arising with similar concerns. The Children's Aid Society (CAS), founded in New York in 1853, turned away from the adult and focused its attention, as earlier programs had done, on slum children.

CAS founder Charles Brace rejected the enthusiasm of previous decades for children's asylums and houses of refuge.[34] The tough individualism and autonomy of the slum urchin and street wanderer was to be rechanneled. A special feature of the CAS's methodology was the institution of the home visit. Middle-class volunteers, convinced about the value of the home as the nurturer of morality, entered dwellings that were not homes at all.

Motivated by those visits the CAS set up dormitories, reading rooms, and "industrial schools" where skills were taught. Young adolescent boys were to be moved to towns and settlements in the West. Spread over the vast expanding continent, the individualism and shrewd opportunism of the boys would become a major social resource. "Scatter them broadcast over the land," came the message; "give their ambition . . . scope for exercise."[35]

32. Ibid., 90–91.

33. Ibid., 93.

34. Charles L. Brace, *The Best Method of Disposing of Our Pauper and Vagrant Children* (New York: Wynkoop, Hallenbeck and Thomas, 1859).

35. *New York Children's Aid Society, Annual Report* (1860), 86.

By the mid-1890s, the CAS vision had transported some 90,000 boys to the West, started up twenty-one industrial schools, thirteen night schools, and six lodging houses in New York. CAS branches were operating in nine cities from Boston to San Francisco.

The Young Men's Christian Association (YMCA) provided still another new urban model in this same direction. Brought to the United States from its English home in 1851, the organization quickly drew to its side revivalists, Sunday school pioneers, and tract society supporters from earlier decades. Non-Christians' endorsements commended them, fearing "lest the religious culture of this generation" should "leave very few traces on the next."[36] By 1860 over 200 local YMCAs were serving some 25,000 members.

The Y would erect a "wall of iron" between young newcomers to the city and the city's evil underside. As its influence percolated downward to all levels of the city, the whole of urban society would be "purified and lifted up."[37]

The Church Speaks to Large-Scale Urban Issues

Voluntarism, however, was not the only avenue to reform in these days. And poverty was not the only social issue to which the evangelical gave attention in the first half of the nineteenth century. Linked to it in the minds of leaders like Lyman Beecher and Charles Finney was drunkenness; to banish drunkenness was to destroy pauperism. Of all the causes of poverty, commented one reformer in 1834, "there is none more prominently conspicuous than that of alcohol."[38] By 1858, even the *Atlantic Monthly* linked the two problems and joined in commending those churches and ministers battling against "drunkenness and want, ignorance, idleness," and "lust."[39]

By the end of the 1830s, most cities had thriving temperance societies. Not content simply to regulate private behavior, the movement aimed at a larger goal, to reform society through law. "For the evangelical mind, a drunken man was a poor example of citizenship in a Christian commonwealth."[40] But when the leaders of the movement

36. Quoted in Smith, *Revivalism and Social Reform*, 39.
37. Verranus Morse, *An Analytical Sketch of the Young Men's Christian Association in North America from 1851 to 1876* (New York: International Committee of Young Men's Christian Associations, 1901), 61.
38. Quoted in Goldfield and Brownell, *Urban America*, 163.
39. Quoted in Smith, *Revivalism and Social Reform*, 168.
40. Handy, A *Christian America*, 45.

pressed to enact prohibition laws in the 1850s, they were thwarted by urban opposition.

Another evangelical call for reform through law, however, proved more successful, though more divisive at the same time. The anti-slavery crusade that culminated in the Emancipation Proclamation of 1863 was fed by revivalist Christianity, both black and white; Aboli-tionism was, for the Northern evangelical, "spiritual warfare."

On the second day of the nineteenth century, Philadelphia's free black community, led by Absalom Jones and James Forten, fired one of the first full-scale shots in the battle. They submitted a petition to Congress to end the foreign slave trade and "prepare the way for the oppressed to go free." The petition was set aside, finally to be ap-proved in 1808.[41]

By 1816, alarmed whites had responded to black demands by or-ganizing the American Colonization Society (ACS) to promote the settlement of free blacks in Liberia and Sierra Leone. The black com-munity responded in disenchantment, seeing the colonization move-ment as anti-black and pro-slavery. "The Colonizationalists," com-mented one black author bluntly, "want us to go to Liberia if we will. If we won't go there, we may go to hell."[42]

With the strong support of the black evangelical community, an al-ternate path for the slave was routed, not to Africa, but to the "prom-ised land" of Canada and freedom. The Underground Railroad was born, carrying between 40,000 to 100,000 fugitives from city to city station. Among "the company of godly men," both black and white, who risked their lives and well-being in the transfer, were a great many "God-intoxicated" women like Sojourner Truth and Harriet Tubman.

From the beginnings of the struggle, in fact, the emerging black churches of this period played a leading role. The congregations of the AME Zion Church (founded in 1892) were typical. Scattered along the Mason and Dixon line, they were known as stations of the Underground Railroad. Frederick Douglass, the great black spokes-person for abolitionism, commented that "it was from this Zion

41. Julie Winch, *Philadelphia's Black Elite* (Philadelphia: Temple University Press, 1988), 73–74.

42. Lerone Bennett Jr., *Before the Mayflower: A History of the Negro in America, 1619–1954* (Baltimore: Penguin, 1966), 131.

church [of New Bedford] that I went forth to the work of delivering my brethren from bondage."[43]

Evangelical whites joined the cause as well. In 1818, the General Assembly of the Presbyterian Church declared,

> We consider the involuntary enslaving of one part of the human race by another, as a gross violation of the most precious and sacred rights of human nature; as utterly inconsistent with the law of God, which requires us to love our neighbor as ourselves; and as totally irreconcilable with the spirit and principles of the Gospel of Christ, which enjoins that 'all things whatsoever ye would that man should do to you, do ye even so to them.'[44]

Within the Holiness stream of evangelicalism, Charles Finney gave his strong voice to the abolitionist cause. Theodore Dwight Weld, one of Finney's converts, brought the anti-slavery gospel to Cincinnati's Lane Theological Seminary in 1834. When disciplinary measures were exercised against Weld supporters, they migrated to Finney's Oberlin College. And soon the college, at first known as a "bivouac in the wilderness," had become the center of revivalism and abolitionism.

In these early decades of the century, a fragile coalition had been formed uniting Methodist perfectionists, New School revivalism, and Quaker and Unitarian radicalism. The American Anti-Slavery Society was the symbol of this alliance. In 1831, William Lloyd Garrison, a Boston Unitarian and an abolitionist militant, joined forces with the society. His journalistic pen and leadership began to threaten evangelical sensitivities.

Trouble began in 1836 and 1837 when the sisters Grimké, Sarah and Angelina, toured New England as agents of the society. "By their example, if nothing more, they gave encouragement to the infant movement for women's rights, about which proponents of abolition were by no means united. Garrison, with characteristic rashness, determined to force the society to accept women on a basis of equality

43. J. W. Hood, *One Hundred Years of the African Methodist Episcopal Zion Church* (New York: AME Zion Book Concern, 1895), 541–42.

44. *Extracts from the Minutes of the General Assembly, of the Presbyterian Church in the United States of America* (1818), 28–29. Though passed unanimously, the resolution may have been motivated by support for the colonization movement. The following year its intent was modified by the passing of an overture favorable to the colonization society.

with men."[45] He was widening the cause from freedom for the slave to the legal equality of the sexes. Evangelicals protested this expansion of the agenda.

Garrison responded with attacks on "the corruption of the church." The church, he repeated continually, "in spite of every precaution, is first to be dashed to pieces." By 1840, Garrison had seized control of the society and evangelicals were withdrawing, ousted by the anti-evangelical sentiments of its new director.

The white evangelical witness against the country's most public evil began to die away. Disagreements within the church ranks— Presbyterian, Methodist, Baptist—would divide region from region, church from church, damaging support even more. The South even more rapidly closed ranks behind support for slavery as a "positive good." And the evangelicals found themselves somewhere "between the upper and the nether millstones of a *pro-slavery* Christianity, and an *anti-Christian* abolitionism."[46]

Middle-Class Identification with the Church

As the church approached 1870, it had a new shape forged by the experiences of the decade before. Increasingly it had come to identify itself and its goals with the emerging middle class.

Even Finney's revivals, though seeking to "gather in all classes," found their greatest success, not in the laboring classes, but among those higher on the social scale. "Such success as urban Protestantism did enjoy in these years was primarily among the more settled and comfortable ranks; the families of professional men, merchants, clerks, and skilled artisans; the more successful of the native-born newcomers."[47]

The middle class provided the leadership for the many reform movements we have charted. As early as 1818, the *Sunday School Repository* noted that the Sunday school movement was supported mainly by "persons of the middle class of society."[48] Behind the working philosophy of the AICP and the CAS and its commitment to environmental heredity and the need for change in social setting lay

---

45. Smith, *Revivalism and Social Reform*, 182.
46. "The Vital Force of the Age," *The Christian Review* 26 (1861): 566.
47. Boyer, *Urban Masses and Moral Order*, 10–11.
48. *Sunday School Repository*, October 1818, 121.

the assumptions of the middle class: "Change the setting and you change the person."

The strategies employed to deal with the "urban crisis" reflected these same commitments. The world portrayed in the tract movement turned the reader to family and values associated with the village lifestyle. The Sunday school movement reflected middle-class perceptions of lower-class life and offered "the best guarantee . . . of moral safety" from what one supporter called "the poorer and vicious class." The slum family from which the Sunday school reformers turned in fearful hostility was perceived as a social failure and a moral disaster. The society they promoted was to be a stable middle-class structure of authority and predictable routine.

This same philosophy sent middle-class reformers on home visits to the slums on behalf of the CAS. "Infuse the slum home with middle class values and the home will become the nurturer of morality." It divided the poor into "deserving" and "undeserving," a distinction growing in importance at this time.

If Robert Fishman is correct, one more urban phenomenon at this time was to identify the evangelical cause with the middle class. We speak of the beginnings of suburbanization. It was more than the expansion of the railroad, more than urban congestion, that began the movement to the edge of the growing cities. The coming of the railroads during the nineteenth century merely gave wheels to a model borrowed from England and the impact of the Wesleyan revival.

Fishman traces the course of suburbanization to the British evangelicals of the late eighteenth and early nineteenth centuries. Outstanding Christians like William Wilberforce, famed for his opposition to the slave trade, and John Thornton, the patron of the evangelical poet William Cowper, championed both the evangelical cause and suburbia. In the village of Clapham, five miles from London Bridge, they settled and drew others to the circle, soon to be dubbed "the Clapham sect."

Here they concentrated their patrician villas around the open setting of the common. Here, they argued, the evangelical ideals of family life and contact with nature would be upheld. Here would be the balance between the public and the private worlds. Here women and children would be removed from the corrupting influences of the city. Here moral purity could be safeguarded "from the dangers, cruelties, bad language, suffering, and immorality that filled the crowded London streets."[49] From here the men would commute to London, soon to be reduced by the journey into a specialized office district. In Clapham the saints would create something close to their ideal of the family in the garden.

Suburbanization would not be a retreat that excluded the world. "On such issues as slavery and child labor the sect really embodied the compassion and benevolence they preached . . . It was in Thornton's library and Wilberforces's drawing room that the great antislavery crusade was planned; here among the children's play and beautiful gardens the antislavery tracts were written; public meetings were organized; and parliamentary forces were mustered for the bitter battle that resulted in the great 1807 bill that banned the slave trade in the British Empire. For the men, at least, Clapham was one pole of their existence, the other being the hard work of political and business commitments in London."[50]

All these traits were to reappear in the American suburb—evangelical commitments to the family; fear of the corrupting influence of the city; obligations toward the poor; the isolation of the public life from the private. But gradually the evangelical roots of the model were to disappear, the sacred overwhelmed by the secular, the obligations of piety by the rights of the individual, privacy by exclusionism.

49. Robert Fishman, *Bourgeois Utopias* (New York: Basic, 1987), 58.
50. Ibid., 60–61.

3

Urban Growth and Decay
1870–1920

In the 1880s, argues Arthur M. Schlesinger Sr., "urbanization for the first time became a controlling factor in national life."[1] The symbolic act of that new reality was the setting aside of Yellowstone as the country's first national park in 1872. In doing that, the nation's political leaders were admitting the wave of the future would be the city; a precedent was being set for preserving uncultivated, nonurban areas for future generations that, the politicians then were assuming, would be urban.

The decades to come affirmed the validity of that assumption. Between the Civil War and World War I the urban population grew from 6,200,000 to 42,000,000. The nation's population tripled between 1860 and 1920, but its urban population grew by ninefold. In the same period "for every urban dweller who moved to a farm there were 20 farmers who moved to a city."[2] By 1920, a majority (51.4 percent) of Americans lived in urban areas, some of these as small as 2,500 in size.

1. Quoted in Charles N. Glaab, ed., *The American City: A Documentary History* (Homewood, Ill.: Dorsey, 1963), 173.
2. A. B. Callow Jr., ed., *American Urban History* (New York: Oxford University Press, 1969), 43.

The City as Radial Center

The closing decades of the nineteenth century and its urban expansion were not without roots. The rise of the great cities, the segregation of urban space into city centers and residential neighborhoods, the political and social implications of urbanization, must all be linked to the history sketched in the previous chapter.

The Railroad and Urban Transformation

The railroad was a rich part of that history. In fact, most of the national urban network was built during the era of rail transportation. In 1970, there were 153 cities with populations exceeding 100,000; fully 75 percent of them had been established after 1840 and the coming of the railroad as the major means of emerging transportation.

During the second half of the nineteenth century, rail lines transformed even the cowboy image of the "wild West." Laid track expanded from 9,000 to 193,000 miles, linking East to West and West to West.

By 1865, Texas population centers like Houston, Galveston, Austin, and San Antonio had come of urban age. They were major centers of cultural, social, economic, and political influence in the state. "They [residents] read urban newspapers, sought out urban society, borrowed money, traded raw materials and purchased goods from urban merchants."[3]

To the west of Texas, the picture was the same. Following the war in 1846 between Mexico and the United States, Anglos increasingly migrated into the Southwest and joined with Hispanics in the development of Albuquerque and Tucson. In 1867, Phoenix was born. By 1880 promoters of these river communities (including El Paso) were involved in the coming of the railroads: the railroad became the key to their emergence as the four principal cities of the Southwest.[4] California joined the urban explosion. By 1885, it had reached the 50 percent urban point, while the United States as a whole was only about 32 percent urban.[5] Rocky Mountain mining camps and Kansas cattle towns became agents of urban civilization.

---

3. Kenneth W. Wheeler, *To Wear a City's Crown: The Beginnings of Urban Growth in Texas, 1836–1865* (Cambridge and New York: Cambridge University Press, 1968), 165–66.

4. Raymond Mohl, ed., *The Making of Urban America* (Wilmington, Del.: SR Books, 1988), 254.

5. Eric H. Monkkonen, *America Becomes Urban: The Development of U.S. Cities and Towns, 1780–1980* (Berkeley: University of California Press, 1980), 85.

At the same time, in the hub cities of the Northeast and the Midwest, the rail lines, like spokes of a wheel, were helping to expand the urban drive to industrialization and to accelerate the changes in its cities already taking place before the Civil War. Rail connections brought coal and iron to Chicago and Cleveland and carried out steel. Birmingham became one of the few Southern cities that benefited from the same combination of rails, coal, limestone, and iron deposits. Between 1880 and 1910 its population jumped from 3,800 to 130,000.

The Impact of Industrialization

In 1780, John Adams prophesied to Benjamin Franklin, "I say that America will not make manufactures enough for her own consumption these thousand years." The prophecy was off by over nine hundred years. By 1830, manufacturing turned from home-produced products to factories. "If there were only 77 patents in 1800, there would be 1000 in 1850, for invention had to keep pace with the demands of machines."[6] By 1920, Adams's prophecy had been fulfilled; the central city was overwhelmed by industrial and commercial activities.

Initially industry depended on steam power. And since steam power was most cheaply generated in large quantities and had to be used close to where it was produced, it encouraged the concentration of manufacturing in a core area near the central business district, with easy access to the rail lines.

Workers had to live close to the factories; only the wealthy could afford to live in the commuting suburbs and residential neighborhoods. On Chicago's periphery, the workforce for her meat plants lived in what came to be called the "back of the yards."

Everywhere in the Northeast and Midwest, the picture was repeated, even intensified as the century came to a close. "Surrounding the factories, slumlords built jaw-to-jaw tenements on every available open space."[7] In Cincinnati, for example, between 1877 and 1882, the proportion of the working class living in tenements housing three or more families expanded from about one-half to 70 percent.

Home ownership was rare in the city. As late as 1900 in Chicago, Baltimore, Pittsburgh, and Minneapolis, only 25 to 30 percent of all

6. Martin E. Marty, *Righteous Empire* (New York: Dial, 1970), 105.
7. J. John Palen, *The Urban World,* 2d ed. (New York: McGraw-Hill, 1987), 73.

homes were owner-occupied. In New York City, the figure was as low as 12 percent. "The great majority of urban Americans, especially those in the working class, rented living space; they could not afford to do otherwise."[8]

New York's conditions received the most attention. Jacob Riis pioneered in the use of photography to reach the conscience of his readers.[9] He found over 300,000 people per square mile living in New York's tenth ward and vividly painted their picture with his camera; today, any concentration over 75,000 a square mile is considered intolerable. The underside of the city and the negative aspects of slum life were there to see clearly.

In 1900, a Tenement House Exhibition was organized in New York by Lawrence Veiller and underlined the call for reform. Veiller used block models to accomplish what Riis did with his camera. The most celebrated item in the exhibit was a model of 39 tenements within a block measuring 200 feet by 400 feet. Here, Veiller said, was a total of 605 dwelling units, housing 2,781 people, with no baths and only 264 water closets.[10]

The pleas of reformers like Riis and Veiller, however, did little more than create sympathy. "Both the organization of municipal government and an underlying confidence in the unique opportunities for self-advancement within American society greatly restrained proposals to adopt more ambitious levels of public intervention."[11]

With the growing decay of downtown housing came also warning signs from the natural environment of the city. The water around Baltimore in the 1880s, said one observer, smelled "like a billion polecats." The Cuyahoga River in Cleveland was "an open sewer through the center of the city."[12] A visitor to the steel-driving city of Pittsburgh in 1884 commented that "a drab twilight hangs over the town, and the gas-lights which are left burning at mid-day, shine out of the

8. Jon C. Teaford, *The Twentieth-Century American City: Problem, Promise and Reality* (Baltimore: Johns Hopkins University Press, 1986), 23.

9. Jacob A. Riis, *How the Other Half Lives: Studies among the Tenements of New York* (New York: Charles Scribner's Sons, 1890).

10. Robert W. DeForest and Lawrence Veiller, eds., *The Tenement House Problem, Vol. 1* (New York: Macmillan, 1903), 112.

11. David Ward, *Poverty, Ethnicity, and the American City, 1840–1925* (Cambridge and New York: Cambridge University Press, 1989), 75.

12. Quoted in John A. Garraty, *The New Commonwealth, 1877–1890* (New York: Harper and Row, 1968), 192.

murkiness with a dull, reddish glare." The sun, when you could see it, appeared "coppery through the sooty haze."[13]

The "New Outsider" in the Industrial City

With the growth of industrialization came the demand for workers. Advances in technology minimized the need for craft and skill. And doors opened wider for ethnic immigrants. From 1870 to 1920, 26,277,565 entered the country, a little less than four times the number from the previous fifty years.[14]

But a new kind of immigrant responded to the call. Economic advance, not primarily religious freedom, pulled them. And this time they came, not so much from Northern Europe and the Anglo-Saxon community, but from the less developed countries of Eastern and Southern Europe. Cities found themselves speaking Italian, Yiddish, Polish. By 1890, New York City had more foreign-born residents than any city in the world. It had half as many Italians as Naples, as many Germans as Hamburg, two and a half times the number of Jews in Warsaw.

There were marked religious differences between the earlier immigrants and the new wave. Except for the Irish, the "old" immigration was about equally divided between Roman Catholics and Protestants. The new arrivals were largely Roman Catholics, Jews, and members of various Eastern churches. In the four decades preceding 1920, one-third of all the Jews in Eastern Europe had moved to the United States.

In overwhelming figures, these immigrants settled in the cities, and predominantly in the cities of the Northeast and the Midwest. By 1920, the city was home to three-fourths of the foreign born. Chicago had seventeen separate neighborhoods that could be called "Little Italy."

Anglo-Saxon reactions to the new immigrants were swift and in keeping with the urban past. The half century after 1880 witnessed what one author has called "another tidal wave of intolerance and racist venom."[15] Nativism, antipopery, and anti-Semitism took

13. Quoted in Glaab, ed., *The American City*, 236–37.
14. Sydney Ahlstrom, *A Religious History of the American People* (New Haven: Yale University Press, 1972), 749.
15. Ibid., 852.

Figure 3
Percentage of Foreign-Born Population in Selected Cities, 1900 and 1920

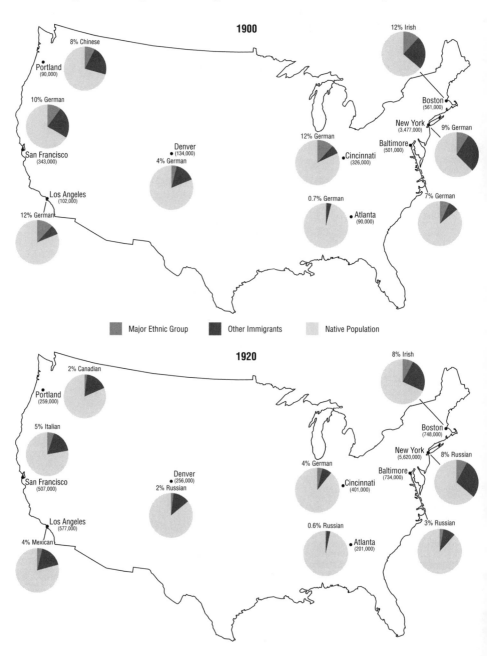

From Eric H. Monkkonen, *America Becomes Urban: The Development of U.S. Cities and Towns, 1780–1980.* Copyright © 1988 The Regents of the University of California. Reprinted by permission.

their place again in American life. "Rum, Romanism, and rebellion" became more than a political antislogan; it pointed its finger at the new immigrants. Even the lines of Emma Lazarus, affixed to the base of the Statue of Liberty (dedicated in 1886), may have given a mixed message. The invitation to the poor, the tired, "the huddled masses yearning to breathe free," added what some have seen also as a condescending reference to "the wretched refuse of your teeming shore."

Meanwhile, similar attitudes were showing up towards "nonwhite" immigrants. In the West particularly, anti-Chinese sentiments grew and Congress passed the Chinese Exclusion Act of 1882. Further immigration from China was effectively blocked by continuing renewal of the legislation until 1943. Large numbers of Chinese returned to their homelands and, by the turn of the century, their number had dwindled from a high of 107,000 to fewer than 90,000.

In the Southwest there were similar conflicts and fears over the growing number of Mexicans crossing the border. From 1921 to 1930, almost one-half million had entered as legal immigrants. But, in this case, the need for unskilled labor won out over vigorous opposition. And when Congress enacted an immigration quota system in 1921, Mexico was excluded from its restrictions. Not until 1965 did it come under the quota limitations.

By the close of the century, Southern blacks were beginning their move north, pushed by bigotry and poverty into the slums that would increasingly be called ghettos. By 1900 there were thirty-two cities with more than 10,000 blacks. In 1910, Washington, D.C. had the largest black community of any city in the country. New York was close behind. "Teeming, decaying residential districts became the womb of black urban culture."[16]

With more intensity than in the past, exclusivism increasingly linked the city's woes to the new immigrants. The sins of the new immigrants were tied to the sins of the city and its festering downtowns. Slum housing, poor health conditions, and high crime rates were all blamed on the newcomers.[17] Even reformers like Josiah Strong, speaking out of the Christian tradition, were proclaiming that "the

16. Howard P. Chudacoff, *The Evolution of American Urban Society,* 2d ed. (Englewood Cliffs, N.J.: Prentice-Hall, 1981), 111.

17. For a sample of these judgments, consult Samuel L. Loomis, *Modern Cities and Their Religious Problems* (New York: Baker and Taylor, 1887), 86, 91–92, 99.

first city was built by the first murderer, and crime and vice and wretchedness have festered in it ever since."[18]

These problems were not without their vocal opponents at this time. The first two decades of the twentieth century have often been labeled the Progressive Era for that reason. It was "an age of enthusiasm for reform as many Americans sought to right the wrongs of a newly industrialized society. Nowhere was this flowering of reform so evident as in the large cities."[19]

One of the most idealistic and most influential of the reform models was the settlement house. Community centers in the slums, they also provided living accommodations for middle-class volunteers. Behind the arrangement, as the constitution of the New York City's University Settlement put it, was the desire "to bring men and women of education into closer relations with the working classes for their mutual benefit." Hull House, the Chicago creation of Jane Addams, was one of the best known of the settlement houses.[20] By 1900 there were more than one hundred of the centers across the country; by 1910 there were over four hundred.

Reformers pressed in other areas—upgrading bad housing, fighting for stricter housing codes, constructing model tenements, campaigning against the vice districts of the downtown areas and against corrupt city officials.

But while individual enterprise fought for a middle-class remodeling of the city, the middle-class community was being reshaped and voting against the city in another way.

Streetcar Suburbs and the Middle Class

The electric street trolley, not the ballot box, carried the middle-class votes. From its experimental operation on the streets of Richmond, Virginia, in 1888 to its adoption in the 1890s and its triumph in the 1920s, it began to reshape the city.

By 1900, only 2 percent of the nation's cities had not converted their horse railway lines to electricity. By then every major street in inner Philadelphia carried an electric streetcar line. In 1908, the sub-

18. Kenneth Jackson, *Crabgrass Frontier* (New York: Oxford University Press, 1985), 70.

19. Teaford, *The Twentieth-Century American City*, 30.

20. Jane Addams, "Hull House, Chicago: An Effort toward Social Democracy," *The Forum* 14 (October 1892): 226–41.

way was added to the Quaker City's mass transit system.[21] By 1902, New York City had almost four hundred miles of streetcar track and was transporting more than 400 million passengers annually. Chicago had over seven hundred miles of track and almost 300 million passengers in the year. The residential neighborhoods, hitherto open only to the elite, now were in economic reach of middle-class whites. Now the middle class could participate in the process of urban decentralization begun decades before.

From the window of the street trolley car, they saw the city divided, "the creation of a two-part city, an old inner city and a new outer city, a city of slums and a city of suburbs, a city of hope and failure and a city of achievement and comfort—this remains the central event of the 1870–1900 era."[22]

Real-estate speculators were quick to see the possibilities also. In the suburbs of Roxbury, West Roxbury, and Dorchester, immediately surrounding Boston, over 23,000 new houses were built between 1879 and 1890. In 1850 Boston was a tightly packed seaport; by 1900 the trolley car had stretched its borders over a ten-mile radius enveloping thirty-one cities and towns. Between 1900 and 1915 the population of Manhattan in New York City increased less than 16 percent; in the suburban borough of Queens it soared 160 percent. Downtown businesspeople were excited by the possibilities. In the early 1900s, Rich's Department Store in Atlanta boasted that no fewer than five trolley lines terminated near its doors.

The streetcar provided wheels to the suburbs for the fears of the city as a hotbed of moral dangers. And the writings of men like Josiah Strong and Samuel Loomis reinforced the concern. The city had become a "serious menace," "social dynamite" in the form of "roughs, gamblers, thieves, robbers, lawless and desperate men of all sorts." "Skepticism and irreligion" abounded, came the message.[23]

Out of all these concerns came the growing identification of the middle class with the streetcar suburbs. The streetcar became the transportation system of the middle class. As late as 1900 and the five-cent fare for a ride, streetcar transportation was still too expensive for

21. Sam Bass Warner Jr., *The Private City* (Philadelphia: University of Pennsylvania Press, 1968), 191–92.

22. Sam Bass Warner Jr., *Streetcar Suburbs*, 2d ed. (Cambridge: Harvard University Press, 1978), vi–vii.

23. Josiah Strong, *Our Country* (1891), quoted in Andrew Lees, *Cities Perceived* (New York: Columbia University Press, 1985), 166.

even a highly-paid skilled workman with a large family. And for the lowly-paid laborer or sweatshop worker it was virtually impossible.

But for the emerging middle class, the fare bought a ticket to paradise. Like the working class and unlike the very wealthy, they enjoyed no independent means. They had to go to work. But unlike the working class, they held white-collar positions. They were doctors, lawyers, smaller merchants, and modest manufacturers. They had sufficient income to purchase their homes convenient to transit lines.

In the suburbs they found a safe environment, new houses that fit their new perceptions of a family life isolated from the work place, neighbors sharing a similar perception of lifestyle. Well-kept lawns, neat streets, freshly painted houses, new schools and parks, communities with names like "Heights," "Woods," and "Gardens" all spoke of safety and new beginnings.

The earlier suburbanization of the elite had begun the process of urban fragmentization, leaving the city in the hands of professional politicians and city government in the hands of second- and third-string echelons. Beyond the municipal borders of the city, the elite lost their interest in the urban quality of life.[24]

With the beginnings of the suburban move of the middle class, that fragmentation was accelerated. And at a special point in American history. Suburban decentralization, promoted by individualism's desire for something better, began to mark urbanization at the very time where census reports indicated that the majority of the population were now living in cities. Urban concentration and suburban decentralization in 1920 had found centrifugal and centripetal forces merging into one point in time.

24. James F. Richardson, "The Evolving Dynamics of America's Urban Development," in *Cities in the 21st Century*, ed. Gary Gappert and Richard Knight (Beverly Hills: Sage, 1982), 41–42.

4

The Evangelical in the Radial Center
1870–1920

The years surrounding and immediately following the Civil War were the prime years of the evangelical empire. Protestant church growth from that point was to continue its accelerated climb—from 4.5 million in 1860 to 12.5 million in 1890. And a key part of that growth was in the emerging city.

As we have said, this was the time when the city became the center of American expansion.

Between 1860 and 1900, the United States experienced explosive urbanization. Cities grew at a phenomenal rate. During these four decades, for example, Detroit and Kansas City increased fourfold, Memphis and San Francisco fivefold, and Cleveland sixfold. Los Angeles grew twentyfold during the same period, while Minneapolis and Omaha each increased fiftyfold and more. Even already established urban centers such as New York, Baltimore, and Philadelphia more than doubled in size. Chicago, incorporated in 1837 as a frontier outpost with seventeen houses, was the fifth largest city in the world by the turn of the century, with a population of nearly 1.7 million.[1]

During this time there began to appear on the main streets of cities churches with names like First Baptist, First Presbyterian, First

1. Timothy P. Weber, *Living in the Shadow of the Second Coming: American Premillennialism, 1875–1920* (Grand Rapids: Zondervan, 1983), 52.

Methodist. Historically they became the center of power and life in a community, guardians of the values and morals of a nation. Their pastors spoke for a nation—Henry Ward Beecher (1815–1887) in Brooklyn, Phillips Brooks (1835–1893) in Boston.

A hundred years later, these same congregations would become "Old First" churches. By 1970 they usually would symbolize a different place for the church in the city. Rewarded in the intervening years through bequests and wills, many remain open today because of these endowments and trusts. Their once thriving membership is gone, disappeared with the American dream into the suburbs. "The few worshipers who do return on Sunday out of a sense of loyalty must now pass sullen neighbors who, despite living in close proximity to the church, do not feel that it is 'their' church."[2] This chapter and the next will tell the story of this change.

Dwight L. Moody and the Changing City

The great urban revival campaigns of Dwight L. Moody and Ira Sankey that reached their peak in 1885 provide us with a clue to this massive change in the relation of the church to the city.

Moody had begun with enthusiasm over the church's role in the city. "Waters run downhill," he cried, "and the highest hills in America are the great cities. If we can stir them we shall stir the whole country." But by the 1870s, his strategy and his tone had changed. His campaigns were avoiding the largest cities, confined to the smaller interior cities (still predominantly American-born and Protestant). Increasingly he was concentrating his attention on the Bible schools he had founded in Chicago and Northfield, Massachusetts.

"'We cannot get the people we are after,' he lamented, when urged to resume urban revivalism. 'The city is no place for me,' he wrote his family in 1896 on a rare visit to New York. 'If it was not for the work I am called to do, I would never show my head in this city or any other again.'"[3] "I look upon this world," he had announced in 1880, "as a wrecked vessel. God has given me a lifeboat and said to me, 'Moody, save all you can.'"[4]

2. Raymond Bakke and Samuel Roberts, *The Expanded Mission of "Old First" Churches* (Valley Forge: Judson, 1986), 14–15.

3. Paul Boyer, *Urban Masses and Moral Order in America, 1820–1920* (Cambridge: Harvard University Press, 1978), 136.

4. Dwight L. Moody, *New Sermons* (New York: Henry S. Goodspeed, 1880), 535.

Moody's revivals were not reaching the poor in the cities. "His audiences were essentially middle-class, rural-born native Americans who had come to the city to make their fortunes; they believed that he spoke God's truth in extolling hard work and free enterprise. But he was not a spokesman for those who were becoming discouraged or disillusioned with the success myth; nor did he reach the foreign-born or Catholic poor who made up so large a proportion of the labor class. His revivals represented an effort to reassure the middle class (or those rising into it) that urban industrial problems were minimal and temporary."[5]

In the decades ahead, the same patterns and attitudes reflected in the Moody campaigns would be seen more clearly in the halls of "Old First" churches. Like Moody, they were linked, perhaps too closely, to the powerful and wealthy in the city. When the powerful began to move to the suburbs in the last half of the nineteenth century, "Old First" churches began their slow decline. Like Moody, their identification with the middle class was another blow as the suburbs opened to receive this class as well. The evangelical ambivalence about cities that Moody reflected hurt more and more as the new century dawned and the anti-urban theme grew stronger.

Anti-urbanism even took theological reshaping within the evangelical camp during these fifty years. Dispensationalist Bible teachers like A. J. Frost would join Moody and warn that cities were "becoming plague-spots of moral and political leprosy, the hotbeds of lawlessness and crime . . . "[6] In the face of the city as threat, the earlier optimism of the Puritan legacy of postmillennialism was fading and dispensational premillennialism was ascending.

This theological change had its positive side. As Timothy Weber indicates, dispensationalism's individualistic, moralistic, and short-term view of social reform played a creative role in the city. Urban revivalism linked side by side the evangelical welfare movement and the new premillennialism in the last half of the nineteenth century.[7]

At the same time, it also may have played a part in breaking the spirit of urban change. "Its hopeless view of the present order left lit-

5. William G. McLoughlin, *Revivals, Awakenings, and Reform* (Chicago: University of Chicago Press, 1978), 144–45.

6. Quoted in George M. Marsden, *Fundamentalism and American Culture* (New York: Oxford University Press, 1980), 66.

7. Weber, *Living in the Shadow of the Second Coming*, 52.

tle room for God or for themselves to work in it. The world and the present age belonged to Satan, and lasting reform was impossible until Jesus returned to destroy Satan's power and set up the perfect kingdom. As Martin Marty has said, premillennialists often gave up on the world before God does."[8] And, we quickly add, they defined that world as the city.

Older Ministry Patterns Continued

Many of the urban ministry patterns displayed by the evangelical church in this period were not new. They continued the models of voluntarism begun in the earlier nineteenth century. Revivals, sometimes coupled with the perfectionist aspirations of the Holiness theological tradition, sometimes with "New Light" from the Presbyterians, continued to infuse a compassion for poor and needy sinners that was the "drive shaft of social reform" in the cities. Augmenting it now was the theme of the immanent appearing of Christ provided by the growing impact of premillennialism.

Coupled with the unique optimism of America's cultural "can do" mentality,[9] evangelical organizations continued to appear—rescue missions; "shelter" homes for children and women; cheap "hotels" for the impoverished; a continuing crusade against alcohol, "the cup of fury."

Springing up everywhere were model ministries, copied repeatedly. The Five Points Mission, begun in New York in 1850, set up a working women's home in addition to seven buildings for welfare work. New York's Howard Mission for Little Wanderers, founded in 1861, erected model tenements and a children's hospital. The Water Street Mission opened in 1872, the outcome of an anti-prostitution campaign; under the leadership of Jerry McAuley it set a pattern for "rescue ministries" repeated across the country.[10] By the 1920s, nearly 3,000 city missions from coast to coast were following its lead.

Other institutions also came into being in this period, seeking to combine social awareness with an evangelical commitment to Bible-

8. Ibid., 234.

9. William A. Dyrness, *How Does America Hear the Gospel?* (Grand Rapids: Eerdmans, 1989), 70.

10. Aaron I. Abell, *The Urban Impact on American Protestantism, 1865–1900* (Hamden, Conn.: Archon, 1962), 35–36.

based theology and strict moralism. One of the most powerful was the Salvation Army, founded in England by Methodist minister William Booth. It crossed the Atlantic in 1880 and by 1900 the Army had seven hundred corps (congregations) in cities throughout the United States, staffed by 3,000 officers.

With a single-minded focus on the urban masses, the Army incorporated earlier urban strategies into its program. Its street meetings and soup kitchens were supplemented with day nurseries, a junior corps for children, homes for prostitutes, secondhand stores providing employment and provisions for the destitute, maternity hospitals (fourteen by 1920 in the Eastern United States). "Slum brigades" carried the message of the gospel and its healing for the city into tenements, saloons, brothels, and dance halls.

In a time when very few people saw the poor as "worthy," the Army symbolized one of those major strengths among evangelicals in the welfare movement; "no matter how troublesome the person they helped—former prisoners, prostitutes, unwed mothers, vagrants, or the unemployed—revivalists accepted them with openness and warmth."[11] The Army lived one of its well-known mottos, "Go for souls, and go for the worst."

Promoting this same fervor for evangelism and welfare work was the journal, the *Christian Herald*, begun in 1878. By 1910, it had a circulation of about a quarter of a million, making it one of the largest religious magazines in the world. And beyond its promotional work for the evangelical welfare movement, it provided direct financial support for such undertakings. Besides channeling its funds largely into non-Western lands, it provided a "Food Fund" for city missionaries in the winter of 1894 and staffed a summer home for tenement children begun that same year. A year later it assumed control of New York's Bowery Mission, supporting other similar programs as well.[12]

The Larger Urban Challenges

As the nation moved past the 1880s, however, it was apparent that the urban situation was calling for more response than simply that of

---

11. Norris Magnuson, *Salvation in the Slums: Evangelical Social Work, 1865–1920* (Grand Rapids: Baker, 1990 repr.), xvii.
12. Ibid., 25–29.

individual or group charity. Two problems especially appeared to demand more than voluntarism could solve alone.

Immigration was one. In the single decade of the 1880s immigration brought over five million newcomers. And few were Protestant or Anglo-Saxon. The *New York Tribune* spoke of them grimly as "masses of ignorant foreigners congregated in many cities," "magazines of explosives" waiting to be lit by the match of radicalism.

Poles, Italians, Russians, most of them Jews or Catholics, poured into the industrialized areas. "Although only one-third of all Americans lived in cities in 1890, two-thirds of all immigrants did. By 1910 about 80 percent of all new arrivals at Ellis Island were remaining in cities, as were 72 percent of all of those 'foreign born.'"[13] By the turn of the century, the immigrant vote was electing mayors for New York, Chicago, and Boston and increasing the attractiveness of the suburbs for the middle-class evangelical.

The second problem came with the growth of industry and the widening social and economic gap between owner and worker; in the words of one merchant, American capitalists were as independent of workingmen "as the imported slaves made Roman patricians independent of Roman laborers."[14] Working-class discontent created strike after strike in the 1880s as armed encounters hit Chicago, Cincinnati, Milwaukee, New York, and St. Louis. The 1890s brought no relief. The nation, declared Attorney General Richard Olney, was "at the ragged edge of anarchy."

The evangelical welfare movement was not silent in the face of these needs. Nor did it call only for charity. "We must have justice— more justice," cried Ballington Booth, commander of the American Salvation Army. "To right the social wrong by charity," he argued, "is like bailing the ocean with a thimble . . . We must readjust our social machinery so that the producers of wealth become also owners of wealth."[15]

The *Christian Herald* underlined the call for justice. During the 1886 railroad strike in New York, it defended the strikers by affirming that "they have been oppressed and cheated out of their earnings."[16]

13. Kenneth Jackson, *Crabgrass Frontier* (New York: Oxford University Press, 1985), 70.

14. Francis B. Thurber, "Lay Criticism on the Ministry and Methods of Church Work," *Homiletic Review* 8 (April 1884): 412.

15. Quoted in Donald W. Dayton, *Rediscovering an Evangelical Heritage* (New York: Harper and Row, 1976), 118.

16. *Christian Herald* 9 (29 April 1886): 17.

Over the years its editor argued for better pay and working conditions for miners, denounced the seven-day work week in the steel industry, endorsed regulation of the trusts. The Army's periodical, *The War Cry*, supported President Woodrow Wilson's call for the humanizing of industry through legislation that would reduce work hours, provide the right to organize unions, and offer protection against industrial accidents.

Accompanying these words were deeds flowing out of the models from the welfare movement's history. Rescue institutions provided temporary work for the unemployed—Salvation Army "woodyards" in Boston, Houston, San Francisco, and Seattle; a Bowery Mission-run three-hundred-acre farm outside of New York intended as a training school for prospective farmers; employment bureaus to obtain positions outside of rescue institutions. By mid–1899, Frederick Booth-Tucker, son-in-law to William Booth, had inaugurated three farm colonies to encourage migration back toward the land, the project slogan being "the landless man to the manless land."

But for all these noble sentiments and innovative twists, the evangelical welfare movement was still offering the old pre-industrial forms of ministry. Voluntarism was no match for the growing size of industrial problems. And lurking behind the farm colonies and the training school for prospective farmers remained a rural romanticism that still could not come to grips with the cities as anything other than "tainted spots in the body-politic."

Growing Urban Frustrations

Outside the evangelical welfare movement the church's commitment to an expanding urban society was even dimmer. Anglo-Saxon immigration movements in an earlier day had prompted compassionate ministries and church planting efforts; these efforts were renewed again toward groups of German and Scandinavian arrivals at the end of the century.[17] And in the West missionary efforts had been initiated toward the Chinese and were bearing some fruit. By 1892, eleven denominations had planted ten Chinese churches and 271 Sunday schools and missions.[18]

17. Sydney Ahlstrom, *A Religious History of the American People* (New Haven: Yale University Press, 1972), 749–62.
18. Horace Cayton and Anne Lively, *The Chinese in the United States and the Chinese Christian Church* (New York: National Council of the Churches of Christ in the U.S.A., 1955), 40.

But towards the southern Europeans a different spirit arose. Fear grew that the "new immigrants" would threaten traditional American values. Didn't the immigrants, after all, congregate in city slums? Didn't they refuse to keep the sabbath? Didn't they prefer to send their children to parochial schools? How could society escape their corrupting influence? Nativism and racism closed formerly open doors.

Industrialization was also reinforcing the Protestant church's identification with the Anglo-Saxon middle class. And no matter what the theological boundary, the church crossed it to the suburbs to affirm that identification. The alienation between the working class and traditional Christianity was growing.

"During the eighties several clergymen carefully investigated the religious habits of the various occupational groups, invariably finding that wage-earners attended Protestant services in much smaller proportions than other classes."[19] An 1888 survey in Pittsburgh and Allegheny reached the same conclusion; business, professional, and salaried men who formed less than 10 percent of the population made up over 60 percent of the male membership in Protestant churches.[20]

Samuel Gompers of the American Federation of Labor underlined that perception on behalf of trade union leaders: "My associates have come to look upon the church and the ministry as the apologists and defenders of the wrongs committed against the interests of the people simply because the perpetrators are possessors of wealth." Methods found by labor to be successful, he argued, "have been generally frowned down upon with contempt, treated indifferently or openly antagonized by the ministers and the apparently staunch supporters of the church."[21]

In 1885 a book appeared to sum up the growing frustration and fears both evangelical and otherwise. *Our Country: Its Possible Future and Its Present Crisis*, was written by Josiah Strong (1847–1916). Second only to *Uncle Tom's Cabin* in popularity during the century, it was penned by a leading figure in what came to be called the Social Gospel movement.

19. Abell, *The Urban Impact on American Protestantism*, 61.

20. Alexander Jackson, "The Relation of the Classes to the Church," *Independent*, 1 March 1888, 258–59.

21. Samuel Gompers, "The Church and Labor," *American Federationist* 2 (August 1896): 119–20.

Listing the perils that threatened the manifest destiny of American Anglo-Saxon culture, Strong dwelt on the cities and the "new immigrants." In the urban storm center lurked every serious threat to American life, "multiplying and focalizing the elements of anarchy and destruction." Protestant church life in the city was decaying, he asserted. Boston, the original Puritan city, could claim only one for 1,778 people, Chicago only one for every 3,601 citizens.

Where would it end? Soon, he replied, when "our Cincinnatis have become Chicagos, our Chicagos New York, and our New Yorks London," when the "igorant and vicious power" of urban Americans had "fully found itself," then would "the volcanic fires of deep discontent" explode with terrible force.[22]

The Social Gospel Movement

During this troubled period, a new urban response was making its appearance among Protestants. Dubbed "Social Christianity" in some circles, "the Social Gospel" in others, it traced its roots to many sources. In its earliest stages, its leaders (like Josiah Strong) made common cause with evangelical concerns.[23] But differences were to grow as the church moved into the twentieth century.

Fed by the evangelical reform spirit vital to the millennial expectations of earlier decades, the Social Gospel underlined the here-and-now realization of the kingdom of God. Heir to the American dream that a new world was about to dawn, it optimistically affirmed that any "social crisis" could be overcome by "faith enough to believe that all human life can be filled with divine purpose."[24] And into this mix it added increasingly the antisupernatural skepticism of the "New Theology" emanating from Ritschl and Schleiermacher in Germany. Sociology and a theology stressing the immanence of God were merged in the watchwords of the movement: "the Fatherhood of God and the brotherhood of man."[25]

22. Josiah Strong, *Our Country: Its Possible Future and Its Present Crisis* (Cambridge: Harvard University Press, 1963 reprint of 1885 ed.), 177, 182, 186.

23. Ronald White Jr. and C. Howard Hopkins, *The Social Gospel: Religion and Reform in Changing America* (Philadelphia: Temple University Press, 1976), 5–13.

24. Walter Rauschenbusch, *Christianity and the Social Crisis* (New York: Macmillan, 1907), 355.

25. Susan Curtis, *A Consuming Faith: The Social Gospel and Modern American Culture* (Baltimore: Johns Hopkins University Press, 1991), 5–6.

The place where the mix took place was the city. And here too the movement's spokespeople spoke with the same fears that haunted evangelical sentiment. Washington Gladden (1836–1918), called the father of the Social Gospel, wrote thirty-six books out of the pain of a seven-year pastorate in industrial Springfield, Massachusetts, and thirty-two years in Columbus, Ohio. Walter Rauschenbusch (1861–1918) carried to his teaching responsibilities at Rochester Theological Seminary a theology shaped in a pastorate in the "Hell's Kitchen" district of New York from 1886 to 1897. This place, he concluded, "is not a safe place for saved souls."[26]

Not content with what it perceived as a growing evangelical emphasis on the more private outlook of Christianity, the Social Gospel movement swung strongly in the other direction, toward the public, the political. Increasingly, early collaboration with the evangelical was left behind and the only test of truth was said to be action in the public square of the city. What can we say about the validity of truth? Nothing, replied the pragmatist movement, until we see what they do.

Supporting the Social Gospel was the institutional church movement.[27] While many urban churches followed their members to the suburbs, these congregations and missions stayed behind, expanding their ministries to offer a variety of what looked like "secular" activities and programs. St. George's Episcopal Church in New York, under the leadership of its rector, William S. Rainsford, and with the financial backing of J. Pierpont Morgan, modeled the new approach. Its parish house, created to foster the new direction, became the center for a boys' club, recreational facilities, and an industrial training program.[28]

Others were to follow in the North—Judson Memorial Church and Madison Avenue Presbyterian Church in New York; Grace Church in Philadelphia under the leadership of its pastor, Russell Conwell; Wesley Chapel of Cincinnati. By 1894 the Institutional Church League had been formed to multiply the model. And by the turn of the century there was said to be at least 173 congregations committed to urban philanthropy and Christianizing society.

26. Quoted in Ronald C. White Jr., *Liberty and Justice for All: Racial Reform and the Social Gospel (1877–1925)* (San Francisco: Harper and Row, 1990), xviii.
27. Curtis, *A Consuming Faith*, 72–74, 258–62.
28. Abell, *The Urban Impact on American Protestantism*, 147–50.

Even in the South, still overwhelmingly rural, concern over urban problems was growing. "Most Methodists and Baptists at the turn of the century feared the city and believe it corrupted morals and loosened family ties. One Baptist leader captured the spirit of most Evangelicals when he wrote: 'Men, like hogs, are bred in the country to be consumed in the towns.'"[29]

Here too, the Social Gospel and the institutional church movement arose to respond to those fears. In Birmingham, the Independent Presbyterian Church helped organize the Jefferson County Children's Aid Society, hired a female staff member to assist the jobless, a nurse to aid the poor, and a social worker for the Northside Community House. Women in the Methodist Episcopal Church, South, began a settlement-house ministry in 1893. By 1920, there were at least forty-four such houses serving whites and blacks in the urban South. Their activities included day schools where working women could leave children, night literacy programs for working boys, and free medical dispensaries.

Strong summarized well the philosophy of ministry of these institutional churches in *The Challenge of the City*:

> Inasmuch as Christ came not to be ministered unto but to minister, the open and institutional church, filled and moved by his spirit of ministering love, seeks to become the center and source of all beneficent and philanthropic effort, and to take the leading part in every movement which has for its end the alleviation of human suffering, the elevation of man, and the betterment of the world.[30]

The "new immigrants," virtually forgotten communities for the evangelicals, were not always so for these churches. New York's Lodging House Missionary Society, an institutional church spinoff, organized churches for Germans, Italians, and Jews. Its Italian congregation soon became the largest of its kind in the world. Generally the majority of the Jewish community welcomed only the philan-

29. Wayne Flynt, "One in the Spirit, Many in the Flesh: Southern Evangelicals," in *Varieties of Southern Evangelicalism*, ed. David E. Harrell Jr. (Macon, Ga.: Mercer University Press, 1981), 39–40.

30. Quoted in Howard P. Chudacoff, *The Evolution of American Urban Society*, 2d ed. (Englewood Cliffs, N.J.: Prentice-Hall, 1975), 179; see also Dorothea R. Muller, "The Social Philosophy of Josiah Strong: Social Christianity and American Progressivism," *Church History* 28 (1959): 183–201.

thropic work of the society. But, for those Jews who had professed the Christian faith, the society erected a home in 1891 to support those converts experiencing difficulty from Gentiles in areas of employment and social interaction. St. Bartholomew's Church, a fashionable church in central Manhattan, "specialized in caring for Oriental peoples, being equipped for ministration in three languages: Armenian, Syriac and Turkish."[31] Converts formed similar churches in other cities and the example was followed in other denominations.

The Emerging "New" Evangelicalism

By the end of the century the institutional church movement was reaching its peak. Only about 15 percent of the churches of New York City were engaged in community programs. And in other cities the percentage was still lower. The enthusiasm for the Social Gospel was to peak in the first and second decades of the new century.

In the meantime, white evangelical thinking in the North was turning against the movement, its horizontalism, and more. And in the process, the evangelical church itself was being transformed. The increasing migration of the church to the suburbs, rapidly transforming the cities into a "radial center," was pushed along its way by what the evangelical saw as a Social Gospel capitulation to reform, not regeneration.

Before them was the spectacle of a church they saw as overcome by the needs of the city, compromised by an urban setting that spelled chaos and despair. Where should the evangelicals put their time? Saving souls or trying to salvage a social order they saw crumbling in the cities?

"For much of the nineteenth century most evangelical Protestants had never felt compelled to choose between those two enterprises. They had seen them as complementary parts of the Christian gospel."[32] But now their past fears of the city rose again, this time encouraged by the institutional church's failure to keep its balance.

Evangelical thought in the South had yet to pass through this stage of urban phobia. As late as 1916, 82 percent of the total 44,300 white Baptist and Methodist churches located there were rural. And, in turn, 80 percent of these were served by absentee pastors.

31. Abell, *The Urban Impact on American Protestantism*, 151.
32. Weber, *Living in the Shadow of the Second Coming*, 86.

Figure 4
Total Number of Cities over 2,500 Population (1790–1980)

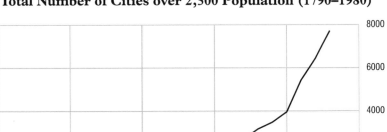

From Eric H. Monkkonen, *America Becomes Urban: the Development of U.S. Cities and Towns, 1780–1980*. Copyright © 1988 The Regents of the University of California. Reprinted by permission.

But, even without the urban backdrop, Southern evangelicalism fit rather well alongside the new drive for modifications from the North. Mainstream Southern evangelicals "were individualistic and felt more comfortable with a religion that consoled the heart than with one that troubled the mind." Their faith, like that emerging in the North, functioned "to help them understand the world they lived in, to comfort them in times of trouble, to provide a sense of personal worth."[33]

North and South, the stage was set for change. The evangelical church moved to survive by forming a subculture that would protect itself against the perceived monstrous power of the city and its secularizing effect on the church. A new worldview took shape that provided an alternative to the dominant urban ethos. The hymnody of revivalism reflected it in imagery that contrasted faith drawn in rural hues to the turmoil and strife painted in terms of the city.[34] And the preacher who symbolized it was Billy Sunday (1862–1935).

In a revival career that crossed over the "urban year" of 1920, Sunday in many ways remained rooted, as did the evangelical cause, in rural America. The farmers transplanted to the city were the people

33. Flynt, "One in the Spirit, Many in the Flesh: Southern Evangelicalism," 44.
34. Sandra S. Sizer, *Gospel Hymns and Social Religion* (Philadelphia: Temple University Press, 1978), 122–23, 127.

Figure 5
Total Number of Cities over 100,000 Population (1790–1980)

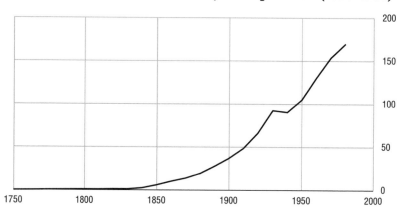

From Eric H. Monkkonen, *America Becomes Urban: the Development of U.S. Cities and Towns, 1780–1980*. Copyright © 1988 The Regents of the University of California. Reprinted by permission.

that Sunday targeted. His crude language and homely sermons were delivered with the vocabulary of the simple theological affirmations of millions of rural migrants.[35]

But if his strength was the old rural America, his failure, like that of the evangelicalism he exemplified, was his inability to be attuned to the growing pluralism of the American city. Though supportive of, and supported by, the black community, he "did not appeal to the immigrant masses, especially those from southern and eastern Europe who comprised the bulk of the immigrants in the 1890s and early twentieth century. Many of them were Roman Catholic or Jewish, with little understanding or sympathy for Sunday's call to return to the oldtime religion of Protestant America."[36]

It was especially in Sunday's message that the "new" evangelicalism began to show itself. He occasionally echoed the revivalists of the earlier nineteenth century when he spoke for women's rights and promoted child labor legislation. His support of prohibition also reflected earlier themes. But his definition of the righteous life had a strongly individualistic tint to it.

35. Lyle Dorsett, "Billy Sunday: Evangelist to Urban America," *Urban Mission* 8, no. 1 (September 1990): 10.

36. Ibid., 11. For his relationship to blacks, consult Lyle Dorsett, *Billy Sunday and the Redemption of Urban America* (Grand Rapids: Eerdmans, 1991), 96–97.

Sunday's vision of the "American way" had shifted from the larger Puritan scale of much earlier times. With other evangelicals, he was reducing it to "regular church attendance, sexual purity, abstinence from drugs and alcohol except for medicinal purposes, honesty, hard work, avoidance of tobacco, dancing, and gambling, and more time for Bible study and prayer. Sunday and his supporters were convinced that if this moral posture was embraced, more than souls would be saved: entire communities would be restored to what God intended them to be, to what they were like in the days before the Civil War."[37]

Like Moody before him, Sunday, as his ministry peaked, spent increasingly less time in the large cities and more time in smaller and medium-sized cities such as San Diego, Wichita, and New Haven. Evangelicalism among whites was moving away from its original stance of urban engagement and more and more toward a socially passive Christianity. A functional Christian social ethic was dimming, quiet in the suburbs to which evangelicals increasingly withdrew, drawing its wagons around a narrowing theological circle it found itself necessary to defend.

37. Dorsett, *Billy Sunday and the Redemption of Urban America*, 112.

5

A Changing Center and an Exploding Fringe
1920–1970

New urban demographic patterns were to emerge between 1920 and 1970. The growth of the medium-sized and large cities accelerated. In 1860, only six cities in the country had a population of exceeding 100,000; by 1900 38 cities could claim this distinction. By 1980, there were 173. In 1850, only one city surpassed 500,000; in 1980, there were 22. In 1800 there were over four times as many small cities as large ones; by 1980 "this ratio had fallen to only one-third its former size."[1]

Larger cities, in fact, have had a longer and more dramatic history of growth. For the past two centuries the number of U.S. cities over 10,000 has grown 28 percent faster than those under 9,999. And some of the most dramatic changes following 1920 have taken place in the largest cities. In 1880, only 3.4 percent of the population lived in cities over a million. By 1930, this number had peaked at 13.3 percent. Then it began a steady decline to 7.7 percent in 1980.

In the meantime, the large cities were spilling over into the adjoining neighborhoods, becoming metropolitan areas. The U.S. Census Bureau began looking for new ways to classify them. In 1950, these areas extending beyond the boundaries of central cities were dubbed

---

1. Eric H. Monkkonen, *America Becomes Urban: The Development of U. S. Cities and Towns, 1780–1980* (Berkeley: University of California Press, 1988), 76.

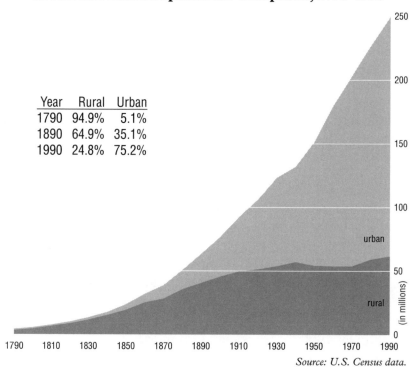

Figure 6
Urban and Rural Populations Compared, 1790–1990

Year	Rural	Urban
1790	94.9%	5.1%
1890	64.9%	35.1%
1990	24.8%	75.2%

Source: U.S. Census data.

Standard Metropolitan Areas. In 1959, they were given the current title of Standard Metropolitan Statistical Area (SMSA).[2] By the early 1980s some twenty-nine of these SMSAs each had more than one million residents.

The First Suburban Decade

Through the 1920s more technological and demographic changes were to underline these shifts. For the first time in American history the suburban areas beyond the city grew faster than the city itself. And "automobility" and Henry Ford helped to do it.

The car became the principal means of expressing individualism

2. To be classified as an SMSA, an area has to have a central city with a population of at least 50,000 and surrounding counties with considerable economic and social ties to the central city. According to the 1980 census, there were 284 SMSAs in the United States.

and self-reliance. In 1915 there was one automobile in Chicago for every sixty-one residents; by 1920, it was one for every thirty. By 1930 it was one car for every eight people in the Windy City; in Detroit and Seattle the ratio was one car for every four residents. And in Los Angeles, the ratio was one to three.

Nationwide, the average was more startling. By 1927, more than one out of every two families in urban America owned a vehicle. Ridership on public transit declined for the first time during the decade. And the *Literary Digest* was complaining that "the American public is thinking more about where to park its cars than about the League of Nations."[3]

The impact of the automobile on the metropolis was far-reaching. Suburban boom was part of the picture. Housing reformers like Lawrence Veiller, Jane Addams, and Jacob Riis welcomed the growth. For them overcrowding in the downtown areas was the handmaiden of crime and poverty. Henry Ford predicted, "The city is doomed," and exclaimed, "We shall solve the city problem by leaving the city."[4]

Everywhere new suburbs sprouted in support of these prophecies. "Of the seventy-one new municipal incorporations in Illinois and Michigan in the 1920s, two-thirds were in Chicago, St. Louis, or Detroit suburbs. Between 1920 and 1930, when automobile registrations rose by more than 150 percent, the suburbs of the nation's 96 largest cities grew twice as fast as the core communities."[5] Grosse Pointe, near Detroit, grew by 725 percent in ten years. Connecticut's nineteen fastest-growing towns of the decade were all suburbs. In suburban Cleveland, the population of Shaker Heights increased 1,000 percent. And in southern California the picture was the same. Glendale's population rose over 360 percent, Beverly Hills almost 2,500 percent.

Meanwhile, in the central city, the automobile was bringing gloom. Traffic jams and parking congestion overpowered the originally residential streets. An Atlanta shopkeeper observed that "traffic got so

3. Jon C. Teaford, *The Twentieth-Century American City: Problem, Promise and Reality* (Baltimore: Johns Hopkins University Press, 1986), 64.
4. Morton White and Lucia White, *The Intellectual Versus the City* (New York: Oxford University Press, 1977), 201.
5. Kenneth Jackson, *Crabgrass Frontier: the Suburbanization of the United States* (New York: Oxford University Press, 1985), 175.

congested that the only hope was to keep going. Hundreds used to
stop; now thousands pass."[6]

Retailers began to follow the factories and the families to the suburbs. In Kansas City in 1923, J. C. Nicols, a developer, pioneered in
the opening of a suburban shopping center, the Country City Plaza.
Ample parking spaces in front of the stores ensured instant success
for the shopping center and new models for business. Others quickly
followed.

Growing Urban Fears

Other pressures also minimized the attractiveness of the city. Gang
wars in Chicago and Detroit made crime entrepreneurs of Al Capone
and the Purple Gang and established the cities in the public mind as
America's capitals of organized crime. Ethnic stereotyping continued
to hurt the reputation of the downtown cities. Fed by the flames of
the conflict in Europe, anti-immigration laws appeared in 1921, setting quota limitations and restrictions. One more step was taken in
the isolation of the central cities.

Adding to the white fear of the cities was the outmigration of
Southern blacks to the North. It was the beginning of the largest single migration movement within the country. Northern industrial
firms encouraged it by recruiting laborers in the South during World
War I. And the mechanization of Southern agriculture and the inva-
sion of the boll weevil helped as well. By the end of the war well over
a half-million blacks had moved North. By the end of the 1920s, that
number had increased to 749,000. And by mid-century it would total
almost 3 million.[7]

Northern cities welcomed these laborers with race riots in East
St. Louis (1917) and five days of violence in Chicago (1919). Washington, D.C. and Omaha followed, Tulsa in 1921. Throughout the
nation there were over twenty serious racial incidents or riots recorded during the summer and fall of 1919. A white neighborhood
association dedicated to the residential segregation of blacks declared, "There is nothing in the make-up of a Negro, physically or
mentally, which should induce anyone to welcome him as a neigh-

6. David Goldfield and Blaine Brownell, *Urban America: A History*, 2d ed. (Boston:
Houghton Mifflin, 1990), 297.

7. Charles Glaab and Theodore Brown, *A History of Urban America*, 3d ed. (New York:
Macmillan, 1983), 283–84.

bor . . . Niggers are undesirable neighbors and entirely irresponsible and vicious."[8]

By the close of the decade, the Roaring Twenties had earned their nickname. American life in city and suburb was taking on new shape and new lifestyles. In a dozen major cities of the North immigrant populations from Europe and blacks from the South had already become the majority. And adding to their number was the growing Mexican community—15,000 in Detroit and Chicago by 1928, one-third of San Antonio's residents by 1930.

On the northern, countryside fringe of New York's Manhattan Island, a predominantly white, middle-class community by the name of Harlem in 1890 symbolized the shift. By 1920, it was a black ghetto and much more besides. It gave its name and vitality to a national flowering of black intellectualism, music, poetry, social activism and spirit—the Harlem Renaissance of the "New Negro."[9]

But the suburbs were dividing the metropolis and winning the demographic war. Another city, Los Angeles, represented that emerging outcome. From its beginnings as a sleepy market town before the 1880s, Los Angeles became a conglomerate of spread-out neighborhoods in search of a city center. Its suburban geographical spread went further, earlier and quicker than anywhere else. Though it early possessed the world's largest mass transit system, it just as soon was disowning that system for the automobile. A major road-building program after World War I was initiated. And by 1925 this tenth largest city in the nation had the highest ratio of cars to people in the world.

The Middle Class and the Suburbs

The earlier images of the suburbs as an elite-class safety zone had expanded to include the middle class. The suburban dream of an estate and a well-manicured lawn had been socially miniaturized to a bungalow and a garage. Zoning restrictions had been introduced to keep out unwanted persons, architectural styles, and businesses. Regional enthusiasm for incorporation into the expanding city municipalities had turned to resistance; neighborhoods were no longer en-

8. Teaford, *The Twentieth-Century American City*, 57.
9. C. Eric Lincoln and Lawrence Mamiya, *The Black Church in the African American Experience* (Durham: Duke University Press, 1990), 167.

thusiastic about incorporation into what they were perceiving as the decaying city.

The suburban neighborhoods quickly were becoming white, Gentile preserves of good taste. "The motor age permitted white, middle-class Americans not only to escape from the congestion, soot, and clatter of the central city, it allowed them to isolate themselves from those ethnic and economic groups deemed incompatible with their way of life."[10]

Reginald Bibby has described the ideology of Americanism as a combination stressing "rugged individualism" and a group commitment to "we, the people."[11] The emerging worldview of the suburb in American life was redefining "we, the people" to "the suburbs, the people." Americans were voting for an anti-urban restrictivism with their automobiles.

Depression and War: 1930–1945

In some ways the 1930s and early years of the 1940s represented an interlude in urban development and change. The skyscraper skylines appearing in the downtown districts of the 1920s looked the same in 1945. Few new suburban housing tracts appeared.

But a major shift was underway that would change the future in a radical way. The great depression had hit the cities in the 1930s. And with it came urban intervention from a new source—the federal government.

By 1932 the nation's cities were so overwhelmed with human need that their limited resources could not respond adequately. In one-industry steel towns like Gary, Indiana, unemployment hit 90 percent. In Chicago 40 percent of the workforce was jobless, and over 15,000 home foreclosures had taken place in the previous four years. The governor of Pennsylvania looked at Philadelphia and estimated that nearly a quarter of a million people "faced actual starvation."[12] Authorities in Denver ran out of money in 1931. The situation was even worse in the South, where cities traditionally allocated few reserves for public welfare.

10. Teaford, The Twentieth-Century American City, 70.
11. Reginald Bibby, Mosaic Madness (Toronto: Stoddart, 1990), 94.
12. Bayrd Still, ed., Urban America: A History with Documents (Boston: Little, Brown, 1974), 421.

By 1933, during the depth of the depression, an estimated 25 percent of the workforce was jobless. In cities like Detroit and St. Louis, unemployment topped 30 percent. Some city payrolls were slashed by 50 percent. The national income in 1929 was $83 billion; by 1932, it had dropped to $40 billion.

Hardest hit were the black and Hispanic newcomers to the city. In both the South and the North there was invariably discrimination. Norfolk in 1933 retained its daily relief allocation for whites at $2 and reduced it to blacks from $2 to $1.25. Houston refused to accept relief applications from blacks or Mexicans. Unemployment rates for blacks were consistently higher than those for whites. In St. Louis, the overall rate was over 30 percent by 1933, and 80 percent for blacks. A New York paper in 1930 reported that the 1929 stock market crash had "produced five times as much unemployment in Harlem as in other parts of the city." Before the decade was over, almost 500,000 Mexicans in desperation had migrated southward across the border.

Government Intervention

President Franklin D. Roosevelt inaugurated a whirlwind of federal "alphabet agencies" beginning in 1933 to respond to urban needs. PWA, WPA, FHA, HOLC, FEHC, USHA—all poured money and federal expertise into an effort to meet more immediate needs, put the cities back to work, and build low-cost housing.

The record was impressive. The Works Progress Administration (WPA), during its eight-year existence, built, repaired, or improved 650,000 miles of streets and highways, 125,000 public buildings, and 8,000 parks. Eight and a half million people were employed. The Public Works Administration (PWA) spent $4.5 billion, much of it in cities. With funds from the Civil Works Administration (CWA), New York's park commissioner Robert Moses employed 68,000 workers in a six-month period.

Housing needs were not forgotten. By unofficial estimate, more than 5 million urbanites were homeless at any time between 1933 and 1937. Between 1933 and 1936 a million mortgages were renegotiated and funded. The Federal Housing Association (FHA) insured low-interest, long-term mortgages. The building of low-cost housing was initiated and, in the four years from 1933 to 1937, 22,000 dwelling units were completed. By 1941, the figure had reached 130,000 units in 300 housing projects across the country.

The legacy of federal intervention into the cities met with mixed reviews. In the South, these federal intrusions were looked on with much suspicion. But the unemployed were working now, and their salaries in turn were bringing profits to others.

In significant respects, however, the urban policies of the New Deal perpetuated the divisions of city and suburb.[13] Their commitments seemed directed, as before, to decentralize the metropolis.[14] Highway construction provided work for thousands but expanded access to the edges of cities. And low-interest mortgage rates encouraged the middle class again to travel those highways to suburban settings.

In the meantime, the renewed cries of reformers for better living conditions for the poor went unheeded. Only a few sections of the worst slums were demolished and replaced with public housing. The racial composition of the neighborhood in which the project was built was undisturbed. If a neighborhood was all white, then only white tenants would be eligible to live in the new units.

Above all else, for good or ill, a precedent had been set: the future of America's cities turned, and would turn, to Washington, D.C. New York's mayor, Fiorello LaGuardia, spoke for then and now when he said, "If it weren't for the federal aid, I don't know what any of us could have done."[15] There was an increasing pessimism about cities and their potential.

World War II and the City

Then came World War II, adding its own boost to the cities. Industry converted to manufacturing for the war machine and employment soared. Public transit enjoyed a wartime boom; gasoline and tire rationing halted "automobilization."

With the dispersal of military bases throughout the country and the awarding of defense contracts to industry, the West, the South, and the Southwest found themselves the recipients of the urban advan-

13. Leonard Wallock, "The Myth of the Master Builder: Robert Moses, New York, and the Dynamics of Metropolitan Development Since World War II," *Journal of Urban History* 17, no. 4 (August 1991): 348–53.

14. Zane Miller, *The Urbanization of Modern America: A Brief History* (New York: Harcourt Brace Jovanovich, 1973), 162–68.

15. Mark Gelfand, *A Nation of Cities: The Federal Government and Urban America, 1933–1965* (New York: Oxford University Press, 1975), 46.

tage. By 1943, southern California was the aircraft capital of the world. Five major aircraft builders were scattered about the Los Angeles metropolitan area. In the San Francisco Bay area and in Portland, Oregon, Henry Kaiser employed hundreds of thousands in his shipyards. In Seattle, the Boeing Aircraft Company jumped from 4,000 employees in 1939 to 50,000 in 1944.

Military bases changed the face of Charleston and Norfolk. Mobile, with two major shipyards and an Alcoa plant, was the fastest growing city in the country between 1940 and 1943; Norfolk was second. Air corps training installations and the aircraft industry took advantage of the sunny desert climate of the Southwest. Cities like Phoenix, Tucson, and Albuquerque exploded with growth. Between 1940 and 1960, the high-tech industry increased by 180 percent in the South, compared with a national rate of 92 percent.

Wartime opportunities and labor shortages encouraged again ethnic and minority migration to the cities. Reversing the depression-era policy of movement back to their homeland, the Bracero Program of contract laborers welcomed thousands of Mexican workers to harvest crops in the Southwest. Between 1940 and 1943, roughly 600,000 blacks left the rural South, more than half finding their way to the North and the Midwest. Detroit's black population grew by 65,000, the largest increase in the country. They were welcomed, as before, with 1943 race riots in Detroit and Harlem, in Oakland and San Francisco. In Cincinnati, 10,000 white workers at the Wright aircraft plant commemorated D-Day, June 6, 1944, with a wildcat strike protesting the integration of the machine shop. "Urban Americans were not only at war with Germany and Japan, they were also at war with each other."[16]

Suburbia Triumphant: 1945–1970

In 1920, city dwellers became a majority of the population. In 1970 another milestone was marked; more Americans were living in suburbs than in cities. "Of two hundred million people, seventy-six million lived in areas around but not inside cities, sixty-four million in cities themselves."[17] The urban fringe was no longer a fringe.

16. Teaford, *The Twentieth-Century American City*, 96.
17. Howard P. Chudacoff, *The Evolution of American Urban Society*, 2d ed. (Englewood Cliffs, N.J.: Prentice-Hall, 1981), 264.

The suburban shift was not a sudden one. The process had been underway for a century. But from 1945 to 1970 it was a boomtime. During the 1950s the aggregate population of America's twenty largest metropolitan areas inched upward by 0.1 percent; the suburban population in those same regions soared 45 percent.

Almost everywhere the pattern was the same. In 1950, Warren, a Detroit suburb, had 727 inhabitants; in 1960 it had reached over 89,000. The St. Louis suburb of Florrisant had grown in the same period from 3,700 to 38,000. In southern California, Anaheim moved from 15,000 to 104,000 people, Garden Grove from 4,000 to 84,000.

It was the South, however, that benefited the most. The urban transformation of the South was virtually a post–1950 phenomenon. Far more new and more suburban than Southern, the late-blooming, "new urban South" could skip much of the historical developments in the industrial North. It had no aging industrial plants, no decaying sewers and bridges. It leaped "from their anachronistic eighteenth-century governments right into the late twentieth century."[18] Fueled by the military connections of World War II and a heavy increase in its share of postwar federal government expenditures,[19] the South erupted in automobile cities. Less densely settled, the Southern city experienced little of the downtown/suburban dichotomy of the North.

Another major change was to reshape the suburban boom of this period. A third group, the blue-collar middle class, was to find its American dream fulfilled. And the man who opened the door to that dream was William J. Levitt.

A housing developer, Levitt used 1,400 acres of Long Island potato fields to apply Henry Ford's assembly-line method of building cars to the prefabrication of housing. By using his own coordinated workforce and by manufacturing and supplying his own materials, he began erecting houses at breakneck speed. By 1948, he was producing 35 houses a day and 150 a week. Levittowns were sprouting up all over the Northeast. Other builders followed quickly and by 1952, prefabricated homes accounted for 8 percent of the nation's housing. FHA-VA-backed mortgages provided indirect subsidy and by 1970 nearly two out of every three Americans owned their own homes. The

18. Monkkonen, *America Becomes Urban*, 235.
19. Randall Miller and George Pozzetta, eds., *Shades of the Sunbelt* (New York: Greenwood, 1988), 6.

suburb was fulfilling dreams for more than elite or white-collar professionals. Now the white lower-middle class had found a place to satisfy its transplanted urban hopes and images.[20] And by 1955, there were 1,000 shopping centers to accommodate their needs.

That dream still had no place for minorities. Suburbia would remain largely white with few black enclaves until after 1970. In New York's Levittown each homeowner's contract included a clause stating that "no dwelling shall be used or occupied by members of other than the Caucasian race." Suburbia was still to be a white haven, Levittown a representative of similar racial attitudes in other neighborhood communities like it.

Center City Change and Crisis: 1945–1970

Suburbia's gain was center city's loss. Industry and manufacturing increasingly followed retailer and resident to the growing edges of the city. Between 1947 and 1954 suburban Detroit saw a 220 percent increase in the number of factories; Chicago's suburban industry doubled. Freeways and interstate highway systems encouraged the shift.

Central city population figures began to decline sharply for the first time in U.S. history. The Northeast and Midwest were particularly hard hit. Between 1945 and 1980, St. Louis lost 50 percent of its population, Boston 30 percent, Philadelphia 18.5 percent. In smaller cities the decline was similar: losses in Buffalo, Providence, Minneapolis, Rochester, and Newark fell between 25 and 37 percent.

The short-lived transit system boom of the war years died quickly. By 1965, commuter patronage had dropped 64 percent. The airplane replaced the train for longer trips. And for every new hotel downtown, there were ten Holiday Inns opening along the interstate highways.

The growing loss of the middle class to the downtown area now began to show its effects. "As the urban whites fled for the suburban frontier, the shrinking central city came to be more heavily populated by poor and low-income people, by blacks, Hispanics, and other new immigrant groups."[21]

The strongest presence came to be that of the black community. By 1970, over 93 percent living in the North were living in cities. In

20. Herbert Gans, *The Levittowners* (New York: Vintage, 1967), 288.
21. Raymond Mohl, ed., *The Making of Urban America* (Wilmington, Del.: SR Books, 1988), 191.

the decade of the 1950s, New York's white population declined by 7 percent but its black population grew by 46 percent. In Chicago the black growth rate was 65 percent. By 1960, Washington, D.C. had become the first American city with a black majority. By the mid–1970s, five other cities joined the capital to claim a black majority—Newark, New Orleans, Baltimore, Atlanta, and Gary.

Other newcomer groups joined the blacks. Puerto Ricans, American citizens since 1917, formed the first airborne migration. New York became their mecca as they sought to escape the poverty of their island. In 1940, there were only 61,000 Puerto Ricans in New York; by 1960, there 430,000. By 1970, the total was over 800,000. And, in south Florida, came Cubans escaping Fidel Castro's 1959 island revolution. Miami welcomed more than 200,000 in the early 1960s.

Flowing into Midwestern cities like Cincinnati and Chicago came almost 1,600,000 migrants from the southern Appalachian region during the 1950s. Nearly one-third of eastern Kentucky abandoned coal mines and eroded farmland and moved to the Northern cities.

Unlike earlier immigrants, all these newcomer groups, refugees from rural poverty, arrived in the cities when demand for unskilled labor was declining and industry was suburbanizing. The net result was the impoverishment of the central city and continued patterns of social, economic, and racial isolation of city from suburb.

Federal Intervention Again: 1945–1970

Once more, federal and local governments turned to the issue of urban renewal, at first with much more optimism about the city than in the past. Federal legislation in 1949 and 1954 authorized and helped fund urban slum clearance projects and the proposed construction of 800,000 civic centers, office complexes, and university campuses.

New pressures for government action came in the 1960s. Under the leadership of Martin Luther King Jr. and Malcolm X, the black community was radicalized into action; the civil rights movement was born.[22] And it was born in the city. In the South King turned, not to the farms, but to the key locales of cities and towns—Little Rock, Birmingham, Selma, Montgomery. And in the North, Malcolm X stirred the ghettos of Chicago, New York, and Detroit.

---

22. For a fascinating comparison of the message and methodologies of these two men, consult James Cone, *Martin and Malcolm and America* (Maryknoll: Orbis, 1992).

In partial response, the federal legislature, guided by President Lyndon Johnson, rediscovered poverty and inaugurated war on it in 1964. Affirmative action in hiring, a Job Corps aimed at training blacks for the marketplace, a day-care program for preschool children (Project Head Start) followed in quick succession. The Community Action Program (1964) sent nearly $2 billion into center city "target area" neighborhoods, the majority of which were black.

In 1966, the Model Cities program, to be administered by the new Department of Housing and Urban Development (HUD), was launched. Originally intended to target the worst neighborhoods in a few cities, the program was expanded to 150 cities. Available funds were spread too thin to have a significant impact. And, as before, the program was linked also to the larger metropolitan area. "The hope was to encourage suburban jurisdictions to build facilities at federal expense—housing, training centers, industrial parks—that would attract blacks away from central cities."[23] President Richard Nixon terminated the Model Cities program on taking office in 1969. The urban crisis, he announced, was over.

The war on poverty left a large array of measured achievements. By 1969, it had spawned over five hundred federal grant programs and was spending over $14 billion. By 1974, that figure would reach $26.8 billion. It had provided job training for thousands of urban unemployed and, in the creation of HUD, had given the city a cabinet role in government. Its community action programs gave blacks the opportunity for wielding power and legislative skills that they would use as they moved more and more into the political arena. From here on, urban politics would see an increase in black and Hispanic power voices.

Finally, the war on poverty represented a shift in how to handle urban problems. The urban renewal programs of the 1950s, with their demolition derby mentality toward human displacement and neighborhood destruction, would not return.

But the problems of the city would not go away. By the late 1960s America's greatest cities seemed on the verge of breaking up. City and suburb, minority and white, poor and middle class represented two metropolitan worlds, not one. Where had the church been in all this? Where should it be?

23. Ibid., 365.

6

The Church and the Vital Fringe
1920–1970

The 1920s marked the demographic shift from a rural America to the beginning of an urban era. It also marked the triumph of suburbanization. For the first time in the nation's history the areas beyond the city grew faster than the city itself. Between 1910 and 1950 suburban population had increased 210 percent while the population as a whole increased 64 percent.

How will we evaluate the history of the evangelical church in this period? Observed one writer in the 1960s, it is a record of "notable successes in the growing suburbs" and "dismal failures in the central areas of the metropolis."[1] Was it? The purpose of this chapter is to look for that answer.

The "Great Reversal"

A major shift in perspective shaped the white evangelical church as it moved through the first three decades of the twentieth century. It was a retreat "from active social involvement into private prayer and personal evangelism as the primary means of coping with the problems

1. Gibson Winter, *The Suburban Captivity of the Churches* (Garden City, N.Y.: Doubleday, 1961), 15.

of the city."[2] The revivalistic, millenarian movement that had appeared in the cities of the nineteenth century flourished now under the banner of a narrowing fundamentalism in the early twentieth century.

In this regrouping under a narrow evangelical subculture, social activism found itself in decline. Earlier cooperative church efforts devoted to the needs of the community shifted to more exclusively church-centered purposes. Prohibitionism, to cite one example, lost its focus on social regeneration and was reinterpreted in terms of personal salvation. It was time to restructure ecclesiastical, not urban, goals.[3] The opening doors of many evangelical institutions for women in public ministry began to close.[4] Strength turned inward to rebuilding institutions lost to liberalism.[5]

The Holiness theological tradition provides a sampling of this change. At the urban forefront of social activism in the nineteenth century, it took another direction now. Out of its roots came the Pentecostal churches of the new century, its formal birth usually traced to a Los Angeles revival movement in 1906. By 1926 five of the major denominations it spawned had a combined total of 2,426 congregations and 117,406 members.[6]

A significant part of the reason for that growth was a strong urban orientation. The movement "began as a city phenomenon, with many major events occurring in Los Angeles, Chicago, Topeka, Dunn, North Carolina, Portland and Indianapolis. Aimee Semple McPherson's settling in Los Angeles foreshadowed dozens of 'Temples' and 'revival centers' which came to dot the nation's largest cities."[7]

Also unlike the rest of its evangelical counterparts, the early constituency of the Holiness tradition was drawn from the ranks of the urban poor and underprivileged; through the middle of the century its members continued to occupy the social cellar. This, in fact, may be one of the reasons it quickly attracted large numbers of African-Americans. And why from its earliest informal beginnings in 1890 to

2. Robert D. Linder, "The Resurgence of Evangelical Social Concern (1925–1975)," *The Evangelicals: What They Believe, Who They Are, Where They are Changing,* rev. ed., ed. David Wells and John Woodbridge (Grand Rapids: Baker, 1977), 212.

3. David O. Moberg, *The Great Reversal* (Philadelphia: J. B. Lippincott, 1972), 31.

4. Janette Hassey, *No Time for Silence* (Grand Rapids: Zondervan, 1986), 137.

5. Joel Carpenter, "Fundamentalist Institutions and the Rise of Evangelical Protestantism, 1929–1942," *Church History* 49 (1980): 62–75.

6. Vinson Synan, *The Holiness-Pentecostal Movement in the United States* (Grand Rapids: Eerdmans, 1971), 203.

7. Ibid.

1920, "Negros and whites worshipped together in virtual equality among the pentecostals."[8]

But with fundamentalism, Pentecostalism shared also an "other-worldly" orientation. Its catalogue of "social sins" often sounded to the non-Pentecostal as more individual than social. They included "tobacco in all its forms, secret societies, life insurance, doctors, medicine, liquor, dance halls, theatres, movies, Coca Cola, public swimming, professional sports, beauty parlors, jewelry, church bazaars and makeup."[9]

Reaction to the "Social Gospel"

A major theological factor in the shift was the widening battle between evangelical and Social Gospel advocates. By the time of World War I "social Christianity" was becoming thoroughly identified with antisupernaturalism and the "New Theology" of modernism or liberalism. Evangelicals saw more at stake than simply the issue of social concern, whether public or private. Their concern was an "emphasis on social concern to the exclusion of the spiritual dimensions of faith."[10] And behind that issue was another, a radical hermeneutical rearrangement of historic Christianity itself.

A. C. Dixon is representative of those who made this connection. During a Boston pastorate that began in 1901, his church administered a million-dollar endowment. At first Dixon reasoned "that if they fed the hungry, paid their rent, and gave them a good doctor and medicine, it would be good preparation for preaching the gospel. But when, at the end of three years, Dixon realized that soul-winning did not follow body healing, he decided to 'dispense with the whole business and get back to first principles' . . . He learned that it 'is immensely easier to reach a man's body through his soul, than his soul through his body.'"[11] An associate of Moody, Dixon was echoing Moody's frustrations over the limited effects of social ministry and his reductionist commitment to a "simple gospel."

By 1910, Dixon was pastoring Moody Church in Chicago and serving as the first editor of a series of twelve paperbacks to be issued

---

8. Ibid., 165.

9. Ibid., 190.

10. James D. Hunter, *American Evangelicalism: Conservative Religion and the Quandary of Modernity* (New Brunswick: Rutgers University Press, 1983), 30.

11. Brenda M. Meehan, "A. C. Dixon: An Early Fundamentalist," *Foundations* 10, no. 1 (January–March 1967): 53.

through 1915, *The Fundamentals*. The books, intended as a broad defense of the faith, received little notice in academic or popular theological journals. They may have served more as "a symbolic point of reference for identifying a 'fundamentalist' movement."[12]

Two-thirds of the published essays focused on issues surrounding the defense of Scripture and traditional theological topics, an agenda that would cause debate into the 1930s. But the practical essays and personal testimonies included were pointing to the new social direction that evangelicals would take under the flag of "fundamentalism." These "display an overwhelming emphasis on soul-saving, personal experience, and individual prayer, with very little attention to specific ethical issues, either personal or social. Political causes—even prohibition—were studiously avoided. Sabbath observance was urged, but not as a political issue. A few writers alluded to the dangers of communism and anarchy . . . Charles Trumball warned against too much 'social service' at the expense of creating 'victorious soul-winners.'"[13]

Later years would underline even further these agenda issues in the debates and church conflicts to follow. Out of the struggle evangelicalism would form a new subculture, "fundamentalism." And opposition to "social Christianity" would be enlarged to antimodernism. The theological side of the controversy would dominate the church through the 1920s and 1930s, splitting especially Presbyterians and Baptists.[14]

Other factors also played a part in the growing isolation of evangelicals from active involvement in the city and its struggles.

Among these are the diversion of fervor into anti-evolutionary conflicts and battles with theological liberals, the feeling that Prohibition would solve all social ills, the premillennialist doctrine that all social conditions would inevitably and irreversibly grow increasingly worse until the Second Coming of Jesus Christ, the belief that only the establishment of the millennial Kingdom of Christ could cure social problems, the false doctrine that New Testament admonitions to Christian love apply to the material welfare of only brethren in Christ, the dichotomistic fallacy that the Christian message must be either personal or so-

12. George M. Marsden, *Fundamentalism and American Culture: the Shaping of Twentieth-Century Evangelicalism, 1870–1925* (New York: Oxford University Press, 1980), 119.
13. Ibid., 120.
14. The apologetic work of J. Gresham Machen, *Christianity and Liberalism*, appearing in 1923, remains the high-water mark of the debate.

cial, either spiritual or social, and either this-worldly or other-worldly and cannot be both, "the gospel of individual piety" which has led many selfishly to try to escape from the world and live lazily in separation from it . . . [15]

Retreat from the City

We need to remember here a forgotten or at least minimized dimension in this increasingly theological debate. The battleground on which this theological struggle began was not simply the social demands of the gospel. It was the social demands of the gospel in the city. And the effects of the struggle were to play a heavy role in the social conscience of the evangelical church. That conscience experienced a moratorium that was not broken until the late 1940s.[16]

Reinforcing the moratorium was the continued retreat of the evangelical church to its suburban home.[17] Not only was liberalism rejected by the evangelical in the struggle. So was a working Christian social ethic and the city in which to practice it. Critics like H. L. Mencken, reflecting on the 1925 Scopes "monkey trial" in Tennessee, would identify fundamentalism with rural and small-town America. But that judgment needs modification.[18] It forgets the expanding suburban base of fundamentalism in the Northern and Eastern sections of the country. The anti-urban dichotomy from which fundamentalism operated was more one of suburban-urban. And it was one shared by the "New Theology."

The "Outsiders" and Their Great Reversal

In the closing half of the nineteenth century the black church had moved rapidly toward separate identity. By 1870, there were nearly 500,000 blacks associated with independent Baptist congregations. The African Methodist Episcopal (A.M.E.) Church had grown from a modest 20,000 members at the beginning of the Civil War to over 450,000 by 1896, the A.M.E. Zion Church to 350,000.

15. Moberg, *The Great Reversal*, 37.
16. Marsden, *Fundamentalism and American Culture*, 85–93.
17. H. Paul Douglass, *The Suburban Trend*. New York: The Century Company, 1925.
18. Gregory Singleton, using some rather complicated definitions, examines this thesis in some detail in "Fundamentalism and Urbanization: A Quantitative Critique of Impressionistic Interpretations," in *The New Urban History*, ed. Leo Schnore (Princeton: Princeton University Press, 1975), 205–27. Unfortunately, he makes no sharp differentiation between city and suburb in his otherwise careful analysis.

With the opening years of the twentieth century, blacks had become part of the beginnings of the Great Migration to the North and
to the cities. From 1910 to 1930, 1.2 million blacks had left the South
and were joining those already in the (largely Northern) cities. Even
those blacks remaining in the South (never less than 52 percent of the
total population) moved in larger numbers to the city.

The churches multiplied, though membership growth was mainly
by transfer from rural areas. In Chicago, Detroit, Cincinnati, Philadelphia, and Baltimore, the number of black Baptist congregations
showed a 151 percent increase. The A.M.E. churches in those same
cities showed an increase of 124 percent.[19]

But, as the black churches proliferated, they entered into a "Great
Reversal" of their own. Unlike the white churches, the realities of slavery and racism had never allowed the black church the luxury of iso-
lating its life and place in the community from social issues. Its very
existence had always demanded a marriage of the gospel and social
concerns. Those issues followed the church wherever it went.

But with the proliferation of black churches in the twentieth-
century city came some measure of deradicalization. The economic
and political viability of congregations was threatened. Educational
and financial resources were already strained by white barriers to
learning and power. Now they were strained even more by the planting of urban churches to meet the urban black newcomer from the
South. The great depression added to the burden. "The vast majority
of black churches were stretched to their financial limits and strapped
with large debts."[20] One estimate suggests that about 71.3 percent of
urban churches sampled were indebted.

"During the 1920s and 1930s most black churches retained a ba-
sically rural orientation and retreated into enclaves of moralistic, revivalistic Christianity by which they tried to fend off the encroaching
gloom and pathology of the ghetto. As far as challenging white society, or seeking to mobilize the community against poverty and oppression, most churches were too other-worldly, apathetic or caught
up in institutional maintenance to deal with such issues."[21]

19. Benjamin Mays and Joseph Nicholson, *The Negro's Church* (New York: Russell and
Russell, 1969 reprint), 96.
20. C. Eric Lincoln and Lawrence Mamiya, *The Black Church in the African American Experience* (Durham: Duke University Press, 1990), 120.
21. Gayraud S. Wilmore, *Black Religion and Black Radicalism*, 2d ed. (Maryknoll: Orbis,
1983), 161.

This change did not happen easily. Nor did it isolate the black church that radically from its call to social protest.[22] Two contradictory voices arose in the church to offer it two different paths to that protest. One voice, that of Booker T. Washington, called for change through gradualism and accommodation; self-help was the key to integrationism. The opposing response came from W. E. B. DuBois (1868–1963). His 1903 book, *The Souls of Black Folks*, was a blistering anti-Bookerite protest against racism and oppression, an aggressive call for white repentance.

In fact, two organizations formed during this time symbolized the choices these two men offered the community. In 1909, the National Association for the Advancement of Colored People (NAACP) was formed and in 1910 the National Urban League. The League adhered closely to Washington's schedule of priorities, concentrating its major efforts on the expansion of employment opportunities and providing social services for the influx of blacks to the urban centers. The NAACP, by contrast, moved in the orbit of DuBois in its early stages, abandoning amelioration for protest.

In the critical years from 1895 to 1915, Washington's voice was heard the loudest by both whites and blacks in America. His moderatism provided the rationale for the black church's Great Reversal, for what Carl Ellis calls "the neo-Colored movement."[23]

Besides the social roots of its origins in response to white racism, the Great Reversal of the black church differed in still another area. By and large, its theological commitments to supernatural Christianity were not withered by commitments to the "New Theology" as was true of the white church. The Social Gospel movement found few supporters among its constituency. And, within that movement itself, allegiances shifted and there were divisions over solutions to the race problem. Washington Gladden, for example, moved from Bookerite accommodation to the reform demands of DuBois.[24]

As the great depression pursued its course, support for Washington's course of action, combined with continuing Northern racism, froze the black church into the ghettos of the city. Battered by the

---

22. Albert J. Raboteau, "The Black Church: Continuity within Change," in *Altered Landscapes: Christianity in America, 1935–1985*, ed. David Lotz, Donald Shriver Jr., and John Wilson (Grand Rapids: Eerdmans, 1989), 85–86.

23. Carl Ellis, *Beyond Liberation* (Downers Grove: InterVarsity, 1983), 54–56.

24. Ronald C. White Jr., *Liberty and Justice for All: Racial Reform and the Social Gospel (1877–1925)* (San Francisco: Harper and Row, 1990), 146–47.

pressures of economic decline and harassed by the brutality of prejudice, the black church was silent.

The Great Depression Wipeout

The depression also played its part in silencing urban hope for the
larger evangelical community. It was a time of "religious depression"
that correlated closely with the great depression.[25] "These were
hardly years to launch a movement of recovery from within the
churches."[26] The 1920s saw a sharp downturn in the winning of converts and the reception of new members.[27] Traditional Sunday
evening services were closing, especially in the cities. The confidence
of Catholic, mainline Protestant, and evangelical alike was shattered.
Even the Social Gospel began to slump by the late 1920s.

"Outwardly the churches suffered along with the rest of the nation.
Memberships dropped, budgets were slashed, benevolent and missionary enterprises set adrift, ministers fired, and chapels closed."[28]
How was Christian voluntarism, itself reeling economically and insti-
tutionally, to help in the face of such massive need?

Least affected theologically may have been the fundamentalist
subculture. James Hunter suggests rather strongly that the socioeconomic conditions of the depression fit more easily the pessimism of
fundamentalist premillennial eschatology.

> The Great Depression was in their view a sign of God's vindictive pun-
> ishment on an apostate America as well as a sign of Christ's imminent
> return. Their nearly exclusive orientation toward spiritual salvation
> proved adaptive to the deprivation they experienced as well. Personal
> salvation and the variable degrees of holiness attainable by the believer
> served as compensations for the privileges denied him in the social and
> economic spheres.[29]

25. Robert T. Handy, "The American Religious Depression, 1925–1935," *Church History*
29 (1960): 3.

26. Martin E. Marty, *Protestantism in the United States* (New York: Charles Scribner's Sons,
1986), 229.

27. H. C. Weber, *Evangelism: A Graphic Survey* (New York: Macmillan, 1929), 181ff. The
decline, beginning about 1925, did not show a significant upturn until the mid-1930s.

28. Robert M. Miller, *American Protestantism and Social Issues, 1919–1939* (Chapel Hill:
University of North Carolina Press, 1958), 63.

29. Hunter, *American Evangelicalism*, 39. See also Liston Pope, *Millhands and Preachers*
(New Haven: Yale University Press, 1965), 86.

The voice of Billy Sunday echoes a somewhat similar refrain. Commenting in 1931, he said: "Sometimes I'm glad God has knocked over the heavens to put America on her knees before she became too chesty . . . Our great depression is not economic, it is spiritual and there won't be a particle of change in the economic depression until there is a wholesale revival of the old time religion."[30]

At the same time, others sounded less vindictive and acted with what concrete help they could muster. Aimee Semple McPherson set up a commissary in her Angelus Temple. From 1927 to 1936 she fed 99,520 families and 355,158 people. By the end of the depression she had met the physical needs of over 1.5 million people.[31] She also set up an employment office that supplied 4,850 jobs between 1935 and 1936.

Suburbanization and the White Church

Reinforcing the Great Reversal and extending its impact on the evangelical church was the shift to suburbanization that began its triumphant march in the 1920s. By the middle of that decade, more than 15 million persons were residing in the fringe neighborhoods of the city. Slowed down by a depression and a world war, the great push continued after 1945. By 1955, approximately 1,200,000 Americans were moving to the suburbs annually.[32] And scholars were predicting that 85 percent of city growth during the 1960s and 1970s would be suburban.[33]

The churches followed, giving primary attention to their suburban expansion. The amount spent on new churches rose steadily, the bulk of it concentrated on the suburbs. Between 1946 and 1960, money spent on church building moved from $76 million to $1 billion, 16 million.[34]

"A Return to Religion"?

Was suburban growth a "return to religion," signs of another revival? As early as 1925, H. Paul Douglass had predicted optimistically

30. *The Boston Herald*, 2 March 1931, 1.
31. Stanley Burgess and Gary McGee, eds., *Dictionary of Pentecostal and Charismatic Movements* (Grand Rapids: Zondervan, 1988), 10, 570.
32. Frederick A. Shippey, *Protestantism in Suburban Life* (Nashville: Abingdon, 1964), 20.
33. John C. Keats, *The Crack in the Picture Window* (Boston: Houghton Mifflin, 1957), 173.
34. Winthrop S. Hudson, *Religion in America*, 2d ed. (New York: Charles Scribner's Sons, 1973), 382.

that such a suburban trend would "genuinely lead out into an evangel of hope . . . the gyroscope for the next Great Experiment" of the church.[35] Some were claiming the fulfillment of his prophecy by the mid-1960s.

Others were far more reluctant. Herbert Gans in his 1967 research reported that for 60 percent of his suburban respondents the move to suburbia entailed no change in church or synagogue attendance.[36] Dennison Nash pointed out that the impressive increases in church membership statistics in suburbia were only a reflection of the increased number of families with school-aged children in the country, the postwar "baby boom" that had helped to produce the suburban migration itself. As the number of school-aged children declined, so did the alleged revival.[37] Suburban Americans, concluded some, are no more prone to religiosity than their urban counterparts.[38]

As a matter of fact, if Robert Handy is correct, the opposite direction had already been taken. America decades before had entered a "second disestablishment" of religion far more devastating than the formal breaking of church-state links in the colonial era. The buoyant expectations of the church following the "great crusade" of World War I had dimmed. "The idealistic hopes for a Christian America as envisioned by nineteenth-century evangelicals were fast fading in the face of the realities of postwar America; the enthusiasm and morale needed to sustain the crusade were undermined."[39] Disillusionment over the church as the moral conscience of the nation, fed by the weight of the economic depression, left the old talk of the Christianization of the country and its cities no more than talk.

Robert Lynd and Helen Lynd had sensed this change early in their sociological studies of the city they called Middletown, USA (Muncie, Indiana). Their original study in the mid-1920s had found a wide gap between religious theory and actual practice. Ten years after their initial research, they saw the gulf widened: "the gap between reli-

35. Douglass, *The Suburban Trend*, 326–27.

36. Herbert Gans, *The Levittowners: Ways of Life and Politics in a New Suburban Community* (New York: Random House, 1967), 264.

37. Dennison Nash, "And a Little Child Shall Lead Them: A Test of an Hypothesis That Children Were the Source of the American 'Religious Revival'," *Journal for the Scientific Study of Religion* 7 (Fall 1968): 238–40.

38. William M. Newman, "Religion in Suburban America," in *The Changing Face of the Suburbs*, ed. Barry Schwartz (Chicago: University of Chicago Press, 1976), 267–68.

39. Robert T. Handy, *A Christian America: Protestant Hopes and Historical Realities* (New York: Oxford University Press, 1984), 169.

gion's verbalizing and Middletown life has become so wide that the entire institution of religion has tended to be put on the defensive; and the acceptance of a defensive role has tended to mean that it is timid in jeopardizing its foothold in the culture by espousing unpopular causes"[40]

The Impact of Suburbanization

Roosevelt's New Deal reforms in the 1930s and 1940s filled the role that church voluntarism had lost. The school, not the church, would now Americanize ethnic minorities and culturally deprived groups. The federal government, not the church, would now plan and program America's urban society. And suburbanization, among other things, symbolized that change. Earlier commentators in the 1920s had seen it as the church's unfinished task in the metropolis; now many were becoming suspicious it was a symbol of faith's irrelevance and the church's disestablishment in the urban world.

Suburbanization did mean other things for the Protestant church, and for the city in particular. The flight to the suburbs represented a flight from trapped urban populations, from urban social problems, and commitments to both.

Gibson Winter signaled it in the title of his 1961 book, *The Suburban Captivity of the Church*. He predicted accurately the white abandonment of Christian witness and mission to the inner city. The church, he argued, in moving to the suburbs, was dividing along racial lines and between blue-collar and white-collar populations; alienation from the city was aligning the white branches of the major denominations "with the middle-class, suburban side of the social-class and racial schism."[41] Decentralization of the metropolis would bring church disengagement from central city and from its mission to working-class people; once again the church was in danger of identifying with the middle and upper classes and surrendering to the demands of the American ladder of achievement. Introversion and the deformation of Protestantism could be expected. Suburbanization was a flight from social responsibility.

Suburbanization had still another effect on the churches and particularly the evangelical segment. For the first time in American his-

---

40. Robert L. Lynd and Helen M. Lynd, *Middletown in Transition: a Study in Cultural Conflicts* (New York: Harcourt, Brace, 1937), 311.

41. Winter, *The Suburban Captivity of the Church*, 31.

tory, the "urban crisis" was in danger of being isolated from the issues of social responsibility. In the past, they had been inextricably linked together in the evangelical mind. The church, after all, was an urban institution. To speak of the city was to speak of the church's context. And the needs of that context were defined in terms of housing needs, of political corruption, of ethnicity and racism.

But now suburbanization allowed the church to deal with these problems (or not) without wrestling equally seriously with the city. Earlier problems of privatization and "spirituality" could now be affirmed or denied at arm's length from the central city location. "The world of daily work, of urban politics, or racial tensions, or stark poverty is miles away at the other end of the commuter route. And this is true by choice and determination. Not a very likely set of social forces in which to generate social change!"[42] Or, we add, to feel the press of involvement in the pain of the city.

Mainline Responses to the Urban-Suburban Dichotomy

Mainstream white Protestantism, suffering from "fundamentalist" schisms but embracing a theological pluralism within its ranks that left room for nondissenting evangelicals, was not as quick to desert the urban setting.

"Transitional ministries," as they came to be called, stayed in the racially changing cities and sought to shift the church's membership to fit the new ethnic neighborhood mix that was emerging. Experimental ministries, often with white clergy and nonwhite members, were set up in the old church buildings.

But results were disappointing. Pastors were more willing than white church members to seek integration.[43] Cultural differences loomed too large, along with the high costs of maintaining ministry in poverty-stricken neighborhoods. Hopes for integrated congregations dimmed and some began to see that a word like "transitional" focused too much on the church as an interim institution.[44] The reality came to be less than the process of integration and more like the end of the process, a black church that once was white. The less pain-

42. Quoted in Moberg, *The Great Reversal*, 92.
43. Lyle Schaller, *Planning for Protestantism in Urban America* (Nashville: Abingdon, 1965), 187.
44. Gaylord B. Noyce, *Survival and Mission for the City Church* (Philadelphia: Westminster, 1975), 78.

ful solution, and one often taken, was to sell buildings to black or Hispanic congregations.

Other mainstream church models developed holistic community programs that sounded strongly reminiscent of the Social Gospel's institutional church movement. The East Harlem Protestant Parish, started in 1948 as an experimental, storefront ministry in New York, was one.[45] Deliberately spurning ecclesiastical buildings, it aimed its ministry to, and with, the powerless of the city. Service-oriented to the community's needs, with a commitment to group ministry, the Parish spurned the idealistic optimism of the institutional church model.[46] Similar patterns can be seen in the Detroit Industrial Mission and the Church of the Saviour, Washington, D.C.

A New Theological Basis

The 1950s and 1960s articulated more clearly the new theological basis for these church models. The superficial optimism of the Social Gospel had faded away under the impact of neo-orthodoxy. And with it went also the earlier fear of urban secularism as an enemy. A new emphasis on the vocation of the church in and for the world began to dominate. Secularization was being embraced as the key to the heart of the urban world.

Fed by the celebration of secularization in Harvey Cox's 1965 best seller, *The Secular City,* and the more cautious call to servanthood in a secularized world by Gibson Winter's *The New Creation as Metropolis* (1963), the church was displaced by the world as the object of God's first concern.[47]

Linking together the church and this new orientation to the world were the "urban training programs" that sprang up around the country from 1962 to 1976. Twenty-seven such programs came and went during this period. Cities like Chicago, New York, and Atlanta, Denver, St. Louis, and Minneapolis, Richmond, and Seattle hosted them. Often white in leadership, and originally more oriented to the needs of the "transitional churches," increasingly they placed a heavy emphasis on neighborhood action geared to political and social change.

---

45. Bruce Kenrick, *Come Out the Wilderness* (London: Fontana Books/ William Collins and Sons, Ltd., 1962).

46. The philosophy of ministry of the Parish is outlined in George W. Webber, *God's Colony in Man's World* (Nashville: Abingdon, 1960).

47. Colin Williams, *Where in the World?* (New York: National Council of the Churches of Christ in the U.S.A., 1963), 76.

Evangelical Reactions

Institutional white evangelicalism by and large avoided them. The programs operated "within the theological assumptions of the liberal and neo-orthodox traditions of North American Protestantism."[48] And the evangelical churches, already slow to join the cause of civil rights that the action training centers supported, were slower still to join programs that sounded too much like the Social Gospel *redivivus*.

Any number of reasons closed the centers by 1976.[49] Geared to innovation and experimentation, the centers were not able to communicate well their findings to the sponsoring denominations and in the face of a growing focus on more localized black and ethnic ministries. By the mid–1960s, the term *urban* had begun to be understood as a synonym for "black" and "minority." And the centers were shifting their emphasis from the more comfortable strategies of integration to "black power." The shift was a strategy more fearful and misunderstood in a white constituency. By the mid-1970s, the centers' interest in race relations and civil rights began to fade with the majority society's decline of interest in these issues.

Churches were also uncomfortable with the strong stress of the centers on social action. Traditionally, this focus in previous decades had been tied also to evangelization and church development. All these emphases were seen as complementary strategies. But with the centers' emphasis on involvement in social action, the churches found themselves with a message more difficult to understand and justify to their constituency.

In addition, the theology of secularization that provided one component in the basis for the centers was fading fast as a permanent foundation. A later self-reflection of Cox, one of its advocates, admitted that the theology had misjudged the persistency of human religiosity and had minimized the evil side of secularization as a process that could destroy as well as heal. It was also, Cox affirmed, a perspective on the city "of a relatively privileged urbanite. The city, secular or otherwise, feels quite different to those for whom its promise turns out to be a cruel deception."[50]

---

48. George D. Younger, *From New Creation to Urban Crisis: A History of Action Training Ministries, 1962–1975* (Chicago: Center for the Scientific Study of Religion, 1987), 186.

49. An extensive analysis of both the strengths and weaknesses of the center movement is found in Younger's study, 152–91.

50. Harvey Cox, "*The Secular City* 25 Years Later," *The Christian Century* 107, no. 32 (7 November 1990): 1028.

Unanswered Questions

The end of the 1960s left the mainstream white churches in an ambivalent position over the city. On the one hand, social activism had been an invigorating experience for them. Churches and leaders had become involved with the civil rights movement and the war on poverty.

> Inner-city black churches demonstrated to their white suburban counterparts the interconnections between personal and social salvation, churchly and political ministry, justice for poor people and obstructions to justice in the unequal opportunities of American society. The incorporation of white Christians into the civil rights movement, rooted in the black churches, was a major breakthrough for white consciousness of these very connections. It was natural for some white and black churches, for example, to support the War on Poverty of the Lyndon Johnson years and to sense, with Martin Luther King, Jr., the incompatibility of that war with the one in Vietnam. Sargent Shriver, then Director of the Office of Economic Opportunity, considered the churches an important ally in the fight against poverty. That office, in the late 1960s, funnelled an estimated $90,000,000 annually through the churches for community action programs.[51]

On the other hand, there were those evangelicals within the mainstream with theological questions that appeared to be going unanswered. They wondered if social activism was the major responsibility of the church or of the federal and urban governments. *Who really speaks for the church and where?* they asked. What has happened to evangelism and church planting? Has the mission of the church lost its balance?

These questions combined with a growing lethargy infecting the nation and its churches. The black momentum for social change, slowed by resistance in Northern cities like Chicago, had been devastated by the deaths of Martin Luther King Jr. and Malcolm X. Sentiment against the Vietnam war had accelerated. The white mainstream churches, for all their social concerns and talk, still showed no real move from their own geographical captivity in the suburbs.

51. Ronald D. Pasquariello, Donald W. Shriver Jr., and Alan Geyer, *Redeeming the City: Theology, Politics and Urban Policy* (New York: Pilgrim, 1982), 4.

By 1972, national mainstream church efforts to fight poverty, racism, and other urban problems had all but died. "As national interest waned, the responsibility for urban mission reverted to local congregations with little or no support from national or judicatory offices. In most cases, efforts to grapple with urban problems consistently simply stopped. In many churches, the fight against poverty and racism gave way to the struggle to survive as a congregation."[52]

An Evangelical Social Conscience Reawakens

Not until the late 1940s was there a stirring from the quiet sleep of the white evangelical isolated largely from mainstream efforts.[53] It began with the pen of a young theologian named Carl F. H. Henry. Frustrated over the negativism and social disinterest, the theological reductionism of what had come to be called "fundamentalism," Henry vented his anger in a little book, *The Uneasy Conscience of Modern Fundamentalism* (1947). As in-house self-criticism, the book, to quote one historian, "exploded in the field of evangelical thought . . . like a bombshell."[54]

Lamenting what he called "the evaporation of fundamentalist humanitarianism," Henry called for a return to the world-changing message of the evangelical past. He traced that message to the theme of the kingdom of God and to the biblical philosophy of history it embodied. He feared that fundamentalist interest in the future of the kingdom, apprehensive over Social Gospel abuses of this theme in the recent past, was not paying sufficient attention also to the establishment of the "*now* kingdom."

In its revolt against the Social Gospel, fundamentalism was becoming known also as a revolt against the Christian social imperative; it had developed a theological reputation for social impotence. "For the first protracted period in its history," he argued, "evangelical Christianity stands divorced from the great social reform movements." [55]

52. Ibid., 5.
53. The idealized category of "evangelical" used in this discussion has been examined more carefully in recent literature. It is still, in my judgment, a generalization that bears meaning, even past the theological discussions and divisions of the 1920s and 1930s. But readers will find a more sophisticated analysis of it in Donald W. Dayton and Robert K. Johnston, eds., *The Variety of American Evangelicalism* (Knoxville: University of Tennessee Press, 1991).
54. Linder, "The Resurgence of Evangelical Social Concern (1925–1975)," 221.
55. Carl F. H. Henry, *The Uneasy Conscience of Modern Fundamentalism* (Grand Rapids: Eerdmans, 1947), 36.

Henry's book may not have been the key factor in reawakening the evangelical social conscience. But it most certainly spoke with power of the logjam that would begin now to shift. Once again social concerns became a legitimate part of the evangelical study and action agenda.

NATIONAL ASSOCIATION OF EVANGELICALS

An important organization in legitimizing this agenda was the National Association of Evangelicals (NAE), founded in 1943. Fearful of ecumenical agencies both to its right and its left, it called on evangelicals both inside and outside the mainstream churches to join in a constructive and aggressive "program of evangelical action in the fields of evangelism, missions, Christian education and every other sphere of Christian faith."[56]

The NAE's commitment to humanitarian concerns quickly became apparent. "The new Association promptly organized committees on varied social services which included programs of war relief in Europe and Korea. Committees were also organized to consider political problems, management-labor relations, and race issues."[57] By 1951, a permanent Commission on Social Action had been created with Henry as its chair.

These early years of the NAE reflected a very moderate posture on such issues. Many of its actions seemed closely oriented to the NAE's concerns over religious liberty and the separation of church and state, its sense that "evangelicals do not want the Church in politics."[58] Its permanent Office of Public Affairs, located in Washington, D.C., was the voice of many of these concerns. Its stand on Native American rights was defined in terms of pleas for religious liberty of non-Catholic Indians. It argued for Bible reading and for released time for religious instruction in the public schools, for "the preservation of reasonable limitations on the type and number of immigrants to be admitted to American citizenship."[59] Traditional agenda interests from the evangelicals' recent past, those linking morality and religion—liquor control, communism and socialism, governmental regi-

---

56. James D. Murch, *Cooperation Without Compromise* (Grand Rapids: Eerdmans, 1956), 62.
57. Louis Gasper, *The Fundamentalist Movement* (the Hague: Mouton, 1963), 122.
58. Murch, *Cooperation Without Compromise*, 140.
59. Ibid., 151–52.

mentation—reflected the more conservative mindset of evangelicals at this time.

By the early 1970s, social ministry in evangelicalism would come into its own and move further into an activist stream. And the NAE would reflect that change as well.[60] Approximately one-third of its member denominations by then would have formalized their social ministries in terms of "commissions" or a committee. And joining the NAE's World Relief Commission and the interdenominational World Vision International (founded in 1947) would come World Concern, Food for the Hungry, Samaritan's Purse, and International Christian Aid. These four parachurch agencies, it is argued, were to typify a new direction for evangelical social relief agencies; in them evangelism, still acknowledged as a distinctive part of the church's mission, had only a tangential concern.[61] In a time when the orbit of mainstream church interests in social concerns was decaying, evangelicals were catching their second wind.

The "Young Evangelicals"

Pressing the "establishment" evangelical represented in the NAE in this new direction were the "young evangelicals" of the 1960s and 1970s. Socially awakened by the protest movements over civil rights and Vietnam, angered by evangelical identification with politically conservative approaches and its relative quiet over contemporary issues of war and race, a new generation espoused "a truly Evangelical Social Gospel—one that meets the deepest needs of the heart and the urgent demands of a society in turmoil as well."[62]

Though linked to evangelical orthodoxy of the past, the movement's agenda was more social-action-oriented than the fundamentalism of the past. Gone also was the former ideology of "Christian civilization" stamped on evangelical thinking of former days. Identifying, as in the past, sometimes with the theological flavor of Calvinism, sometimes with Anabaptism or Arminianism, the "young evangelical" sounded more radical, more leftist, than the middle-class evangelical could sometimes appreciate.

Often charismatically based, the movement called for a new sense of community among evangelicals, a view of mission that would pay

60. James D. Hunter, *Evangelicalism: The Coming Generation* (Chicago: University of Chicago Press, 1987), 42.

61. Ibid., 42–43.

62. Richard Quebedeaux, *The Young Evangelicals* (New York: Harper and Row, 1974), 101.

as much attention to justice as to charity. And frequently that call to community took concrete shape in shared living or house church models, Christian adaptations of the communal models popular in the sixties. Out of such communities originating in places like Berkeley, California, and Chicago came new periodicals in the seventies to give voice to their vision—*Radix, Seeds, Inside.*

The Peoples Christian Coalition has been one such community with the longest history and the most influence. Its periodical, *The Post American*, first appeared in 1971 to announce its mandate: "Radical Christians seek to recover the earliest doctrines of Christianity, its historical basis, its radical ethical spirit, and its revolutionary consciousness."[63] Moving its community to the inner city of Washington, D.C. and changing the name of its periodical to *Sojourners* did not change its social vision. But it has widened considerably the ecclesiastical circle of its influence.

Numerous signs point to the impact of this widening agenda on evangelicalism's centrist core. But perhaps one event more climactic than others was the Thanksgiving Workshop on Evangelical Social Concern held in Chicago in 1973 and the organization it eventually spawned, Evangelicals for Social Action.

The declaration issued by the workshop underlined the evangelical faith of the signers, pointed to that same faith's past sins, and called for a total Christian discipleship that requires both love and justice. "We call our fellow evangelical Christians," it pled, "to demonstrate repentance in a Christian discipleship that confronts the social and political injustice of our nation."[64]

How deep do these commitments go? From 1981 to 1983 James Hunter surveyed 1,980 students from nine evangelically-related colleges and 4,280 students from seven evangelical seminaries.

When asked to rate the relative importance of the pursuit of social, economic, and political justice in the world and "telling the world about the claims of Christ," Evangelical collegians and seminarians held a similar view. Over half (54%) of each group claimed that the pursuit of justice was "just as important" or "almost as important" as evangelism . . . Of no little consequence was the fact that a large number choosing

63. Jim Wallis, "Post-American Christianity," *The Post American* 1, no. 1 (Fall 1971): 3.
64. The text of the declaration, and an analysis of the gathering's significance, will be found in Ronald Sider, ed., *The Chicago Declaration* (Carol Stream Ill.: Creation House, 1974).

evangelism as the chief focus of missionary activity were not comfortable with an unqualified choice of evangelism distinct from the social and economic issue.[65]

Dangers of Relapse

Balancing this perspective, however, is the concern of some commentators who see evangelicalism in danger of once more identifying its destiny with America's destiny, of moving again toward a public posture defined by an individual, private ethic.

Grant Whacker, for example, contends there is a structural tension between current evangelicalism and modernity. And in that tension, those evangelicals who are more fearful of cultural pluralism may be merging with southern strains of evangelicalism and borrowing from it its self-understanding as "the last great bulwark of Christianity."[66] Whacker fears a coalescence of more centrist and Southern evangelical outlooks for the purpose of clinging to the South's lingering concept of some sort of custodial responsibility for society.

The argument has some resemblance to the thesis of Martin Marty as he tries to explain the prominence of the South, and Southern leadership, in the current evangelical revival. The South after all "was a reservoir where the old-time religion had remained intact amid the challenges of the twentieth century. Threatened by an intensified modernity in the postwar years, Americans looked for religious answers and Southerners had them. The South's role will remain large in the immediate American religious future, says Marty, 'the real power and greater share in American destiny will probably emerge from the course southern Evangelicals take.'"[67]

An Evangelical Urban Conscience Reawakens

The slow emergence of a white evangelical social conscience, however, did not necessarily mean a parallel concern for the city. With all the problems raised by Henry in 1947, nowhere is there mention of an "urban crisis." His societal concerns are abstracted from the city.

65. Hunter, *Evangelicalism: The Coming Generation*, 43–44.
66. Grant Whacker, "Uneasy in Zion: Evangelicals in Postmodern Society," in *Evangelicalism and Modern America*, ed. George Marsden (Grand Rapids: Eerdmans, 1984), 24–28.
67. David J. Harrell Jr., ed., *Varieties of Southern Evangelicalism* (Macon, Ga.: Mercer University Press, 1981), 3–4, 7–21.

As we have argued earlier, that lack may be tied to the geographical identification of the white evangelical movement with the suburbs. It is another case of "out of sight, out of mind."

That suburban identification base is apparent in Hunter's statistical survey among students. Of those surveyed, only 3 percent of the college students and 10 percent of the seminarians came from cities with a population of more than a million people. By comparison, 12 percent of the collegians and 14 percent of the seminarians came from the suburbs of such metropolitan areas. Totaling up participation from rural areas (under 2,500), towns (2,500–10,000), and small cities (10,000–50,000), the number of college students reaches 50 percent and the seminarians 40 percent.[68]

The Black Church's Contribution

How then do we explain a growing sensitivity to the city? The reawakening of the black church from its Bookerite days of accommodation to the activism of the civil rights movement and the period of black pride and black power that followed it. When Rosa Parks refused to give up her seat on a Montgomery, Alabama, bus on December 1, 1955, a new day dawned for the black community and its churches. The South, and then the nation, experienced a revival of black faith—"a revival that did not break out with sawdust trails and mourners' benches, but with picket lines, boycotts, and marches through the downtown sections of scores of southern towns and cities."[69]

The voice of the black church as a cultural broker for its people, its constant critical posture against racism, spoke loudly in the fifties and sixties. Not the general community but the black church became the major point of mobilization for mass meetings and demonstrations.

Black church members fed and housed the civil rights workers. "Most of the local black people, who provided the bodies for the demonstrations, were members of black churches acting out of convictions that were religiously inspired. Black church culture also permeated the movement from oratory to music, from the rituals and symbols of protest to the ethic of nonviolence. It is estimated that several hundred churches in the South were bombed, burned, or at-

---

68. Hunter, *Evangelicalism: The Coming Generation*, 10.
69. Wilmore, *Black Religion and Black Radicalism*, 177.

tacked during the civil rights years, with ninety-three of those occurring between 1962 and 1965, with more than fifty in Mississippi
alone; the white opposition understood the importance of the black
churches."[70]

Out of the struggle came a new pride for the black churches. And
it came, significantly enough, at a time when the massive black mi-
grations from the rural South to the urban North and West were coming to an end in the late 1950s. In this expanding commitment to the
city, the civil rights movement played yet another role.

The movement gave the black church a sense of "urban place,"
providing many of the black churches with a mission less rural and
more urban in orientation. The black church was putting roots down
in the cities abandoned by white flight to the suburbs. And a sign of
that shift was the theological reflection that began in the urban North
and came to be called Black Theology.[71] An authentically indigenous
theological movement that was specifically urban in context had been
born. And though few black clergy acknowledged its impact,[72] it said
loudly to the black church, "The city is our mission."

White Evangelical Response

"Establishment" evangelicals in the white community were slow
to participate in or support the civil rights movement. But there
were some signs of sensitivity. In the early 1950s Billy Graham was
refusing to speak to segregated urban audiences. And in 1956 he declared that prejudice and racial disharmony constitute the greatest
social evil in the world.[73] He integrated his staff and spoke in favor
of the Civil Rights Act of 1964. In 1967, he traveled to Washington
to give his full support to the antipoverty program of the Johnson
administration.

Graham's associate at the time, Leighton Ford, moved in a similar
direction. He used the occasion of the 1969 U.S. Congress on Evan-

70. Lincoln and Mamiya, *The Black Church in the African American Experience*, 212.

71. For a full taste of the dialogue that goes on within this theology, consult James Cone,
For My People: Black Theology and the Black Church (Maryknoll: Orbis, 1984) and J. Deotis
Roberts, *Black Theology in Dialogue* (Philadelphia: Westminster, 1987).

72. A national sample of 1,531 urban black clergy taken by Lincoln and Mamiya asked if
they had "been influenced by any of the authors and thinkers of black liberation theology." 65.1
percent said no and 34.9 percent said yes. See Lincoln and Mamiya, *The Black Church in the
African American Experience*, 169.

73. David Lockard, *The Unheard Billy Graham* (Waco: Word, 1971), 118–19.

gelism in Minneapolis to appeal for a more holistic shape to the gospel. And in his 1970 book that expanded the Minneapolis message, he elaborated in more detail the need for both personal evangelism and social concern.[74]

The new white awareness of the city, however, did not come from those evangelicals identified, as were Graham and the NAE, with Middle-America conservatism. It came from the sixties generation of emerging evangelicals who saw the rightness of the civil rights movement and called not simply for integrated revivals but for justice. They, more than their suburban predecessors, saw the city as the place where this was happening.

Black Leadership Orientation

Among them, some saw something else: the black churches would take the leadership role in that urban social renewal. The white evangelical role would have to become an urban posture more of learner than teacher. The "transitional ministries" of the postwar years did not sufficiently recognize that behind the "melting pot" mythology of American life was a subtle racism that had failed to acknowledge the authenticity and integrity of cultural diversity.

Some saw this early. In the mid-1960s appeared the little magazine, *Freedom Now*, edited by a white pastor, Fred Alexander. The journal, later to be called *The Other Side*, sought to awaken white fundamentalists to their racism and to stimulate corrective Christian action about the "forgotten Americans" of the city. Books began to appear highlighting the urban dimension of evangelical mission to America.[75] "Our twentieth century target," they proclaimed, "was a city."

Similar to the evangelical past, calls came again for urban alliances on a large scale, for lifelines linking not rural and urban but urban and suburban connections. By the late 1960s Detroit had spawned the Central City Conference of Evangelicals. Out of Boston appeared the Evangelical Committee for Urban Ministries (ECUMB) and its periodical, *Inside*.

---

74. Leighton Ford, *One Way to Change the World* (New York: Harper and Row, 1970). See also his article, "Social Action Through Evangelism," *Christianity Today* 11, no. 19 (23 June 1967): 970.

75. Three of the earliest to appear were David McKenna, ed., *The Urban Crisis* (Grand Rapids: Zondervan, 1969); George Torney, ed., *Toward Creative Urban Strategy* (Waco: Word, 1970); Craig Ellison, ed., *The Urban Mission* (Grand Rapids: Eerdmans, 1974).

Churches and ministries began to appear oriented to the city and seeing themselves, with the black church, as co-belligerents with those in secular society fighting for compassion and justice. More deeply connected to community needs, they combined a high level of social concern with the traditional evangelical emphasis on the personal gospel. The University Church in Athens, Georgia, LaSalle Street Church and Circle Church in Chicago modeled this new direction, though not always successfully.[76] And adding their support to these more institutionalized structures were "the hundreds of neighborhood Bible study groups, prayer and discussion sessions, 'house churches,' coffeehouse ministries, communitarian societies, underground churches, and other ventures both within and outside of religious institutions."[77]

Modifying the model of the mainstream urban training centers (and sometimes cooperating with them), evangelicals sought to find ways to awaken "urban consciousness" through a "schooling" approach. In an effort to avoid the paternalistic white approach of the past, they sought to build (some more successfully than others) leadership for their programs out of the black community as well as their own white constituency.

In Chicago was born the Seminary Consortium for Urban Pastoral Education (SCUPE), providing one year of residential education in the inner city for its cooperating theological institutions. Evangelicals in Boston inaugurated the Emmanuel Gospel Center. Westmont College in Santa Barbara, California, offered an urban semester in the city-as-campus. Messiah College, a rural-located institution, opened an urban satellite campus in inner-city Philadelphia.

Perhaps the most striking symbol of this new direction came in the address of a black evangelist, Tom Skinner, to the 12,300 students gathered at Inter-Varsity Christian Fellowship's triennial conference, Urbana '70. Skinner's message was a blazing indictment of white evangelical hypocrisy over the race issue. Repudiating what he called the god of the American civil religion, he called for a new focus on Christ as liberator. Christ, he pled, invites all men and women to join his revolution by committing themselves to him and by both proclaiming and demonstrating to the world and its cities that the divine

76. Manuel Ortiz, "Circle Church: A Case Study in Contextualization," *Urban Mission* 8, no. 3 (January 1991): 6–18.

77. Moberg, *The Great Reversal*, 172.

liberator has come to loose those who are bound spiritually, mentally, and physically.[78]

Skinner was given a standing ovation by the students. The planning leadership of Inter-Varsity were apparently more alarmed by Skinner's radical tone. The "young evangelicals" had had their urban conscience reawakened. The older generation, still cautiously conservative, were not so sure. The "outsider" had become an urban "insider." And the "young evangelicals" were recognizing in repentance now their own suburban status as the new "outsider."

78. Tom Skinner, "The U.S. Racial Crisis and World Evangelism," *Christ the Liberator* (Downers Grove: InterVarsity, 1971), 189–209. The same themes would reappear in Skinner's other writing. See his *Words of Revolution* (Grand Rapids: Zondervan, 1970); *How Black Is the Gospel?* (Philadelphia and New York: J. B. Lippincott, 1970).

7

The "New" Urban America
1970–1990

By 1970, the central city core was reflecting the effects of the continuing change we have chronicled. Its industrial and retail functions were reduced, shifting to the suburbs with the growing middle class. And in place of the factories came the corporate economy—banking, insurance, accounting, education, and legal services. Federal intervention in the central core had become a new reality. And the poor were more and more identified by the suburbanite with what some were now calling "the inner city." One commentator has described it as "a city trying to escape the consequences of being a city and still remaining a city."[1]

By the 1980s, America had been turned into an urban world of "supercities." The city had been replaced by the larger metropolitan area as the major urban unit. The New York City area contained more than 16 million people spread over 3,600 square miles. The urbanized area of Los Angeles was home to almost 12 million. According to one study, the urbanized Northeastern seaboard of the United States, now dubbed the "Rust Belt" by scholars, would contain about 60 million, or one-fourth of the nation's population by the year 2000.[2]

1. Quoted in Robert Lee, ed., *The Church and the Exploding Metropolis* (Richmond: John Knox, 1965), 20.
2. Raymond Mohl, ed., *The Making of Urban America* (Wilmington, Del.: SR Books, 1988), 189.

The New Geographical Shift

Since 1975, population and economic shifts have introduced a new urban power center, the southern half of the United States. In 1920, only one in four Southerners lived in urban areas. By 1980, more than two out of three lived in metropolitan areas. More suburban than their Northern counterparts, their cities smaller with lower population densities, the Southerner has joined the move to the urban center.[3] And, in the process, the word *southern* has been stretched to define an area from the Atlantic to the Pacific shore.

The Expanding Sun Belt

Since 1970, urban areas of the rustbelt Northeast have generally either lost population or made marginal gains. By contrast, more than half the nation's population growth between 1980 and 1982 occurred in three sunbelt states: California, Florida, and Texas. By 1980, five of the ten largest American cities were located in the Southwest: Los Angeles, Houston, Dallas, Phoenix, and San Diego. By the year 2000, the Sun Belt will be said to have 112 million people, 43 percent of the nation's total.[4]

As late as the early 1950s, for example, Miami was a Southern city, marked by its own history of Klu Klux Klan violence and its own patterns of segregation and exclusion. Now Jews constitute 29 percent of its population and a quip in *Rolling Stone* magazine introduces it as "afterlife for Ohio, surrogate for Cuba, landing strip for Colombia, laundromat for the mob, beach for Brooklyn."[5] Uniquely automobile cities, the Southern cities grow—Houston from 160 to 556 square miles between 1950 and 1980, Oklahoma City from 51 to 603, Phoenix from 17 to 324.

In 1980 for the first time in American history the West and the South had more people than the North and the East. A massive shift in economic activity had brought new jobs as well as new people to the Sun Belt while the snowbelt North and Midwest had lost both jobs and people.

3. Randall Miller and George Pozzetta, eds, *Shades of the Sunbelt* (New York: Greenwood, 1988), 2.

4. J. John Palen, *The Urban World*, 2d ed. (New York: McGraw-Hill, 1987), 128.

5. John Rothchild, "Florida: Sunset in the Sunshine State," *Rolling Stone*, 1 October 1981, 20.

Assimilation Struggles

How different were the problems now faced in this new urban expansion? Old refrains appear to emerge.

Miami struggles as vigorously with its exploding Cuban population as Cincinnati does with white Appalachians. Black struggles in Chicago and New York sound strikingly similar to Texas' border problems with unregistered Mexican aliens. Northern cities like Cleveland, Detroit, and Philadelphia are not far from insolvency. But Houston moves from growth to oil bust in the 1970s to slow recovery.

Poverty and social divisions continue to strike at both Sun Belt and Rust Belt alike. "Residents of southern urban slums are poorer, based on per capita income, than slum dwellers in northeastern cities, yet almost one-half of the northeastern poor are unemployed, compared with only one-quarter jobless in poor southern urban neighborhoods."[6] The number of those earning salaries below a government-defined living wage is significantly higher in Southern inner cities than those in the North.

Crime statistics offer few alternative choices between cities. "Crime rates do not indicate that Sunbelt cities are safer than any other metropolitan areas in the United States, and perhaps they are even less so. Gangs roam at will in Los Angeles. Downtown Atlanta and New Orleans are as murderous as central Detroit. And the cities of southern Florida are among the nation's prime conduits for illicit drugs. Though civil disturbances on the scale of the 1960s are rare, the two major uprisings between August 1988 and February 1989 occurred in Shreveport, Louisiana, and Miami, respectively."[7]

Decentralization, most visible spatially in suburbanization, is seen everywhere. The modern central city, says Michael Conzen, is "locked in the grip of a vast suburban 'noose.'"[8] Left behind in the Northern rush to the suburbs are aging housing stock, an increasing proportion of minorities and poor, particularly blacks and Hispanics, and a deteriorating infrastructure of utilities, urban services, and public schools.

Decentralization also dominates in the South. The "New South" is the new suburban South where the real growth and development

6. David Goldfield and Blaine Brownell, *Urban America: A History*, 2d ed. (Boston: Houghton-Mifflin, 1990), 406.

7. Ibid., 406–7.

8. Mohl, *The Making of Urban America*, 283.

are taking place. Atlanta's history exemplifies the trend. In the midst of Atlanta's downtown building boom in the 1960s and 1970s, the city's population grew only slightly during the 1960s and suffered a net loss of approximately 70,000 residents during the 1970s. In the same period, her suburban population doubled and between 1960 and 1980, the city's share of the metropolitan area's office space declined from 90 percent to about 42 percent. "In sum, growth in the southern Sunbelt, like that in the Far West and elsewhere in urban America, remained suburban."[9]

The New Urban Core

From the 1970s, the steady dripping of inner-city decay began hemorrhaging. As in the last half of the nineteenth century, the heart of the crisis once more revolved around the divisions of urban center and urban periphery. But this time there were differences.

For the first time in American history, the 1970 census counted more suburbanites than city dwellers or farmers. "In 1960 the American population lived in almost exactly equal proportions in central cities, suburbs, and nonmetropolitan areas. By 1975 the suburban component had risen to 39.1 percent, but the central city portion had fallen to 29.6 percent. If one considers only population residing within official metropolitan areas, by 1980 six out of every ten inhabitants lived in the suburbs."[10]

Urban Population Loss

By 1980, of the fifteen largest metropolitan areas, only Houston could count a larger majority of residents living in the central city. Major cities in the Northeast and Midwest began to experience serious accumulative population loss. Detroit had experienced a 9 percent loss in the 1960s; in the 1970s decline reached 21 percent and in the 1980s 14.6 percent. St. Louis lost 27 percent of its population in the 1970s. And by 1980 its population was the same as in 1890. Ten years later another 55,919 had left, for a decadal percentage loss of 14.6 percent.[11] From 1950 to 1980 eighteen of the nation's twenty-five largest cities suffered a net loss.

9. Miller and Pozzetta, eds., *Shades of the Sunbelt*, 8–9.
10. Raymond Mohl, ed., *The Making of Urban America*, 281.
11. "The Census Bureau's Report on Cities," *New York Times*, 27 January 1991, A20.

Figure 7
Black–White Suburban Population Trends, 1900–1980

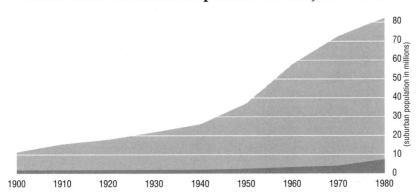

Adapted from Truman Hartshorn, *Interpreting the City: An Urban Geography*, 2d ed., copyright © 1992. Reprinted by permission of John Wiley and Sons.

A massive percentage of that loss was the white community. White flight has continued unabated. In the ten-year period from 1970 to 1980 Chicago lost 33 percent of its white citizenry, Los Angeles 16 percent, Houston 12 percent.[12] Philadelphia's white population in 1990 accounted for 54 percent of all residents, down from 58 percent in 1980 and 66 percent in 1970.

Black Middle-Class Exodus

A new feature in this long-standing outmigration from the city was the departure from the cities of the growing black middle class. In the years since 1968, the African-American community has become two societies—the underclass in which nearly a third of black families live below the poverty line and the emerging middle class.

Between 1970 and 1990, the percentage of black families earning more than $50,000 (in 1990 dollars) has increased 46 percent. The percentage of African-Americans holding college degrees has doubled. Between 1960 and 1990 the percentage of black men holding white-collar jobs has jumped from 12.1 to 30.4 percent, women from 18.2 to 57.7 percent.[13]

12. Charles Glaab and Theodore Brown, *A History of Urban America*, 3d ed. (New York: Macmillan, 1983), 351.

13. Vanessa Williams, "Blacks, Too, Are Becoming Two Societies," *Philadelphia Inquirer*, 4 April 1993, C1, C3.

This disparity is great in the comparison of city and suburb. According to the 1990 census reports, 62 percent of America's black households have incomes of less than $25,000, compared with 40 percent of whites. But by contrast, in metropolitan areas of one million or more, black suburban families average $32,000 per year. This figure is 55 percent higher than the average income of African-American families living in the center city of these metro areas. Middle- and upper-class blacks are a growing force in the suburban marketplace.

In pre–1960 African-American suburbs like Cleveland's Chagrin Falls Park and among the 17,000 blacks who occupied Detroit's Eight Mile-Wyoming District by 1950, the American dream was a shared reality. It was too often shaken by racism but it was still a dream. From 1960, as the black middle class grew, so did the black suburbs. The city began to experience black flight. "Between 1960 and 1980, more than three and one-half million African-Americans found their way to suburban communities."[14]

The migration has assumed significant proportions. In Chicago, for example, the number of African-Americans grew 65 percent in the 1980s. But the total population of the Chicago metro area increased a scant 0.2 percent in that same period. By 1990, there were 40 metropolitan areas with at least 50,000 black suburbanites. Washington, D.C. is the largest, with 619,239 living outside of the central city.

Just over half of all blacks (53 percent) live in the South; along with the capital city, four other Southern metros are in the top ten for suburban blacks: Baltimore, Atlanta, Houston, and Miami. The proportion of African-Americans is, in fact, high in the suburbs of medium-sized Southern metros, probably related to the South's high proportion of rural blacks.

Northern cities also on the top ten list include Philadelphia, Newark, Chicago, and St. Louis.[15] During the decade of the 1980s, to cite one example, Philadelphia's African-American population declined by 6,942 to 631,936 (−1 percent). But six of its seven surrounding suburban counties recorded black percentage growths from a low of 10 percent to a high of 28 percent.[16]

14. Andrew Wiese, "Places of Our Own: Suburban Black Towns Before 1960," *Journal of Urban History* 19, no. 3 (May 1993): 30.

15. William O'Hare and William Frey, "Booming, Suburban, and Black," *American Demographics* 14, no. 9 (September 1992): 32.

16. Neill Borowski, "Minorities Accounted for Area Population Gain," *Philadelphia Inquirer*, 20 February 1991, 1A, 13A, 15A.

In general, the largest black suburbs are found outside the largest cities. Atlanta added a quarter of a million in the 1980s; Miami, 100,000. The fastest growing African-American suburbs are found in rapidly growing Sun Belt cities, Riverside-San Bernardino, California and San Diego almost doubling their black population, Dallas and Houston following suit.

In this shift, however, some things have not radically changed. Nationally, nearly 30 percent of the nation's blacks—or about 9.1 million—live in neighborhoods that are at least 90 percent black.[17] And the suburbs would appear to follow this intractable pattern. Suburban blacks often live in counties still characterized by a high degree of segregation at the neighborhood level. Housing discrimination still continues. Blacks and whites are still treated differently when they buy houses. At the same time, there is also evidence that this segregation is a choice affluent blacks make for themselves.[18]

From Industry to Service

With the coming of the 1970s and 1980s, the industrial city became an institutional anachronism. Central city manufacturing was being drawn to the suburbs, attracted by local and federal tax breaks and the proximity of interstates and freeways for easy access to transportation; industrial parks were popping up everywhere. "As early as 1963, industrial employment in the United States was more than half-suburban based, and by 1981, about two-thirds of all manufacturing activity took place in the 'industrial parks' and new physical plants of the suburbs."[19]

The impact of this on the center city was devastating. Earlier job decline accelerated. "From 1947 to 1967 New York City had lost 175,000 manufacturing jobs, but during the next ten years it lost almost 266,000. Between 1950 and 1967 manufacturing employment in Boston dropped 21 percent; from 1967 to 1977 it fell 36 percent."[20] Buffalo's employment rate dropped by 30.4 percent; that of Minneapolis, 24.9. Between 1970 and 1980 Philadelphia lost

17. Neill Borowski and Murray Dubin, "Black Segregation Up in Philadelphia, Census Shows," *Philadelphia Inquirer*, 11 April 1991, 1B.

18. O'Hare and Frey, "Booming, Suburban, and Black," 36.

19. Kenneth Jackson, *Crabgrass Frontier* (New York: Oxford University Press, 1985), 267.

20. Jon C. Teaford, *The Rough Road to Renaissance: Urban Revitalization in America, 1940–1985* (Baltimore: Johns Hopkins University Press, 1990), 213.

140,000 jobs; by 1977, about 60 percent of the city's metro area employment was outside Philadelphia.

The picture was the same elsewhere. The cities were not simply losing jobs; they were losing blue-collar jobs, the doorway through which poor city dwellers traditionally entered the labor market. "By 1980 almost twice as many persons were employed in manufacturing in the suburbs (10.9 million) as in the cities (5.9 million)."[21]

And in place of manufacturing and industry as the core of center-city commerce came finance, government, and business services. Factories gave way to multifunctional hotels and office buildings. A 1984 survey of 38 large U.S. cities "found that approximately 58 million square feet of office space was built in the 1950s, 132 million square feet in the 1960s, 196 million square feet in the 1970s, and 218 million square feet completed or under construction from 1980 to 1984."[22]

The skylines of American cities have been transformed in the last four decades, primarily by office towers—the 110-story Sears Tower in Chicago, the two towers of Pennzoil Place in Houston, Transamerica's 48-story building in San Francisco. Each structure became a self-contained "downtown," a mix of shopping mall and central business district. Offices, shops, theaters, and restaurants filled Atlanta's Peachtree Center, Detroit's Renaissance Center, the Embarcadero Center in San Francisco. "Once a retail center, the new downtown now specialized in so-called 'knowledge functions'—the acquisition and delivery of information and services."[23]

Downtown and Inner City

This move to a service-oriented economy divided the city into two cities—downtown and inner city. The one opened up its doors to middle-class single persons and childless couples who came to enjoy the pleasures and conveniences a city could offer. The other played host to a growing number of poor and elderly on fixed incomes who now were being called the "underclass." They were excluded by working skills and economics from the high-tech orientation and affluence generated by the new economy.

21. J. John Palen, *The Urban World*, 3d ed. (New York: McGraw-Hill, 1987), 119.
22. John Fondersmith, "Downtown 2040: Making Cities Fun!" *The Futurist* 22, no. 2 (March-April 1988): 9.
23. Goldfield and Brownell, *Urban America*, 411.

Table 2
Manufacturing Employment Shares
in Selected Metropolitan Areas, 1958–1987

City	1958	1967	1977	1987
Atlanta				
City	49.6 59%	54.0 46%	39.9 31%	40.3 20%
MSA	83.5	117.2	128.7	200.4
Baltimore				
City	113.4 56%	106.7 51%	79.9 48%	50 35%
MSA	201.0	209.7	165.9	145.2
Boston				
City	90.2 30%	79.6 25%	50.9 19%	42.5 16%
MSA	301.0	316.2	267.7	272.4
Charlotte				
City	21.2 76.5%	25.6 65.1%	27.8 32%	44.0 28%
MSA	27.7	39.3	87.1	155.4
Houston				
City	68.8 65.8%	97.9 70.9%	147.4 70%	112.8 70%
MSA	104.5	138.1	210.1	160.2
Milwaukee				
City	126.6 64.9%	118.6 54.8%	91.4 45%	63.9 37%
MSA	195.1	216.5	204.1	172.5
Minneapolis-St. Paul				
City of Minneapolis	58.5 43%	69.2 34%	52.0 24%	44.3 18%
City of St. Paul	41.8 31%	54.4 27%	36.9 17%	34.6 14%
MSA	146.0	203.7	216.9	250.9

From Truman Hartshorn, *Interpreting the City: An Urban Geography*, 2d ed., © 1992 John Wiley and Sons. Reprinted by permission of John Wiley and Sons, Inc.

The central city had not died. Under the growing impact of decentralization, it had simply become two more suburbs, still pretending to live as one community on a shrinking tax base. "Downtown" became the center of renovation. The concept of "festival marketplaces" recycled the Faneuil Hall Marketplace in Boston, the waterfront Harbourplace in Baltimore, San Antonio's Pase del Rio. Major performing arts centers were built in Los Angeles, Houston, and Denver. Classic old music halls and movie theaters were renovated in

Richmond, Cincinnati, and Milwaukee. Rehabbed neighborhoods, molded by the gentrification of wealth, provided recovered homes for those "who found newly fashionable inner-city neighborhoods more desirable than child-oriented suburbs."[24]

And isolated from this recycling remains the second city, the "inner city." Beyond the central business districts it lies, a wilderness of vacant lots, persistent blight, and abandoned housing. Its ravaged neighborhoods remain abandoned by federal and local governments, a wasteland of unkept political promises. Public housing becomes a symbol, not of concern, but of "crime, graffiti, garbage, urine-stained stairwells and broken elevators." The giant, high-rise apartment projects of Chicago and St. Louis are "almost universally viewed as failures that devour human lives and tax dollars."[25]

Gentrification is not a blessing, not even a mixed blessing. The middle- and upper-class return to the city drives up housing costs and taxes for the poor, more and more displacing lower-income residents and leaving few housing alternatives.

Pain and anger sink deeper under the malaise of drugs and poverty, occasionally provoked to explosion, as in South Central Los Angeles in 1992. *Time* magazine heralded urban renaissance with a cover article in November 1987: "Bringing the City Back to Life." But they are looking at the wrong city.

The New Urban Poverty

New Jersey's largest office complex is Newark's Gateway Center; by 1987 the city, with a population of 314,000, was drawing nearly one million workers daily to it and its fellow downtown institutions. But there is another Newark beyond the shadow of the Gateway Center. It is a city where one-third of the population is on welfare, where teenage pregnancy rates and drug abuse are among the highest in the nation.

It is a symbol of the urban problem that will not go away—the struggle of poverty. What are the nationwide numbers? "In 1987 there were 32.5 million poor people in America, representing 13.5 percent of the population . . . Minorities remain disproportionately

---

24. Jon C. Teaford, *The Twentieth-Century American City: Problem, Promise, and Reality* (Baltimore: Johns Hopkins University Press, 1986), 153.
25. Quoted in Teaford, *The Rough Road to Renaissance*, 304.

poor—blacks at 33.1 percent and Hispanics at 28.2 percent in 1987."[26]

The ghetto endures, fled now by middle-class blacks as well as by whites. The massive departure of industrial opportunities to the new suburban centers has left behind "garrison cities" where the focus now seems to turn to damage control, not to change.[27] And reinforcing this shift was the disappearance of federal largess, lasting only from the late 1960s to the late 1970s, with the Reagan administration's "new federalism" and its call for redistribution of funds.

Before the federal budget axe had finished its task, HUD's neighborhood self-help fund and VISTA were gone. Budget changes between 1982 and 1985 reduced by more than $20 billion the income of those urban households with incomes under $10,000. Programs hit the hardest were education and training, public-service employment, nutrition programs, Medicaid, and other social services. Federal retreat from urban assistance could not have come at a worse time.[28]

The Feminization of Poverty

Pressed by these circumstances, poverty in the 1980s took new turns from its past, though its breaks with that past can be overdone.[29] Family pattern shifts, for one thing, are creating the "feminization" of poverty.

In 1960, 8.1 percent of white households and 20.9 percent of black households were headed by a woman. By 1981, the percentage for whites had moved to 11.9, for blacks to 41.7. "All of those families headed by a woman were not poor. As a matter of fact," writes Michael Harrington in 1984, "70 percent of them were not, only 30 percent. Even so, the decline in intact families, the epidemic of unmarried teenage pregnancy, the growing number of families headed by a poor woman, significantly changed the structure of poverty in

26. Peter Edelman, "Urban Poverty: Where Do We Go from Here?" in *The Future of National Urban Policy*, ed. Marshall Kaplan and Franklin James (Durham: Duke University Press, 1990), 91.

27. Richard C. Wade, "The Enduring Ghetto: Urbanization and the Color Line in American History," *Journal of Urban History* 17, no. 1 (November 1990): 13.

28. Goldfield and Brownell, *Urban America: A History*, 433–35.

29. John Bauman, Norman Hummon and Edward Muller, "Public Housing, Isolation, and the Urban Underclass: Philadelphia's Richard Allen Homes, 1941–1965," *Journal of Urban History* 17, no. 3 (May 1991): 264–92.

the United States. In 1960, on the basis of the official figures, 65 percent of poor families were headed by a man under sixty-five years of age, 21.2 percent were headed by a woman . . . By 1979, the percentage of male heads had dropped to 42.4, and of female heads had risen to 43.7. Adding to the fact that the aging poor are predominantly female, the feminine percentage of the adult poverty population had doubled in the years after the declaration of the war on poverty!"[30]

This shift has been particularly strong in the African-American community. You can hear it in the informal comment of one long-time black resident in an Eastern inner-city neighborhood: "Ninety percent of the families around here are made up of single women and children. The men are just not around. That's gone [out of style]."[31] During the 1970s, "the number of black families in poverty who were maintained by men declined by 35 percent, while the number maintained by women increased by 62 percent. In the course of one decade, black female-headed families increased from one-half to three-fourths of all poor black families."[32]

Homelessness

In the early twentieth century, the word *homeless* would evoke images of older male derelicts, usually alcoholic and unattached to family or community. "Skid Row" or "the Tenderloin" would be synonyms to paint the picture of street life for the marginal vagrant.

Now in the latter half of the century there are the new homeless. They range in number from 300,000 to 3 million (the estimate of the National Coalition for the Homeless). And the old stereotype of the single, male, adult alcoholic no longer fits. In fact, the fastest growing categories of the homeless are families with a single parent and children. By 1991, 39 percent of the homeless were families, 26 percent were children under the age of 18.[33]

People migrate to the South seeking jobs and fill tent cities in Houston. They set up refugee camps in front of San Francisco's city

30. Michael Harrington, *The New American Poverty* (New York: Holt, Rinehart and Winston, 1984), 195.

31. Elijah Anderson, *Street Wise: Race, Class, and Change in an Urban Neighborhood* (Chicago: University of Chicago Press, 1990), 38.

32. Janice Peterson, "The Feminization of Poverty," *Journal of Economic Issues* 21 (1987): 329.

33. Kevin Lehman, "Homelessness: A Growing National Disgrace," *Washington Memo, Mennonite Central Committee* (July-August 1991): 6.

hall, a community of cardboard condos and shopping-cart traffic jams. By 1992, an estimated 50,000 are sleeping on New York's streets, another 23,000 in city shelters.

What brought this avalanche to the city? The de-institutionalization of the mentally ill is surely one part of the answer. In a social blunder of massive proportions, patients were released from public institutions with no place to go—no community care, no halfway houses, no local clinics. Between 1960 and 1984 the population of mental institutions fell from 544,000 to 134,000.

Some survived in single-room-occupancy hotels (SROs). But in the 1980s half of all the nation's SROs were eliminated by developers. The government cut nearly 500,000 mentally ill people off the welfare rolls. And by 1991, 33 percent of the homeless were mentally ill.[34]

The largest part of the answer, however, probably lies elsewhere. During the decades of the 1970s and 1980s the poor were being squeezed out of the housing market. The average rent during this time grew twice as fast as the average income. Rising rents in a post-industrial time of disappearing industrial jobs and a tight real estate market left the underclass especially prone to borderline disaster.

Part of the problem was lack of housing. In 1970 there were 6.6 million housing units renting for less than $250; a little less than 6 million rental households were seeking such housing. By 1990, the number of available units had decreased to 4.3 million. And the number of households in need of such units had increased to 8.5 million.[35]

Chicago illustrates what we mean. While 1,500 housing units are built there annually (mostly for the middle class), "thousands of units are burned or torn down, not to be replaced. There is a seven- to ten-year wait to get into Chicago's decrepit public housing apartments, home to over 170,000 people."[36]

Another part of the problem is the rental cost of housing.[37] The cost of a medium-priced rental unit (including utilities) was $355 in 1980. By 1989 it had jumped 15 percent to $409. Meanwhile, the average income of the poorest fifth of families fell 6.1 percent. The rent

---

34. Steve Goldberg, "It Wasn't Supposed to Be Like This: Mentally Ill on Streets Signs of a Failed Policy," *Richmond Times-Dispatch,* 29 December 1991, D-5.

35. Lehman, "Homelessness: A Growing National Disgrace," 7.

36. Clinton Stockwell, "The New Urban Reality: Hope for a Remnant," in *Envisioning the New City,* ed. Eleanor Scott Meyers (Louisville: Westminster/ John Knox, 1992), 84.

37. Karin Ringheim, "Investigating the Structural Determinants of Homelessness: The Case of Houston," *Urban Affairs Quarterly* 28, no. 4 (June 1993): 617–40.

burden for young, single-parent families jumped from 35 percent of their income in 1974 to 58 percent in 1987.

What does this mean? Those who must spend 60 percent of their income on rent are only one paycheck away from homelessness. And the poor are often working poor, equipped to work in an urban industrial world that no longer exists.

Drugs

Another plague has come to devastate the inner city in the 1980s and to change the shape of urban poverty. By 1990, it touched the lives of 18 percent of America's infants born in city hospitals. It fills the jails each day with teenagers doing heavy time. It has touched or helped to create a new vocabulary: crack babies, drive-by shootings, AIDS, coke-hookers. We speak of drug abuse.

In one sense, writing about drugs in connection with what we've called "the new urban poverty" doesn't quite fit. The crack-cocaine trade, for example, spells big money. It has become the newest U.S. "job program" for inner-city children, an urban cottage industry that brings in vast sums of wealth. "Whether or not the children involved in the crack trade are in gangs, they often become the primary money-winners in the family, take over the power role in the family, and may even strengthen this role by making their parents crack addicts."[38]

Drug abuse is not limited to the city or to the poor. Cocaine usage, for example, began with the wealthier classes and spread to the poor. In May 1983, the first U.S. cocaine hotline was set up to obtain information and aid callers seeking help. A first survey of hotline callers that year found that most users were well-educated and had an income adequate enough to support a habit of $640 a week on cocaine.

This was to change by the mid–1980s. The price of cocaine dropped and crack, a cocaine derivative and much cheaper, appeared on the scene. Crack, in the language of two faculty members of the Yale University School of Medicine, "is an egalitarian drug; every race and socioeconomic class in the Americas has been heavily impacted by it."[39]

How do we explain, then, the inner-city epidemic? Scholarship

38. David Allen and James Jekel, *Crack: The Broken Promise* (New York: St. Martin's, 1991), 85.
39. Ibid., 13.

finds a multiplicity of factors linked to drug abuse that we can see impacting the inner city of the 1980s. And in these factors we see the genuine poverty of drug abuse. We see the absence of a meaningful relationship to God; unfulfilled expectations; family insecurity; poor self-esteem and frustration; depression and mental instability; low academic motivation; the role modeling of family and peer substance abuse; high community availability of drugs.[40]

And out of these factors comes still more poverty. As Elijah Anderson describes it, the roles of drug pusher, pimp, and hustler become more attractive. The working residents of the community become more cautious, distrustful of anonymous young people. The atmosphere on the street becomes more and more one of estrangement, segmentation, and social distance. Traditional sex codes and family life are battered by new street pressures.[41]

A variety of social supports still exist to withstand the lure of the street/drug culture—strong commitments to the church and the gospel; extended kin networks; however battered, a deeper sense of neighborhood and community than the suburbs can provide. But the struggle grows.

The New Multicultural City

The American city has always functioned as a preview of coming attractions. In the streets and alleys of the early nineteenth-century city sprang up the factories, the first taste of coming industrialization. Major transportation shifts were hinted in the urban rail lines along which horse-drawn trollies clopped to the suburbs. New immigration patterns in the later nineteenth century shifted America's religious demographics to make room for Catholics and Jews. Greek, Yiddish, and Italian became the languages of city streets.

New Immigration Patterns

In the last decades of the twentieth century, another preview of the future is appearing in our cities. In America's traditional past, immigrants have been European and African. New immigration patterns are changing that picture.

40. James Jekel and David Allen, "Trends in Drug Abuse in the Mid-1980s," *The Yale Journal of Biology and Medicine* 60 (1987): 49–50.
41. Anderson, *Street Wise*, 77–111.

Figure 8
Percentage Increase of Minority Groups, 1980–1988

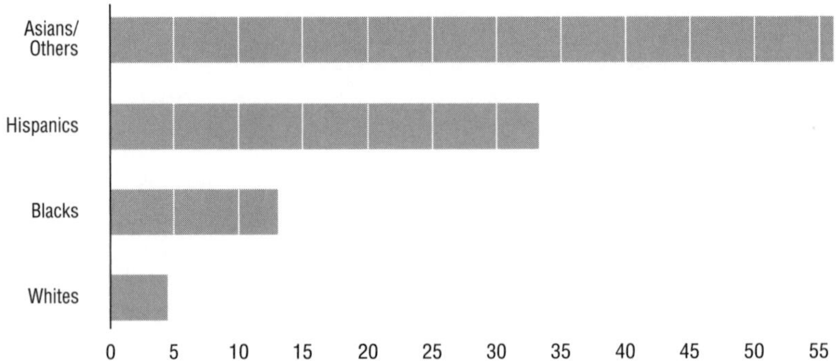

Adapted from Kenneth U. Fong, *Insights for Growing Asian-American Ministries* (Rosemead, Calif.: Ever Growing Publications, 1990), 26. Reprinted by permission.

Whites are becoming one more urban minority group. And the immigrant newcomers are non-Europeans. In the twenty-first century racial and ethnic groups in the U.S. will outnumber Anglos for the first time. Announces a headline from *American Demographics,* "You'll know it's the 21st century when everyone belongs to a minority group."[42]

Immigration will play a large role in this change. During the 1980s, the U.S. received 6 million legal immigrants, a significant jump from 4.2 million during the 1970s and 3.2 million during the 1960s. The future will see an acceleration of the process. The Immigration and Naturalization Service projects that legal immigration will exceed 700,000 per year starting in 1992. That compares with 600,000 per year as recently as the late 1980s.

Few of these immigrants now are of European descent. By 1990, one American in four defined himself or herself as Hispanic or non-white. To be sure, that means 77 percent of America's population of 250 million people are Anglo. But, predicts *Time* magazine, "If current trends in immigration and birth rates persist, the Hispanic population will have further increased an estimated 21%, the Asian presence about 22%, blacks almost 12% and whites a little more than 2% when the 20th century ends . . . By 2056, when someone born today [1990] will be 66 years old, the 'average' U.S. resident, as defined by

42. Judith Waldrop, "You'll Know It's the 21st Century When . . . ," *American Demographics* (December 1990): 23–27.

Census statistics, will trace his or her descent to Africa, Asia, the Hispanic world, the Pacific Islands, Arabia—almost anywhere but white Europe."[43]

Central cities will still be the front line for receiving these new immigrants. Already, in fact, America's cities are exhibiting this shifting. The Latino community is a good sample. Miami follows Havana as the second largest Cuban city in the world, New York the second largest Puerto Rican city after San Juan. It is, in fact, the large cities that continue to attract the Spanish-speaking newcomer. Dallas-Fort Worth's Latino community grew by 109 percent from 1980 to 1990, San Diego's by 86 percent, Los Angeles's by 73 percent, and Miami's, 71 percent.

Los Angeles offers probably the richest sampling. It is the new Ellis Island. By 1983, 117,000 of its 550,000 schoolchildren spoke one of 104 languages better than they did English. By 1990, Afro-Americans, Asian-Americans, and Latinos accounted for about 59 percent of the city's population. Nearly half of the new residents were recent immigrants. Each year the southern California city absorbs something like 110,000 new immigrants.

But the picture can be duplicated elsewhere. In 1980, Dallas was a mostly white town. And now? Comments a Dallas journalist, "A person caught in a time warp for the past 20 years—even the last 10— would not recognize the place today. You walk four blocks and move through five cultures—upscale white, low-income white, black, Hispanic, and Asian."[44]

On it goes. By 1990, there were 12,000 Hmong refugees from Laos settling in St. Paul. The manager of the Sesame Hut restaurant in Houston, a Korean immigrant, trains Hispanic immigrant workers to prepare Chinese-style food for its largely Afro-American customers. The sign is out all over the cities of the United States: "English spoken here."

"The Model Minority"

One ethnic community's history needs special attention in the closing years of this century. Though part of America's immigrant past, the Asian-Americans we highlight now are shaping a direction quite different from their older history.

43. "Beyond the Melting Pot," *Time,* 9 April 1990, 28.
44. "Our Big Cities Go Ethnic," *U.S. News and World Report,* 21 March 1983, 51.

Figure 9
Projected Percentages of Asian-Americans
in the United States by 2000

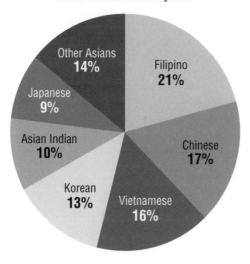

Adapted from Kenneth U.
Fong, *Insights for Growing
Asian-American Ministries*
(Rosemead, Calif.: Ever
Growing Publications, 1990),
45. Reprinted by permission.

For one thing, Asian-Americans represent the fastest growing community. During the 1980s, 2.4 million Asian immigrants arrived, representing an 80 percent increase. That far surpassed the Hispanic gain (39 percent) and was five times greater than the black gain (14 percent).[45]

California remains home to roughly 39 percent of the Asian-American community. And three-quarters of these live in the Los Angeles Basin or the San Francisco Bay area. "Clothing stores in Los Angeles stock petite sizes. Banks in Oakland hire tellers who speak Asian languages. Mainstream American businesses translate their ads into Chinese and Vietnamese for San Francisco's *Asian Yellow Pages*. In California, Asian-Americans have arrived."[46]

The overall size of the Asian-American community is still small. At 7.3 million in 1990, it still makes up only about 3 percent of the national population. But, unlike the Chinese in America's more remote past, these immigrants come as intact families and with the idea of permanent settlement.

Also, unlike the past, Asians come with higher reputations. Popu-

45. William O'Hare, "A New Look at Asian Americans," *American Demographics* 12, no. 10 (October 1990): 30.

46. Dan Fost, "California's Asian Market," *American Demographics* 12, no. 10 (October 1990): 34.

lar writing has some good reason to call them "the model minority."[47] They are the best educated group in the U.S.; 21 percent of them are college graduates, versus only 13 percent of all Americans. In the Silicon Valley south of San Francisco, 40 percent of the jobs in the semiconductor industry are held by Asians.

Also unlike their immigrant past in the U.S., they are more likely to come out of wealth, not poverty. Asian-Americans are more affluent than any other racial or ethnic group, including whites. The median household income of Asians was $31,578 in 1988. For non-Hispanic whites it was $28,661, $20,000 for Latinos, and $16,004 for Afro-Americans. Fully 32 percent of Asian-American households have incomes of $50,000 or more.

Ninety-three percent live in metropolitan areas, with about half of these in central cities and half in suburbs. This contrasts with whites, who are twice as likely to live in suburbs as in center cities.

Central cities will still be the front line for receiving new immigrants. Lower Manhattan and San Francisco, central Los Angeles and Philadelphia will still have their Chinatowns and, increasingly, their Koreatowns. But more quickly than Afro-Americans or Hispanics, they are more likely to integrate into wealthier, even white suburbs. They move more quickly into the suburban stream.

The New Suburbs

Suburban life also is changing. The post–1950s definition of suburbia as the bedroom community for nearby cities is slipping away in the post–1970s. We have already pointed to the significance of 1970. It marked the first time in American life that more people lived in the suburbs than in center cities and rural areas. By 1980, it was even clearer. Forty percent of the U.S. population were there, with 28 percent in the center cities and 32 percent in rural areas.

In this process, the division between the center city as workplace and the suburb as home began to disappear. Corporate life and industry were following the family out of the city, closing the gap between home and work.

In 1960 there were 130 U.S. Fortune 500 companies based in New York City. In 1990, there were 43, an outmigration of two-thirds.

---

47. For a healthy, balanced perspective on this term, consult Bob Suzuki, "Asian Americans as the 'Model Minority,'" *Change* (November/December 1989): 12–19.

Figure 10
Journey to Work Flow

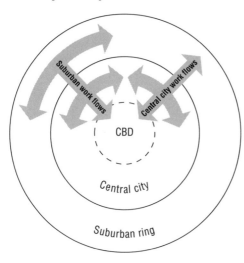

Four flows characterize commuting patterns today: 1) city to city; 2) city to suburb; 3) suburb to suburb; and 4) reverse commuting (city to suburb). Over one-half of the work trips in metropolitan areas today are suburb to suburb flows.

From Truman Hartshorn, *Interpreting the City: An Urban Geography*, 2d ed., copyright © 1992 John Wiley and Sons. Reprinted by permission of John Wiley and Sons, Inc.

Most of them fled to the suburbs. In 1975, for the first time suburban office construction slightly exceeded center city construction. By 1987, the ratio was about 60 percent suburban, 40 percent city.

The effect of this city-to-suburb relocation of the workplace was to further erode the idea of the suburb as a place from which wage-earners commuted daily to work in center city. By 1970, nine of the fifteen largest metropolitan area suburbs were the principal sources of employment. "In some cities, like San Francisco, almost three-fourths of all work trips were by people who neither lived nor worked in the core city."[48] By 1980, 38 percent of the nation's workers were commuting to their jobs, not from suburb to city, but from suburb to suburb. By 1990, almost 62 percent of major metro area jobs were to be found in the suburbs.[49]

The Suburb as "New City"

A variety of names are being given to this new suburban direction—boom town, spread city, slurb, exurb, sprawl. No longer sub-

---

48. Jackson, *Crabgrass Frontier*, 267.
49. Richard L. Forstall, "Going to Town," *American Demographics* 15, no. 5 (May 1993): 44. These reports on the shift of jobs and retailing from central cities to suburbs need to be balanced. Major suburbs still export more workers than they import, and central cities still employ many more workers than they house. Between 1960 and 1990, the number of jobs in the suburbs of major metro areas increased 159 percent. But jobs also grew 24 percent in central cities.

urbs, not quite cities, they are called "urban villages" by some. They spread along the interstate highways or the beltways that surround Baltimore and St. Louis, Columbus or Atlanta. Los Angeles becomes "a network of freeways in search of a city."

Suburbs grow like nodes strung along the highways, groups of interdependent focal points for business, housing, and entertainment. "Each urban village has its core—a kind of new downtown—where the buildings are tallest, the daytime population largest, and the traffic congestion most severe. And each urban village has its outlying districts, which may stretch as far as ten miles from the core."[50]

What makes them different from the post-World War II suburbs? Only some broad generalizations may be made here.[51] To repeat one point we have already made, they are no longer simply where people live; in the new suburbs people now work as well as live. Our jobs, the ways we generate wealth, have now joined us in the suburbs where we live and shop.

In fact, if the thesis of Joel Garreau is correct, jobs may have more of a role to play in the formation of the new suburbs than housing. These "edge cities," as he calls them, rarely have sidewalks, mayors, or city councils. What they do have is millions of square feet of office space like the Galleria area of downtown Houston, an area bigger than downtown Minneapolis. Or thousands of square feet or more of retail space, like the Perimeter Center area north of Atlanta.

Secondly, the basic unit of the suburban new city is no longer the street measured in blocks. The symbol of the new city is not a skyline of skyscrapers but a network of superhighways as seen from the air. The new city is a "growth corridor" stretching 50 to 100 miles. The streetcar created the first suburbs. Highway construction and the automobile have created the new cities. They are linked together not by locomotives and subways but by freeways and jogging paths.

Tysons Corner in northern Virginia is a good sample. An intersection with a beer joint called Tysons Inn in the 1940s, it is still unincorporated. But today it has more office space than either Baltimore or downtown Miami. Along the Route 1 corridor from Princeton to

50. Christopher Leinberger and Charles Lockwood, "How Business is Reshaping America," *The Atlantic Monthly* 258, no. 4 (October 1986): 43.

51. For a more detailed and vigorous defense of one view of the new urban frontier, consult Joel Garreau, *Edge City*. New York: Doubleday/Anchor Books, 1991. A careful review of Garreau's thesis is found in Carl Abbott, "To Boldly Go Where No Data Have Gone Before," *Journal of Urban History* 19, no. 3 (May 1993): 139–45.

northern New Jersey, one finds a ribbon of unincorporated towns, shopping clusters, and office buildings.

Thirdly, the new city is oriented around time, not space or sense of place. People are creating their own urban centers out of the destination they can reach by car in a reasonable length of time. The supermarket is ten minutes away in one direction. The shopping mall is thirty minutes in still another direction. And one's job is an hour away by still another route. The new city suburb is not defined by political incorporation; it is created by the destinations that define each person's movement—household, consumption, and production networks.[52]

Orange County, southeast of Los Angeles, began its evolution with the opening of Disneyland in 1955. It moved from a rural area to a suburb to 26 cities by 1980. No city claims to be center. One resident put it this way: "I live in Garden Grove, work in Irvine, shop in Santa Ana, go to the dentist in Anaheim, my husband works in Long Beach, and I used to be the president of the League of Women Voters in Fullerton."[53]

Changing Lifestyles

What changes in self-understanding has this new city "drive-in" culture made? How does this impact the previous suburban patterns?

Decentralization appears to be reaching to its outer limits. The new suburbs have been called centerless cities. No longer simply places of refuge standing between city and farm, their buffer-zone quality has been lost. They begin to resemble more and more the cities and display the cities' problems. Congestion, labor shortages, crime have all found their way to the new suburbs.[54]

And yet, precisely because of their centerlessness, they are less than cities. The earlier concepts of the suburb as a substitute center of power has evaporated in this new twist to suburbanization. The very concepts of "center" and "periphery" become obsolete.

Family patterns show signs of change. In the older suburban patterns married middle-class women with children were restricted to a life of neighborhood-oriented domesticity. The suburb resembled what William Whyte in his 1956 book, *The Organization Man*, called "sororities with kids."

52. Robert Fishman, "Metropolis Unbound," *Wilson Quarterly* 14, no. 1 (Winter 1990): 38.
53. Quoted in Jackson, *Crabgrass Frontier*, 265.
54. George J. Church, "The Boom Towns," *Time*, 15 June 1987, 15–17.

But in the 1970s, the number of cars doubled, giving families two sets of wheels instead of one. And, given this new mobility, employers realized they could have a tremendous advantage if they located jobs in this "realm of women," the suburbs. Garreau notes that if you ask developers when they first thought it would be a good idea to put a large-size office building in the middle of a cow pasture, many would have said 1978. That, as it turns out, was the greatest year in American history for women walking out of the home and into the work force for the first time.[55]

Now more than half of all women with children aged three years or younger are employed outside the home. Life in the new suburbs appears to be equalizing gender roles in the work force. Is the modern-day women's movement and its complaint against what Betty Friedan calls "domestic ideology" partly a by-product of the new suburbs?

Still another cultural shift in this move toward the new suburbs has been a weakening sense of community in metro America. And this is reflected in several areas. The polarization of suburb and city has grown. Our vocabulary illustrates the shift. The word *suburb* once implied a relationship with the city. Today it is more likely to imply a distinction from the city. Our professional sports teams, up until about 1960, bore the names of cities—the Boston Celtics, the Brooklyn Dodgers, the Vancouver Canucks. Now the designations cover a larger territory—the New Jersey Nets, the Minnesota Twins, the Texas Rangers.

One finds this same lack of community within the suburbs themselves. Centerless, they search for new ways of connecting. Perhaps the shopping mall fulfills that role increasingly. It becomes the center of entertainment and "community" life. Senior citizens gather in them, families stroll through them, and teenagers look for excitement in them. Boosters of the megamalls are arguing that way. "They are taking the place of the old central business districts and becoming the identifiable collecting points for the rootless families of the newer areas."[56]

How has the church responded to all this?

---

55. Garreau, *Edge City*, 111–12.
56. Jackson, *Crabgrass Frontier*, 260.

8

The White Church Faces the New City
1970–1990

Overall, the 1970s began with the apparent promise of a bright future for the church. Membership nationwide had reached its highest peak. In 1776 only 7 percent of the population were church members. By 1850 it had gone to 20 percent, by 1900, 36 percent. And by 1976, it was close to 60 percent. Peter Wagner was commenting in 1978 that "more Americans attend church in an average week than attend all professional baseball, basketball, and football games combined in an average year!"[1]

Suburbanization: Bane and Blessing

The 1970s arrived with many seeing suburbia as the new and challenging frontier for white Protestantism. Churches had followed the growing movement to the suburbs and were tasting the fruits in apparent church growth and massive building programs. "One happy result was the creation of hundreds of large, vital, and strong suburban parishes."[2]

1. Donald Hoke, ed., *Evangelicals Face the Future* (South Pasadena: William Carey Library, 1978), 31–32. Quoted in Howard Snyder with Daniel Runyon, *Foresight* (Nashville: Nelson, 1986), 30.
2. Lyle Schaller, ed., *Center City Churches* (Nashville: Abingdon, 1993), 13.

A small Brethren church in Seattle illustrates this optimistic mood of expansionism. With fewer than fifty members it decided to relocate in the emerging suburbs. "With $39,000 and a great deal of volunteer labor they managed to construct a modest church building and parsonage. Three years later their investment was valued at $150,000 and the church roll listed more than 300 members."[3]

Before World War II, to cite still another example, the single Houston Association of the Southern Baptist Convention had some 130 congregations in an area of some fifty miles in circumference. About 60 of these were in Houston proper. By 1978, four new Associations had been created to cover the same area and the original Association boasted 220 congregations. Sixty-eight churches had memberships exceeding 1,000 people. "Most of the growth has come in suburban areas."[4]

Evangelical Triumphs?

Into the 1980s, evangelical denominations outpaced the older mainline groups. The Southern Baptist Convention grew by more than two million members between 1970 and 1985; the Evangelical Free Church nearly tripled; the Assemblies of God passed that mark. By the end of the 1970s, most of the nation's largest congregations were found within the evangelical orbit.[5]

By contrast, the membership loss in mainline church bodies was staggering. And mainline studies were not afraid to make comparisons and ask why.[6] From 1967 to 1984, the Christian Church (Disciples of Christ) recorded a 40 percent decrease; Presbyterian Church (U.S.A.)—27 percent decrease; Episcopal Church—19 percent decrease; United Methodist Church—16 percent decrease; Lutheran Church in America—8 percent decrease.[7]

3. Robert Wuthnow, *The Restructuring of American Religion* (Princeton: Princeton University Press, 1988), 35.

4. Francis DuBose, *How Churches Grow in an Urban World* (Nashville: Broadman, 1978), 93.

5. Wuthnow, *The Restructuring of American Religion*, 192–93.

6. Two major studies reflecting on these issues and oriented to the mainline churches were Dean Kelley, *Why Conservative Churches Are Growing* (New York: Harper and Row, 1972); and, in response, Dean R. Hoge and David A. Roozen, eds., *Understanding Church Growth and Decline, 1950–1978* (New York: Pilgrim, 1979).

7. Leonard I. Sweet, "The Modernization of Protestant Religion in America," in *Altered Landscapes: Christianity in America, 1935–1985*, ed. David Lotz, Donald Shriver Jr., and John Wilson (Grand Rapids: Eerdmans, 1989), 30.

Table 3
Distribution of Mainliners, Evangelicals, and Catholics per 1,000 Church Members, 1940–1985

Denomination	1940	1960	1985	loss or gain
Mainliners				
United Methodist	124.7	93.0	64.3	–48%
Presbyterian, U.S.A.	41.7	36.4	21.3	–49%
Episcopal	30.9	28.6	19.2	–38%
Christian (Disciples)	25.7	15.7	7.8	–70%
United Church of Christ (Congregationalists)	26.5	19.6	11.8	–56%
Evangelicals				
Southern Baptists	76.7	85.0	101.3	+32%
Assemblies of God	3.1	4.4	14.6	+371%
Church of the Nazarene	2.6	2.7	3.7	+42%
Church of God (Cleveland, Tenn.)	1.0	1.5	3.6	+260%
Roman Catholics	330.0	367.9	368.4	+12%

From Roger Finke and Rodney Stark, *The Churching of America, 1776–1990* (New Brunswick: Rutgers University Press, 1992), 248. Reprinted by permission.

In all this, the evangelicals especially seemed to be gaining in power, if not prestige. *Newsweek* and *Time* billed 1976 "the year of the evangelical" in cover articles. In the same year, a Gallup survey affirmed that a third of the population were willing to identify themselves as born-again Christians. Before the year was out, the country had elected to the presidency Jimmy Carter, a self-declared born-again, evangelical Christian. And before the decade was out, fundamentalists, long silent over political involvement, had created a merger of conservative voices inside and outside the church to reclaim what they perceived to be America's traditional values. Out of a "politics of moralism" was born the New Christian Right.[8]

As one historian claimed, we were observing "one of the most remarkable developments in American religion since 1930 . . . , the re-

8. Robert Liebman and Robert Wuthnow, eds., *The New Christian Right: Mobilization and Legitimation* (New York: Aldine, 1983); Erling Jorstad, *The Politics of Moralism: The New Christian Right in American Life* (Minneapolis: Augsburg, 1981); Robert Zwier, *Born-Again Politics: The New Christian Right in America* (Downers Grove: InterVarsity, 1982).

emergence of evangelicalism as a force in American culture."[9] By 1989, a noted sociologist of religion, Rodney Stark, was predicting that "in the 1990s we will see the evangelicals growing and the oldline mainliners declining."[10]

Evangelical Absenteeism?

But was the evangelical future that rosy? Tex Sample, skeptical of a golden future for the mainline churches outside the social middle, questions also whether the evangelical movement would have the capacity to effect major changes in the culture. "In spite of all the publicity given to conservative and fundamentalist churches in recent years, they are not drawing any greater proportion of the population and are not reversing the trends in the United States."[11]

Evangelicals' triumphs, after all, were limited geographically. In keeping with past patterns, the large majority of white evangelicals continue to gravitate away from the urban centers. By 1979, mainline Presbyterians were abandoning two churches in the city for each one organized in the suburbs.[12] According to one 1987 study spanning a decade of reports, only 18 percent of those "conservative Protestants" surveyed were found in the 100 largest metropolitan areas; 43 percent were located in moderate-to-smaller urban areas.[13]

An earlier study appears to indicate the same general drifts. Evangelicals are strongly represented (43.7%) in rural communities of less than 2,500 people and possess minimal presence (8.6%) in cities of one million or more. "The next greatest percentage of Evangelicals is found in the medium-size cities (28.4%), followed by the small town (population 2,500–50,000) at 19.3 percent."[14]

Too many continued to see the cities, not as centers of positive power and change, but as what Harvey Cox calls spiritual disaster ar-

9. George Marsden, *Understanding Fundamentalism and Evangelicalism* (Grand Rapids: Eerdmans, 1991), 63.

10. Russell Chandler, *Racing Toward 2001: The Forces Shaping America's Religious Future* (Grand Rapids: Zondervan; San Francisco: HarperSan Francisco, 1992), 152.

11. Tex Sample, *U.S. Lifestyles and Mainline Churches* (Louisville: Westminster/John Knox, 1990), 5.

12. Carl Dudley, "Churches in Changing Communities," *Metro-Ministry: Ways and Means for the Urban Church*, ed. David Frenchak and Sharrel Keyes (Elgin, Ill.: David C. Cook, 1979), 78–79.

13. Wade Clark Roof and William McKinney, *American Mainline Religion: Its Changing Shape and Future* (New Brunswick: Rutgers University Press, 1987), 133–37.

14. James D. Hunter, *American Evangelicalism: Conservative Religion and the Quandary of Modernity* (New Brunswick: Rutgers University Press, 1983), 52.

eas. "There is a common suspicion of the city as the most concentrated location of the modern malady. For the fundamentalist, either based in a small-town setting or carrying its ethos to larger cities, the antiurban sentiment sounds forth in hymns about meeting the Lord 'in the Garden' and meeting with Him 'while the dew is still on the roses.' It appears in the folk saying that 'God made the country but man made the city.'"[15]

Reinforcement for this mentality may have come from another geographical source. Evangelicals and fundamentalists, it is true, had been expanding their base nationwide. But the regional distribution is uneven, generally following population shifts from East to West, from Rust Belt to Sun Belt, from North to South. As we have cited earlier, this Southern shift especially may be of some significance.

Not touched by rapid urbanization until post-World War II, the Southern way of life has long reflected regional values of a more rural and small-town character. "The frontier tradition of revivalism and appeal to emotions and a simple faith persisted in the small towns and rural areas within the region long after the course of mainline American religion had begun to change and adapt to urban life and pluralism."[16] Considering the recent trends of urbanization and population movement, one must expect changes in these Southern attitudes.[17] But one must also expect regional blending as evangelicalism found its way through the South, touched by this pro-rural and small-town tradition.

The New Christian Right, some argue, illustrates this influence. Out of fear for what it called "secular humanism," it reinvigorated many of the nineteenth-century evangelical ideals of respectable middle-class culture. And in doing so, it "drew in the natural Anglo-Protestant evangelical constituency of the South, which adopted the renewed Christian America ideal with particular fervor."[18] The shift of the population into the Sun Belt, where evangelical churches predominated, would surely encourage such a merger.[19]

15. Harvey Cox, *Religion in the Secular City: Toward a Postmodern Theology* (New York: Simon and Schuster, 1984), 40–41.

16. Roof and McKinney, *American Mainline Religion*, 128–29.

17. Samuel S. Hill Jr., *Southern Churches in Crisis* (Boston: Beacon, 1968), 176–80.

18. Marsden, *Understanding Fundamentalism and Evangelicalism*, 96.

19. The sociomoral viewpoint of the Southern regions is considerably more conservative than most of the other regions in the United States. For a regional evaluation of these liberal and conservative sociomoral viewpoints and their commitments to the platform of the Moral

In fact, argues Grant Whacker, what was really emerging in all this were two converging ideologies, not one—religious fundamentalism and cultural fundamentalism. "What is growing is not Evangelicalism, conceived as a religious and theological movement, but rather a segment within Evangelicalism defined by its allegiance to a cluster of ideals derived from Victorian middle-class society."[20] Less a list of discrete ideals and more a coherent worldview, the consensus it sought Whacker calls Christian civilization. Evangelicalism in America was seeking to become evangelicalism for America. But was it urban America?

Blended with a strong form of patriotic nationalism, its platform was rarely supportive specifically of emerging urban needs.[21] Individual leaders like Jerry Falwell confessed the racism of his past. But the nineteenth-century advocacy of the black cause did not find its strong place in the agenda of the New Christian Right. "Moral report cards" evaluating congressional voting records, prepared by groups like the Moral Majority and Christian Voice, indicated the same urban disinterest. Critics noted that "the cards omitted issues such as poverty, injustice, hunger, and oppression."[22]

By 1982, Kenneth Kantzer was ready to say that "the single most startling change in evangelicalism is its shift toward political and social involvement."[23] Carl Henry's 1947 indictment of the uneasy conscious of evangelicalism was being heard. But was it being heard too far away from the city to make a difference there?

The "New" Outsiders: Coping Models for Transition

The Anglo-Saxon church has dominated the American city throughout the history we have sketched so far. And standing on the

---

Majority consult John H. Simpson, "Moral Issues and Status Politics," in *The New Christian Right*, ed. Liebman and Wuthnow, 192–94. Simpson also notes a more conservative orientation in the rural hinterland, the smaller cities, and their suburbs.

20. Grant Whacker, "Searching for Norman Rockwell Popular Evangelicalism in Contemporary America," in *The Evangelical Tradition in America*, ed. Leonard I. Sweet (Macon, Ga.: Mercer University Press, 1984), 295.

21. For an extensive listing of such agenda items, consult Robert Zwier, *Born-Again Politics*, p. 57; Anson Shupe and William Stacey, "The Moral Majority Constituency," in *The New Christian Right*, ed. Liebman and Wuthnow, 107–8.

22. Jorstad, *The Politics of Moralism*, 84.

23. Kenneth Kantzer, "Reflections: Five Years of Change," *Christianity Today* 26 (26 November 1982): 14. For a helpful survey of this phenomenon consult Robert Booth Fowler, *A New Engagement: Evangelical Political Thought, 1966–1976* (Grand Rapids: Eerdmans, 1983).

Figure 11
Decrease in Urban White Population, 1920–2056

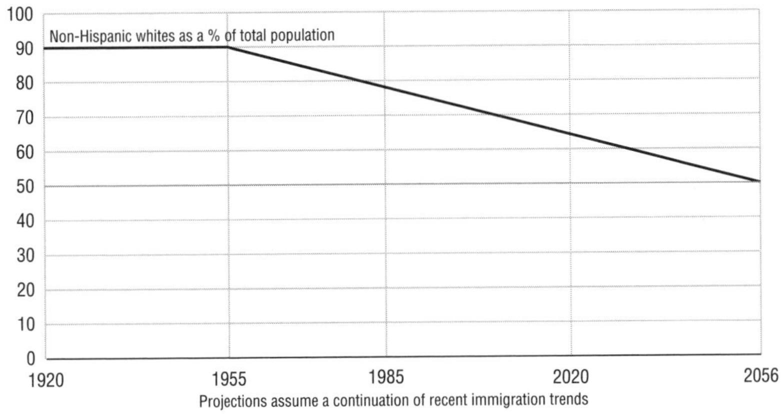

Projections assume a continuation of recent immigration trends

From Kenneth U. Fong, *Insights for Growing Asian-American Ministries* (Rosemead, Calif.: Ever Growing Publications, 1990), 25. Reprinted by permission.

edge of power, close but never inside, have been the Afro-American, Latino, and Asian churches. With the advance of the 1970s that picture began to change in many ways.

For the first time in American history, suburban populations outnumbered urban. And, for the first time in history, suburbanization drew the majority of white churches to the outer edges of inner-city life. Negative images of the city, urban multiethnicity, a growing identification of the church with middle-class success and upward mobility—pictures repeated from the nineteenth century—appeared again to reinforce and accelerate the churches' white flight.

A new urban church outsider was appearing now, the white evangelical community. And the symbol of that shift to the outside could be found in the "Old First" churches that once were centers of power in the life of the downtown urban community.

Formerly shapers of urban morals, the few that remained have tended to move in one of two directions. Some have developed a survivor mentality and become commuter congregations without neighborhood connections or roots.[24] Dependent on a small continuing core of members now living outside the community, they have seen

24. Raymond Bakke and Samuel K. Roberts, *The Expanded Mission of "Old First" Churches* (Valley Forge: Judson, 1986), 10–18.

suburbanization and racial polarization eroding their original sense of mission. A few have become regional churches, minimizing their physical connections with the neighborhood and widening their geographical base of operations. Like the commuter church, they remain predominantly white but with a more viable future, unplugged as they are from a geographical base and the transitions taking place in it.[25]

In 1972, one denomination "estimated that 150 of its churches were in communities 'undergoing ethnic change,' and that 600–800 of its 6,800 congregations throughout the United States would find themselves in changing communities by 1980."[26] They were not alone.

A survey of mainline denominations reported in 1979 that 10 percent of its congregations were directly involved in transition; the same report predicted that another 10 percent would be involved in the next decade. "If a church is to survive this transition, it will cost about $10,000 a year for about ten years, a total of $100,000 or about one-third the cost of starting a new church in the suburbs."[27]

What should they do? To what strategies could the white urban churches turn to deal with a neighborhood in transition? As the 1970s moved on, books began to appear addressing this growing anxiety.[28]

Total abandonment would be too strong a term to describe white evangelical attitudes toward the city. But many did decide that relocation to the suburbs was the only route for preservation. Twenty-eight Methodist churches closed or relocated in thirteen cities. The Lutheran Church in America had 63 congregations in 1973 Chicago and anticipated only 45 by 1983.[29]

Others tried to survive by merging with other weakened churches. This usually resulted in even more shrinking membership. "A surviv-

---

25. C. Kirk Hadaway, "Types of Growing Churches in Transition," *Urban Review* 1, no. 3 (October 1985): 16–18.

26. Walter Ziegenhals, *Urban Churches in Transition* (New York: Pilgrim, 1978), 16.

27. Dudley, "Churches in Changing Communities," in *Metro-Ministry*, 80.

28. Gaylord Noyce, *Survival and Mission for the City Church* (Philadelphia: Westminster, 1975); Lyle Schaller, *Survival Tactics in the Parish* (Nashville: Abingdon, 1977); Donald Shriver and Karl Ostram, *Is There Hope for the City?* (Philadelphia: Westminster, 1977); Carl Dudley, *Where Have All Our People Gone? New Choices for Old Churches* (New York: Pilgrim, 1979).

29. For a full picture of the history of one Lutheran denomination's responses to transitional neighborhoods, consult Harvey S. Peters Jr., "The Lutheran Church and Urban Ministry in North America: An Overview," in *The Experience of Hope*, ed. Wayne Stumme (Minneapolis: Augsburg Fortress, 1991), 23–32.

ing congregation in Kansas City, MO, serves as a typical example. It preserves in its membership the remnants of three congregations, two Presbyterian and one Methodist. In the 1950s, the three as independent congregations had a combined membership of over 5000 people. The merged church had fewer than 350 members by the end of the 1970s."[30]

The most promising models were those that determined to stay in the transitional community and develop ministries that would make the transition with it. And the most common coping model among these has been the homogeneous unit church, the birthing of, and/or transformation into, ethnic churches.

White congregations realized their neighborhood was changing and that deliberate efforts were required to reach the changing community. Sometimes by intention, sometimes not, these churches mothered new ethnic congregations as mission projects, birthing independent ministries in the process. Still others began to shift their own fellowship into an assimilationist pattern, adjusting worship services and style and opening themselves to gradual leadership change. Their expectation was that, as the community continued to change, the church would change with it, eventually becoming a church whose new sociocultural identity would be that of the changed neighborhood.

These changes often were not easily made. The sense of mission that motivated the church was sometimes as much concern for a dwindling financial base as a passion for evangelism and church planting. Untouched racial issues did not make transitions very smooth, especially among those congregations experiencing the assimilation of a new cultural group.

Still another model appeared in the form of the integrated or open church. Unlike the homogeneous unit pattern, the open church model did not have full change or assimilation as its goal. Such congregations saw blacks or whites comprise at least twenty percent of the active membership. "Both races are vitally involved in the leadership and decision making and the worship services reflect to some degree the experiences of both groups. There is also a growing but intangible experience of fellowship."[31]

30. Loyde Hartley, *Cities and Churches: An International Bibliography. Vol. II, 1960–1979* (Metuchen, N.J.: American Theological Library Association and the Scarecrow Press, 1992), 1357.

31. Jere Allen, "Stages of Transition," *Urban Review* 1, no. 3 (October 1985): 9.

How long most integrated churches remained integrated is subject
to some debate. One researcher has noted that "in racially changing
communities, there are few 'integrated' churches. Most so called 'integrated' churches are actually in transition from being a white
church to becoming a black church."[32]

Circle Church in Chicago is one of the more well known evangelical experiments of this kind.[33] It also illustrates the dynamic tensions
and problems linked with this model. Born in the late 1960s as an intentionally integrated congregation, it rejected the goal of assimilation in favor of a genuinely open, multi-ethnic church.

But divisions between black and white members and pastoral staff
began to appear in the early 1970s. Blacks saw a perceived abandonment of the team concept of ministry and a minimizing of the place
of black preaching style in the pulpit. Combined with these concerns
was a sense that the gospel place for the poor was being slighted.
There was also an absence of black members on the church's govern-
ing board. In January 1976, the services of the black pastor were terminated and black members and attenders departed with him. The
concept of the open church had been effectively destroyed at Circle
Church.[34]

The integrated or open church has worked well in stable pluralis-
tic settings consisting of multiracial and multiclass constituencies.
But they are few in number and fewer still of these have crossed class
lines.[35]

A third coping structure, the multicongregational church, has also
appeared to offer integration on a different level. In this model, two
or more ethnic churches, not simply individuals, are joined together
under the umbrella of a single church.[36] The integrated or open
church structure was a model centered around ethnic groups within
a single church. The multicongregational model centers around

32. J. H. Davis, *Dilemmas of Racial Transition: Proceedings of the National Leadership Conference* (Atlanta: Black Church Relations Dept., Home Mission Board, Southern Baptist Convention, 1981), 80.

33. David Mains, *Full Circle* (Waco: Word, 1971).

34. Manuel Ortiz, "Circle Church: A Case Study in Contextualization," *Urban Mission* 8,
no. 3 (January 1991): 12–14.

35. Larry McSwan, "Practical Approaches to Ethnic Ministry: Integrating What Is with
What Should Be," *Urban Review* 1, no. 4 (January 1986): 13.

36. The term *multicongregational* has also been used to describe congregations who simply
share their facilities with ethnic churches maintaining their own autonomy. But this does not
seem an appropriate use of the language to me.

ethnic churches often using separate languages but within a single church.

Much more than just sharing a common building, this model requires a common church membership roll, joint planning and programing, a common budget and, on regular occasions, common worship. But they also retain their own distinctness as an ethnic fellowship within the one fellowship. A joint pastoral ministry team includes pastors from each of the ethnic churches that make up the one church.

One of the oldest examples of this model is the First Church of the Nazarene founded in 1895 in Los Angeles by Dr. B. F. Bresee. Spanish- and Chinese-language congregations were housed then in the original church. But not until 1989, and a six-year journey of experimentation, did the fellowship develop an official charter as a multicongregational church. Now it is made up of English, Korean, Filipino, and Spanish-language congregations.[37]

This model is well suited for large churches located in urban areas where multi-ethnic communities live in geographical proximity. By the mid-1980s nearly 150 churches had adopted the model.[38] The First Baptist Church of Flushing, New York, is still another example of the model. In a nine-block square area of 90,000 people and 104 languages, its century-old building is home to a church of Chinese, Portuguese, and Spanish-language congregations. In addition, it carries on active ministry to the Jewish, Indian, and Afghan communities. "The 'main' congregation (meeting at the Sunday morning worship hour) is itself a multi-ethnic one, in which all the staff participate."[39]

The model is not without problems or issues that must be faced.[40] But the model, it is argued, solves more problems than it creates. "It allows for a unified expression of the diversity of the body of Christ, provides a missionary opportunity for a traditional congregation, and allows the full use of facilities in an otherwise declining situation. More importantly, . . . it has resulted in effective evangelism and growth of ethnic persons and created a consciousness of mission opportunity with ethnic communities."[41]

37. Jerry Appleby, *The Church Is in a Stew: Developing Multicongregational Churches* (Kansas City: Beacon Hill, 1990), 95–96. The charter of the church is found on 96–104.

38. Ibid., 47–48.

39. William Travis, "His Word to His World: First Baptist Church, Flushing, New York," *Urban Mission* 6, no. 3 (January 1989): 38.

40. Appleby, *The Church Is in a Stew*, 65–74.

41. McSwain, "Practical Approaches to Ethnic Ministry," 12–13.

Before we move on, a few concluding comments need to be made at this point. We have surveyed only those models motivated largely by the demands of transitional settings, models that have sought to meet those needs through rollovers from an originally white base.[42] One should not restrict our images of urban congregations to only these. There are other models still to be explored in this chapter.

Further, it is important also not to limit the urban church staying behind, white or otherwise, as exclusively shrinking, financially dependent ministries. "Many, if not a majority, of today's largest congregations are to be found in central cities . . . More than one-half of the forty largest Protestant congregations in the United States are to be found in large central cities as are more than one-half of the forty fastest growing Protestant churches in this nation."[43]

New Pleas for Holistic Mission in the City

As the white evangelical churches, now strongly suburban, moved more and more into the 1980s, coping strategies were becoming less useful and churches committed to the center city were seeing the need for a wider, more aggressive program. What was it to be? A single evangelical pattern of action appears difficult to trace.

Mainline denominations for some time had been calling for a more direct impact by the church on urban development and justice advocacy. And undoubtedly among these churches were evangelical members endorsing such public participation. The church, it was argued, must interact with issues of public policy, with those educational, political, and economic systems that made up the networking complex of the city.[44]

But there were other evangelicals not so supportive. And in many of the more explicitly evangelical denominations there was more reluctance yet. The agenda being proposed by the mainline churches—and in modified form by their fellow evangelicals—may have sounded to them too much like that of the nineteenth-century Social Gospel

---

42. For a wider picture of church models, less limited to this period of time and not originating in exclusively white churches facing transition, consult C. Peter Wagner, *Church Planting for a Greater Harvest* (Ventura, Calif.: Regal, 1990), 59–75.

43. Schaller, ed., *Center City Churches*, 12.

44. For samples of mainline church statements on urban ministry, consult Ronald Pasquariello, Donald Shriver Jr., and Alan Geyer, *Redeeming the City: Theology, Politics and Urban Policy* (New York: Pilgrim, 1982), 182–205.

or the institutional church movement, churches with a commitment to a social agenda and with pluralist theologies too broad to support it. And where was evangelism in it all?[45]

There were evangelicals, however, who had begun to plead for some sort of holistic connection between evangelism and social transformation. The 1974 gathering of the International Congress on World Evangelization in Lausanne was a major impetus. "In emphasizing that 'evangelism and socio-political involvement are both part of our Christian duty,' the Lausanne Covenant marked a turning point in evangelical thinking."[46] A door had been opened again, though not without disagreement.

In the years that followed, some evangelical critics voiced their concern over what they still perceived as a dichotomistic element remaining in the Lausanne Covenant that minimized social responsibility in favor of a priority for evangelism.[47] A 1982 study consultation on that very relationship was called to clarify the issue. It reaffirmed the two are "integrally related in our proclamation of and obedience to the gospel. The partnership is, in reality, a marriage."[48]

It was Lausanne that also promoted a link between these questions and the city. In June 1980, at the Lausanne-sponsored Consultation on World Evangelization (COWE) meeting in Pattaya, Thailand, a Mini-Consultation on Reaching Large Cities sparked a vigorous follow-up program. Ray Bakke was appointed as a Lausanne Associate to lead an extensive program of global consultations on urban ministry. By 1990 he had held such gatherings in over one hundred cities on six continents, drawing on his rich experience in an inner-city pastorate in Chicago.[49] Though not restricted to the United

45. A sample of such concerns may be found in David Hesselgrave, "Holes in 'Holistic Mission,'" *Trinity World Forum* 15, no. 3 (Spring 1990): 1–5; and the rejoinder by John Stott, "An Open Letter to David Hesselgrave," *Trinity World Forum* 16, no. 3 (Spring 1991): 1–2.

46. Athol Gill, "Christian Social Responsibility," in *The New Face of Evangelicalism*, ed. René Padilla (Downers Grove: InterVarsity, 1975), 89.

47. Harvie M. Conn, *Evangelism: Doing Justice and Preaching Grace* (Phillipsburg, N.J.: Presbyterian and Reformed, 1982), 61–63; Orlando Costas, "Proclaiming Christ in the Two Thirds World," in *Sharing Jesus in the Two Thirds World*, ed. Vinay Samuel and Chris Sugden, (Grand Rapids: Eerdmans, 1983), 1–4; Andrew Kirk, *Good News of the Kingdom Coming: The Marriage of Evangelism and Social Responsibility*. Downers Grove: InterVarsity, 1983.

48. *Evangelism and Social Responsibility: An Evangelical Commitment* (Wheaton: Lausanne Committee for World Evangelization, 1982), 34.

49. Ray Bakke with Jim Hart, *The Urban Christian: Effective Ministry in Today's Urban World* (Downers Grove: InterVarsity, 1987).

States, the strength of Lausanne's reputation and the urban focus were not lost on the American evangelical.

The second Lausanne Congress, held in Manila in 1989, reinforced the urban dimension of holistic mission even more. Called by one commentator "an immersion into the urban labyrinth," Lausanne II served as a platform for dialogue and consultation "oriented specifically toward urban mission."[50] "Willingly or unwillingly, mission leaders recognize that they must give cities more attention, and find effective ways to advance Christ's kingdom in the urban world with the same zeal and energy devoted to the rural."[51]

Supporting Lausanne in its urban focus was World Vision International. Prodded by its MARC program (Mission Advanced Research and Communication) in 1980, it began to expand its support of urban evangelism. In addition to its growing involvement in urban relief and development projects, it supported Bakke's involvement in raising the consciousness of Christian leaders through urban consultations.

In 1985 it established urban ministry as one of three new key ministry strategies. Robert Linthicum was called to develop and strengthen the program.[52] And under his direction, World Vision's longtime concerns for both evangelism and community development were focused on the city and the empowerment of the poor.[53]

It was John Perkins (1930–), an African-American from Mississippi, however, who touched the heartstrings of white evangelicals and showed what a fully holistic ministry could be. His autobiographical writings affirmed the authenticity of his evangelical credentials.[54] And his practical commitment to social and economic justice, worked out through the Voice of Calvary Ministries in Jackson, Mississippi, offered a concrete model with which even the moderate evangelical could identify.[55]

50. Samuel Escobar, "From Lausanne 1974 to Manila 1989: The Pilgrimage of Urban Mission," *Urban Mission* 7, no. 4 (March 1990): 22, 24.

51. Roger Greenway, "Reflections on Lausanne II," *Urban Mission* 7, no. 3 (January 1990): 6.

52. Robert Linthicum, "The Urban World and World Vision," *Urban Mission* 5, no. 1 (September 1987): 5–12.

53. Linthicum's theological and strategic vision may be seen in his two books, *City of God, City of Satan: A Biblical Theology of the Urban Church* (Grand Rapids: Zondervan, 1991) and *Empowering the Poor* (Monrovia, Calif.: MARC, 1991).

54. John Perkins, *A Quiet Revolution* (Waco: Word, 1976); *Let Justice Roll Down: John Perkins Tells His Own Story* (Ventura, Calif.: Regal, 1976).

55. John Perkins, *With Justice for All* (Ventura, Calif.: Regal, 1982).

Networking across white and black lines, Perkins's softer voice, backed up by an adult life of grace under brutality and oppression, succeeded in doing what Tom Skinner had articulated earlier. In 1982, he carried the pattern to northwest Pasadena, California, and created the Harambee Christian Family Center. The center was a demonstration model of evangelism, discipleship, education, and enabling on a community level.[56] In 1989 he founded the Christian Community Development Association (CCDA), with a membership of nearly 100 organizations and 500 individual members by 1991.

New evangelical directions in the 1980s were forming against the background of all these pleas. Mainline white churches, with some notable exceptions, continued to withdraw, church extension virtually stopping in both cities and suburbs. And, by contrast, "the number of evangelical Protestant urban missions increased."[57]

Influenced by the more radical evangelical wing of the 1960s and 1970s and a growing evangelical body of urban literature outdistancing the fading mainliner interests,[58] there was a new agenda shaping. The call for justice and for community action, a lesser concern of the nineteenth century, was being picked up again, but more loudly. The program index of the CCDA reflects it.

Traditional evangelical interests in items like evangelism, crisis assistance, alcohol abuse, health care, immigrants, and youth are there from the past. But added to them are larger, more systemic concerns—economic development, education and job training, nutrition, housing and homelessness, legal assistance. The immediate needs of the 1970s and 1980s were not being forgotten either. Three member

56. Benjamin Pierce, "Harambee Christian Family Center," *Urban Mission* 7, no. 5 (May 1990): 45–53.

57. Loyde Hartley, *Cities and Churches: an International Bibliography: Volume III, 1980–1991* (Metuchen, N.J.: American Theological Library Association and the Scarecrow Press, 1992), 1804.

58. Prominent samples of this interest include Roger Greenway, ed., *Discipling the City* (Grand Rapids: Baker, 1979; 2d ed., 1992); Frank Tillapaugh, *Unleashing the Church* (Ventura, Calif.: Regal, 1982); Larry Rose and Kirk Hadaway, eds., *The Urban Challenge: Reaching America's Cities with the Gospel* (Nashville: Broadman, 1982); Tom Sine, *The Mustard Seed Conspiracy* (Waco: Word, 1982); David Claerbaut, *Urban Ministry* (Grand Rapids: Zondervan, 1983); Harvie M. Conn, *A Clarified Vision for Urban Mission* (Grand Rapids: Zondervan, 1987); Roger Greenway and Timothy Monsma, *Cities: Mission's New Frontier* (Grand Rapids: Baker, 1989). Also playing a role was the journal *Urban Mission*, begun in 1983 and published by Westminster Theological Seminary.

associations are focused on questions relating to AIDS. Eight offer help for drug abuse, three reach out to teenage parents.[59]

More Holistic Models for Revitalization

Several flagship churches had already taken the lead in this new emphasis. Long before the agenda found acceptance, even before the later 1960s, the Church of the Saviour, an Episcopal congregation in Washington, D.C., "practiced reform-oriented evangelicalism. It rejected using an imposing church building; it insisted on forging a strong community among its members (and restricted admission to only those who could meet its rigorous standards); and, of course, it practiced Christian service in its local environment."[60]

The congregation's philosophy of ministry was built on a twofold focus, the Christian transformation of the inner person and mission to the outward world. And weaving the two commitments together was the conviction that "the outward journey is determined in part by the gifts discovered in the inward journey."[61]

Out of these convictions came a network of "mission groups," each with specific mandates. These groups worked to restore nearby houses and aid local homeless children. They followed the progress of government legislature of concern to the various groups. A coffeehouse ministry of evangelism and friendship was created, a home for those who needed mental help.[62]

In Chicago came another early flagship model, the LaSalle Street Church. Located in the heart of the original city, it carried the impeccable evangelical stamp of its mother congregation, Moody Church. By the 1960s it stood on the border of the affluent Gold Coast to the east and the impoverished black slums and the Cabrini-Green housing projects to the west. Before the 1960s, it was open to whites only.

In 1961, under the direction of its new pastor, Bill Leslie (d. 1993), the church started down a new road. Its evolving mission, as Leslie described it, was to be "an extension of Jesus' mission. That involves

59. *Christian Community Development Association: 1990–1991 Membership Directory* (Chicago: CCDA, 1991), 106–15. The mission statement and purpose of the CCDA is found on p. 4.

60. Fowler, *A New Engagement: Evangelical Political Thought, 1966–1976*, 112–13.

61. Elisabeth O'Connor, *Journey Inward, Journey Outward* (New York: Harper and Row, 1968), 33.

62. Gordon Cosby, *Handbook for Mission Groups* (Waco: Word, 1975) .

leading people to Jesus Christ, but it also demands that we be involved in the society around us as salt and light."[63]

The transition to a church "that takes on trouble" was not an easy
one. There were conflicts over change with the mother church and
old-time members, fears of the Social Gospel *redivivus* as the church
became involved in community projects with nonevangelical
churches. Would LaSalle Street Church lose its evangelical character?
Its doctrinal statement allayed some of those concerns by affirming its
theological commitments from the past. But it also laid the basis for
their new expression in an urban context of racial tension and need.[64]

Out of those commitments came a more holistic agenda—a "street
academy" for helping high-school dropouts qualify for diplomas; the
opening of a counseling center; a legal aid clinic for the poor;[65] participation with neighborhood churches in a housing corporation that
would erect four apartment buildings for singles, couples, seniors,
and families of different incomes. The spectating church had become
a ministering church.

Others were to follow these spearhead ministries into the 1980s.
The Church of the Nazarene initiated Compassionate Ministries, a
nationwide commitment to the urban poor that now spans the globe.
From its congregations like the Lamb's Church in Times Square,
New York[66] and Golden Gate Ministries in San Francisco have come
community-based services that target the needs of specific neighborhoods and respond to them "in the name of Christ." The list of services includes medical clinics for the homeless, crisis intervention,
client advocacy programs, job counseling, placement, and work skill
training, and halfway house residencies.[67] There is even room for an
off-Broadway theater!

The reader remembering ministry patterns from earlier decades
will quickly recall links with evangelical service from the past—food
and clothing distribution programs, aid for alcohol abusers, overnight
shelters, ministries aimed at youth and new immigrants. But even
these are expanding and changing to fit new needs.

---

63. William Leslie, "The Ministering Church," in *Metro-Ministry: Ways and Means for the Urban Church*, ed. David Frenchak and Sharrel Keyes (Elgin, Ill.: David C. Cook, 1979), 131.
64. Selected portions of the constitution are found in James Hefley and Marti Hefley, *The Church That Takes On Trouble* (Elgin, Ill.: David C. Cook, 1976), 223–25.
65. David Claerbaut, *The Reluctant Defender* (Wheaton: Tyndale House, 1978).
66. Paul Moore, *Shepherd of Times Square* (Nashville: Nelson, 1978).
67. Michael Christensen, *City Streets City People* (Nashville: Abingdon, 1988).

The venerable rescue mission of the Tenderloin is one sample. In the early twentieth century its guests were older men, most of them alcoholics. By 1989 those over 65 years of age accounted for only 6 percent; "the two largest age groups were 26–35 (25%) and 36–45 (23%), with the 18–25 years olds not far behind (17%)."[68] The clients continue to get younger.

Now spousal abuse, drug dependency, or job losses late in life have created a need for extended family shelters to house women with children (46 percent occupancy) and couples (31 percent). Intact families account for 19 percent of the families in such shelters. Ninety to 95 percent of those in women and family shelters had been homeless for almost a year.

Services have expanded—a hospital infirmary using over 100 volunteer physicians and nurses in the Union Gospel Mission of Portland; eighteen-month to two-year residential discipleship training and counseling programs in the 109-year-old Bowery Mission of New York or City Team of San Jose, California; trade skills taught while residing at Our Father's House in Lancaster, Pennsylvania; apartment residences serving as transitional halfway houses for the re-entry program of Bethesda Mission in Harrisburg, Pennsylvania.

Paralleling these new expansions of ministry is the Salvation Army. Building on its past record, the Army's program grows to meet new needs. Its Emergency Lodge in a renovated Holiday Inn in Chicago's Uptown is the city's largest family-oriented shelter. Its model Five-Stage program in St. Louis "provides a network of services which helps families break out of the cycle of homelessness."[69] Eighteen Harbor Light Centers, one of the most well known in Cleveland, offer counseling, work therapy, housing, medical, social, and spiritual help.

With the "graying of America" and the geriatric explosion have come new Army ministries oriented to the elderly. In Oklahoma City a Senior Citizen's Job Bank matches skills with available jobs and provides additional training if needed. Three adult daycare centers serve elderly and disabled adults in Cincinnati. Nutrition programs, health services, and permanent housing are a small part of the ministry of the Army's 249 senior citizens' clubs.

68. Steve Burger, "A Night in the Life of Rescue," *Rescue* 4, no. 4 (Winter 1989): 4.
69. Henry Gariepy, *Christianity in Action: The Salvation Army in the USA Today* (Wheaton: Victor, 1990), 50–51.

And underlying all these programs are the convictions of General Eva Burrows, former international head of the Army: "Some say, 'Social concern or evangelism.' Some say, 'Social concern is evangelism.' Some say, 'Social concern for evangelism.' But I say, 'Social concern and evangelism.'"[70]

Older models for youth ministry are shifting also. In a world of runaways oriented to sex, drugs, and gangs, some are finding that the popular paradigms created to reach the suburban WASP teenager don't work. They require suburban resources to function and perpetuate suburban values at the expense of those healthy values of urban Christians.[71]

Groups like Young Life are moving from programs to relationships on a more personal, incarnational basis.[72] Boston's Cambridge Institute experiments with intergenerational ministries and seeks to shift from professional to lay ministry, building in the process a deeper relationship to the urban church. Organizations like the Fellowship of Urban Youth Ministries arise to provide advice, training, and encouragement to urban youth workers and link caring networks together.

Others move in a still less structured direction. In the Uptown district of Chicago, Mark Van Houten leaves the residential rescue mission behind for a street ministry to homeless youth, gangs, drag queens, and teen prostitutes (male and female). His office a corner bar or a video gameroom, his office hours from late evening to early morning, he brings counseling, help, and a soft-style evangelism to the street.[73]

New Dimensions for Holistic Ministries

Though still, in some sense, following the voluntarist patterns of past years, these models also move beyond them in other ways. Unlike the past, leadership and participation is sought among both blacks and whites, some with more success than others. Racial reconciliation becomes a crucial part of ministry for Harbor House in East

70. Ibid., 20.

71. Chris Wiley, "Toward a New Vision for Urban Youth Ministry," *Urban Mission* 9, no. 4 (March 1992): 6–16.

72. Jean Sanson, "Young Life: A Model for Urban Ministry," *Urban Mission* 9, no. 4 (March 1992): 50–53.

73. Mark Van Houten, *God's Inner-City Address: Crossing the Boundaries* (Grand Rapids: Zondervan, 1988).

Oakland and the Family Consultation Service started in 1978 by Robert Lupton in Atlanta's inner-city Grant Park.[74]

Also unlike the past, these ministries are not carried on by whites from the security of the suburbs. Relocation to the city, a central theme of John Perkins's concerns, is incarnated in a variety of ways. Five people move into what would be called the Oak Street House to build a community for ministry in the Haight Ashbury district of San Francisco. The neighborhood is intentionally chosen in order to focus on the homeless population there. The Bowery Mission in New York opens in 1990 a six-apartment residence for homeless women and children. It is a pilot project to give resident staff members the experience they need to operate the Mission's larger planned residence for up to 70 mothers and children.[75]

Also unlike the past, larger problems demanding larger solutions have been addressed. As we have seen already, housing and homelessness needs have become a dominant concern. And these have been tackled on a large scale. Church- not rescue mission-sponsored shelters have increased dramatically. In New York, a central screening service involved 130 churches that were organized by Here's Life Inner-City to each take their quota of homeless persons for the night. In Los Angeles, two Christian businessmen purchased a 160-unit welfare hotel, the Strand, hoping to see their experiment develop into a model of Christian ministry.[76]

The program of Habitat for Humanity provides an even more permanent solution. Begun in 1976 under the Christian inspiration of Millard Fuller, the program focused on the rehabbing of poverty housing through volunteer labor. Initiating capital is provided through gifts and noninterest loans. And the homes are sold at no profit, with a no-interest mortgage repaid over a 15- to 25-year period. By 1986, there were 171 Habitat projects in the United States[77] and the program had expanded into fourteen developing countries

74. Robert Lupton, *Theirs Is the Kingdom: Celebrating the Gospel in Urban America* (San Francisco: Harper and Row, 1989).

75. "New Women's and Children's Residence Opens," *Ministries in Progress* (Spring 1990): 1.

76. Fletcher Tink, "The Strand Hotel: A Case Study in Faith or Failure," *Urban Mission* 7, no. 5 (May 1990): 28–35.

77. Tim Beidel, "The Lord's Work Cannot Wait for the Bureaucrats," *Sunday Local News*, West Chester, Pennsylvania, 16 November 1986, A15.

with modest projects underway in twenty-five locations.[78] By 1993, there were 800 U.S. affiliates.

Though not specifically evangelical, Habitat has won strong support from the evangelical community. Some churches like New Song Fellowship, a congregation of the Presbyterian Church in America located in what has been called a throwaway neighborhood of Baltimore, have even incorporated Habitat projects as part of their initial church planting strategy.[79]

In the past, obtaining the needed finances for urban ministry depended heavily on the voluntarist compassion of the middle- and upper-class evangelical church constituency. In the closing days of the twentieth century there emerged an additional source of revenue in major metropolitan areas—foundations created to empower the poor and to network between urban churches and available financial resources. The Pittsburgh Leadership Foundation provided an early model. It was soon followed by similar institutions in places like Chicago and Philadelphia.

Typical of these was the Greater Boston Development Coalition. Founded in 1991, it seeks "to maintain the integrity and visibility of the member organizations while creating an environment that fosters effective communication, partnership of available resources, and a common vision of 'Shalom' for our community."[80] Acting as a matchmaker and enabler, the coalition brings together community, church, and funding agencies to work on issues that might not be approached by a single local ministry. With other foundations like it, it desires to be a facilitator of ministries combining a concern for community needs with the message of the gospel.

Advocacy is another new approach by the evangelical. Seldom used in the past, it is directed to the more systemic nature of the city and operates on the principle that prevention is better than treatment. Most comfortable appears to be client advocacy, "to stand beside and speak up for the powerless." The creation of legal clinics, speaking on behalf of the homeless, and the ministry of the Prison Fellowship provide the best samples of this approach.

78. Millard Fuller with Diane Scott, *No More Shacks!* (Waco: Word, 1986), 36.

79. Felicity Barringer, "A Shift for Urban Renewal: Nurture the Grass Roots," *The New York Times*, 29 November 1992, 30.

80. Nick Ramsing, "The Greater Boston Development Coalition," *Urban Mission* 11, no. 2 (December 1993): 50.

Used with much more hesitancy and caution is public-policy advocacy, what some call standing up and speaking up for kingdom principles and values in the face of unjust systems and oppression. It takes many forms. "Social action, political lobbying, letter-writing, phone calls, court appearances, demonstrations, and prophetic judgment are the basic tools of public policy advocacy."[81]

Not all evangelicals are comfortable with any of these forms. Some question the legitimacy of the church's role in the public arena. Others find themselves more comfortable with only some of the forms. More radical communities like Sojourners find little difficulty with demonstrations. Other societies, like the Mennonite Central Committee, keep their wide Anabaptist constituency informed of upcoming political legislation through newsletters and encourage letter-writing responses.

Still other groups, like the National Association of Evangelicals, use the opportunity to speak before congressional subcommittees on more narrow issues they see as related to more traditional evangelical concerns. The Salvation Army follows a similar path in its concerns over poverty, hunger, and homelessness. The Prison Fellowship, under the dynamic leadership of Charles Colson, touches still other channels in its plea for reform of the legal system surrounding incarceration.

As a whole, though, many evangelicals remain slow to move in this area of advocacy, partly due to the lack of a strong sense of "social sin." Like the interaction of *Christianity Today* with the issues of American public life, the evangelical sees "social implications" that flow from the gospel. And flowing from this commitment, again like *CT*'s editors, they prod "Christians to fulfill their duty to the poor, the hungry, the less fortunate than themselves. Yet, they were unable to develop any theological way of addressing the causes of poverty, hunger, and destitution, other than to place the blame on unregenerate individuals and to work toward their redemption."[82]

---

81. Christensen, *City Streets City People*, 170.
82. Mark G. Toulouse, "*Christianity Today* and American Public Life: A Case Study," *Journal of Church and State* 35, no. 2 (Spring 1993): 279.

9

The Minority Churches
Face the New City
1970–1990

As whites and their churches moved to the suburbs, their place was taken by minorities and minority churches. Those who had been geographical and sociocultural "outsiders" for so long found they were now becoming urban "insiders."

For many a major factor in the shift was the abolition in 1965 of a "national origins" quota system that had restricted immigration for four decades. Doors were opened now to a different part of the world.

In 1914, 88 percent (almost nine-tenths) of America's immigrants came from Europe. By 1973, that figure had dropped to 23 percent. And in their place came Latinos and Asians, with 30 percent coming from Asia, 18 percent from Mexico, and 23 percent from Central and South America.[1] The United States, once a microcosm of European nationalities, has become a microcosm of the world.

In the last two decades, that picture has been reinforced dramatically. The United States is undergoing a new demographic transition to a multicultural society. Between 1980 and 1990 the foreign-born population increased by 40 percent, with Mexico the largest contributor (2,369,514 people). The Asian population has jumped from only 877,934 in 1960 to over 5 million by 1985, an increase of 577 percent (compared to 34 percent for the general population).[2]

1. Lyle Schaller, *Understanding Tomorrow* (Nashville: Abingdon, 1977), 68–69.
2. Kenneth U. Fong, *Insights for Growing Asian-American Ministries* (Rosemead, Calif.: Ever Growing Publications, 1990), 27.

The future will see an acceleration of the process. The Immigration and Naturalization Service projects that legal immigration will exceed 700,000 per year starting in 1992. That compares with 600,000 immigrants per year as recently as the late 1980s. Judith Waldrop predicts that by the twenty-first century everyone will belong to one kind of minority group or another.[3]

Central cities will still be the front line for receiving these new immigrants. Based on the 1980 census, four of New York's five boroughs are in the top ten most diverse counties in the nation. San Francisco is the most diverse. On a map, a band of highest-diversity counties extends from San Francisco southward and then across the lower part of the States through the Sun Belt. And the least diverse? "A broad swath stretching from northern New England through the Midwest and into Montana."[4]

New Insider Triumphs: The Black Church

In this multicultural urban society, the black churches, outsiders for such a long time in American history, have "maintained themselves fairly well since the 1950s. None of the mainline black denominations have experienced the kind of severe decline in membership that has affected some mainline white denominations . . . Some black denominations have grown in membership, with the Church of God in Christ showing the most rapid growth from about 800 churches to over 10,000 churches since 1950."[5] From 1980 to 1993, this body has averaged a gain of nearly 200,000 members and 600 congregations per year. It stands now at 5.5 million members, the fifth largest denomination in the country.[6]

Other growth records are less spectacular. The African Methodist Episcopal Church has experienced some measure of growth in some districts and among some congregations, particularly those touched by a neo-Pentecostal or charismatic flavor. Still others, like the Chris-

3. Judith Waldrop, "You'll Know It's the Twenty-First Century When. . .," *American Demographics* 12, no. 12 (December 1990): 23.

4. James Allen and Eugene Turner, "Where Diversity Reigns," *American Demographics* 12, no. 5 (August 1990): 36.

5. C. Eric Lincoln and Lawrence Mamiya, *The Black Church in the African American Experience* (Durham: Duke University Press, 1990), 158.

6. Kenneth B. Bedell, ed., *Yearbook of American and Canadian Churches, 1993* (Nashville: Abingdon, 1993), 8–9.

tian Methodist Episcopal Church and the AME Zion Church, have shown no decline but no rigorous growth either.

As in the white communities, it is among the black Holiness-Pentecostal bodies where one sees dynamic and drive. An integral part of the movement from its beginning, by 1965 over 1 million Afro-Americans were Pentecostal, 5 percent of the total black population then. "This was more than twice the national percentage of all Pentecostals, which was only 2 percent."[7] And sometime in the twenty-first century, predicts *Time* magazine in its issue of November 19, 1990, half of all black churchgoers will be Pentecostal.[8]

The contributions of the black churches, Pentecostal and otherwise, to the Afro-American community of the cities has been rich and diverse. The nature of worship as celebration "afforded tired and downtrodden people a recreative catharsis that helped them face an oppressive and frequently hostile larger world. The values inculcated in the lives of the sanctified church members—honesty, thrift, hard work, and discipline, combined with . . . moral asceticism—structured their daily lives around a coherent system of beliefs and, within the limits of racial discrimination, tended to promote upward mobility."[9] In a world destructive of black community, Afro-Americans found in the church the critical components of that missing community—intimacy, freedom of expression, face-to-face contact, and familiar social and physical surroundings.[10]

Holistic Models

Whether large or small, the black churches have continued to make their contributions. The storefront church, often maligned, opened its doors in hospitality to the Southern black during the time of the Great Migration when established churches would not. And it con-

7. Vinson Synan, *The Holiness-Pentecostal Movement in the United States* (Grand Rapids: Eerdmans, 1971), 179.
8. Russell Chandler, *Racing Toward 2001: The Forces Shaping America's Religious Future* (Grand Rapids: Zondervan, 1992), 176.
9. Albert J. Raboteau, "The Black Church: Continuity Within Change," *Altered Landscapes: Christianity in America, 1935–1985*, ed. David Lotz, Donald Shriver Jr., and John Wilson (Grand Rapids: Eerdmans, 1989), 81.
10. Melvin Williams, *Community in a Black Pentecostal Church: An Anthropological Study* (Prospect Heights, Ill.: Waveland, 1974), 8. A case study underlining this same theme of recovered community will be found in Carolyn Beck, "Entrepeneurs in God's Economy: Christian Stronghold Baptist Church," *Urban Mission* 7, no. 5 (May 1990): 7–19.

tinues to minister as a "walk-in" community to the near neighbor without personal transportation. Small churches in Boston and San Francisco, Cleveland and Dallas, with no tools except evangelism and love, serve as "healing communities" to the ex-addict and single teenage mother, the abused children and battered wives.

And scattered in the inner city are always the large congregations, megachurches before the term was coined—the black charismatic wave of the 1990s including at least a half dozen congregations in the multiple-thousands class; Twelfth Baptist Church serving its 1021 members in the Greater Roxbury and Boston areas; New Shiloh Baptist Church in Baltimore, its weekly program of "food evangelism" taking care of five hundred families yearly, its ministries extending out to senior adults, detention centers, and penal institutions. And balancing all these commitments the conviction of New Shiloh's pastor, Harold Carter: "we must refuse to believe," he argues, "that a social gospel that argues for man to order his own society through legislation and community actions is somehow more relevant than the fundamental message of the gospel declaring, 'You must be born again.'"[11]

Deliverance Evangelistic Church remains the largest Bible-believing church in Philadelphia. Its doors opened in the fall of 1960 with ten persons sharing the Pentecostal vision of a blue-collar worker, Benjamin Smith, its founder and current pastor. By the 1980s its attendance at five worship services was averaging 6,000. In 1992 its 10,000-seat sanctuary was dedicated in the neighborhood where it began.

With a strong Bible-teaching pulpit ministry and a pastor who spends up to five hours a day in prayer, Deliverance defies many white stereotypes of the Pentecostal tradition. Its membership stretches from low- to upper-income residents. Its outreach ministries include "a drug task force, caring for the homeless, a prison ministry, street evangelism, college campus ministries, hospital and nursing home evangelism," and a twenty-four-hour counseling ministry on the telephone.[12] And as a token of its commitment to the neighborhood, before the present sanctuary was erected on the site of the old Connie Mack Stadium, the church had set aside property for the development of a twenty-one-store shopping center, Hope Plaza.

11. B. Carlisle Driggers, comp., *Models of Metropolitan Ministry* (Nashville: Broadman, 1979), 26–27.
12. Andrew J. White, "Reaching the Lost at Any Cost," in *Center City Churches*, 69.

East Oakland, California, a community once predominantly white, is now 90 percent black. Meeting the needs of this neighborhood is the ministry of Allen Temple Baptist Church. A 21-member congregation at its founding in 1919, its membership passed 2,800 by 1983, representing more than 1,100 families. Affiliated with the Progressive National Baptist Convention and the American Baptist Convention, U.S.A., it has combined a vigorous blend of evangelistic enthusiasm and social concern. Since 1970 and the coming of its present pastor, Dr. J. Alfred Smith, more than 100 persons each year have been baptized into membership.

Pastor Smith pleads for a church that will be "the visible manifestation of the invisible Christ." "At Temple Baptist," he says, "the church assembled is concerned about regeneration and racism, hell and housing, justification and justice, evangelism and ecology, prayer and poverty."[13]

In that search for a "harmonious balance between faith and works," the church provides tutorial services for schoolchildren and an annual college scholarship program. Church volunteers work in patient services at a local hospital. Space is provided in the building for dental and medical clinics. Out of a nonprofit housing corporation spun off by the church has come the Allen Temple Arms, a housing facility for the elderly. Financial assistance on a limited scale is ready to pay for rent, medicine, and personal bills, available to both member and nonmember. A credit union began operation in 1979, sponsored by the church.[14]

Linking all this together is an equally vigorous commitment to evangelism. At least two revival meetings a year focus on the unsaved. And in the tradition of the black church, special occasions focus on gospel ministry. Evangelistic street meetings and neighborhood Bible studies are a few of the thirteen areas designated as evangelistic ministry by the church. About 30 percent of all new members come through conversion and baptism.

Some are concerned that the black church is losing its central place in the lives and day-to-day struggles of the Afro-American community.[15] But there are others like William Pannell of Fuller Seminary

13. G. Willis Bennett, *Effective Urban Church Ministry* (Nashville: Broadman, 1983), 36.

14. Ibid., 86–106.

15. E. Franklin Frazier, *The Negro Church in America* (New York: Schocken, 1964), 82; Ida R. Mukenge, *The Black Church in Urban America* (New York: University Press of America,

who still affirm that "the black church is both integrated into the Afro-American culture, and it is a source of strength for leadership and community development . . . It's the one constant."[16]

Lincoln and Mamiya support Pannell's judgment. "The majority of black urban churches are still strong, vibrant institutions and they have continued to attract and to hold the loyalty of a significant sector of the national black community. Gallup Poll data indicate that about 78 percent of the black population in 1987 were 'churched,' that is, claiming church membership and attending church within the last six months."[17]

New Insider Triumphs: the Latino Church

Once the Hispanic population was a pinch of spice for most Americans. Now Hispanics are the fastest growing segment of the U.S. population, the "invisible minority." The Anglo population fell from 83 percent in 1980 to about 80 percent in 1990. By contrast, "Hispanics increased from 14.6 million to 22.4 million, accounting for 9 percent of the population, up from 6.4 percent a decade before."[18] Ninety percent of these live in urban communities.

By the end of the century, some are predicting, Hispanics will be the largest minority, surpassing the African-American community. Depending on your count, their presence marks the United States as the third or fourth largest Spanish-speaking country in the world. By 2025 A.D. they will number over 60 million.

The difficulty of using one term to describe this whole community is apparent by looking at its ethnic and political composition. Mexico accounts for 52 percent (13.5 million). Twenty-four percent (6.2 million), both on the island and the mainland, are of Puerto Rican descent. Twenty percent or approximately 5 million are, to use the language of the U.S. Census Bureau, "other Hispanics." Four percent or approximately one million are Cuban.

1983), 204; Hart M. Nelsen, "Unchurched Black Americans: Patterns of Religiosity and Affiliation," *Review of Religious Research* 29, no. 4 (June 1988): 408–9.

16. Quoted in Chandler, *Racing Toward 2001*, 179.

17. Lincoln and Mamiya, *The Black Church in the African American Experience*, 159–60.

18. David D'Amico, "Evangelization Across Cultures in the United States: What to Do with the World Come to Us?" *Review and Expositor* 90, no. 1 (Winter 1993): 84; Manuel Ortiz, *The Hispanic Challenge: Opportunities Confronting the Church* (Downers Grove: InterVarsity, 1993), 26–27.

With the blacks, the vast majority of Hispanics form a growing and permanent underclass. Less than two-thirds finish high school, compared with nearly 90 percent of non-Hispanics. In 1988, the household net worth of white couples reached $62,390. By contrast, the net worth of black households was $17,640 and Hispanics even lower at only $15,690.[19]

Chronic unemployment continues to plague this community in which, by 1980, 70 percent were unskilled. In New Jersey, the estimated white unemployment rate for 1992 was 7.3 percent, up from 6 percent in 1991. For blacks, it was 11.5 percent. And higher still, the figure for Hispanics reached 15 percent.[20]

A Catholic Community?

And yet, as in the black community, evangelical churches continue to appear in the Hispanic community. Traditional Anglo stereotypes think of the Hispanic community as Roman Catholic. In fact, at least 70 percent of Hispanic Americans profess Catholicism. Nearly a third of the country's 55 million Catholics are Hispanic. And "with immigration and a high birth rate, Hispanic Americans are expected to make up about half of the country's Catholic population in another decade."[21]

At the same time, significant shifts are taking place. A relatively small proportion of the community (perhaps 9 percent) claim to have no religion. Even more striking is the growing number of Hispanics who have turned to the Protestant faith, perhaps more than 4 million. No precise count exists, but several indicators point to a growing constituency, particularly in the 1980s.

In 1986 the Gallup Religion Poll found that 19 percent of Hispanic Americans identified themselves as Protestants. Using data gathered by the University of Chicago, Father Andrew Greeley estimated in 1988 that about 23 percent of all Hispanic Americans were Protestants and that approximately 60,000 from that community join Protestant denominations each year.[22] "Three times as many Hispanic

19. Robert Pear, "Rich Got Richer in '80s, Others Held Even," *New York Times,* 10 January 1991, A1.

20. Neill Borowski, "Joblessness Persisting, Especially for Minorities," *Philadelphia Inquirer,* 9 August 1993, C1.

21. Roberto Suro, "Switch by Hispanic Catholics Changes Face of U.S. Religion," *New York Times,* 14 May 1989, 22.

22. Ibid.

Protestants are enrolled in Protestant seminaries and schools of theology as are enrolled in Catholic seminaries."[23]

In southern California, to cite one example, the number of Hispanic Protestant congregations jumped from 320 in 1970 to 1,022 in 1986 to 1,450 in 1990.[24] In Boston between 1970 and 1980 the Hispanic population doubled, and its Spanish-language churches grew from a handful to more than two dozen. By 1990 there were approximately 150 Spanish churches in Massachusetts, Rhode Island, and New Hampshire. And 43 were Protestant.[25]

The exact number of Hispanic Protestants in the U.S. is very hard to estimate. But "if there are at least 20 million Hispanics (and some researchers think the exact figure should be around 25 million), the number of these Protestants should be no less than 5.4 million or 23 percent in 1990, up from 16 percent in 1972."[26]

Figures on the full strength of the evangelical Latino subcommunity are just as hard to obtain. Some suggest there is a larger body of independent congregations in the community than among the blacks, and therefore harder to find and count. As with the black Christian constituency, there are also some congregations connected with predominantly white evangelical bodies. But these numbers are limited. And, argue some, this is linked in all likelihood to the preoccupation of such Anglo denominations with their own urban survival and to an ultimate disinterest in the evangelism of Hispanics.[27]

By 1988, the Church of the Nazarene had 124 organized Hispanic churches and 71 mission churches. The Church of God (Cleveland, Tenn.) listed 400 Hispanic churches on its rolls, the Evangelical Free Church of America only 18. The Assemblies of God saw a strong rise in the 1980s and counted 2,717 Hispanic ministers and 1,217 churches in its fellowship (a 35 percent increase for the decade).[28] The Southern Baptist Convention appears to have the strongest con-

---

23. David D'Amico, "Evangelization Across Cultures in the United States," 90.

24. Andrés Tapia, "¡Viva Los Evangelicos!" *Christianity Today* 35, no. 12 (25 October 1991): 18.

25. Alderi S. Matos, "Boston's Ethnic Churches," in *The Boston Church Directory, 1989–1990*, ed. Rudy Mitchell (Boston: Emmanuel Gospel Center, 1990), 256.

26. Manuel J. Gaxiola-Gaxiola, "Latin American Pentecostalism: A Mosaic within a Mosaic," *Pneuma: the Journal of the Society for Pentecostal Studies* 13, no. 2 (Fall 1991): 114.

27. Eldin Villafañe, *The Liberating Spirit: Toward an Hispanic-American Pentecostal Social Ethic* (Grand Rapids: Eerdmans, 1993), 67–68.

28. "Outreach Among Hispanics Increasing in NAE Denominations," *Action* (July-August 1988): 10.

stituency with 2,612 Hispanic congregations by 1987; it speaks of itself as "the largest Spanish-speaking evangelistic religious group in the world."[29]

It is outside all these circles, however, where the great growth lies. Unnoticed by mainstream Christianity, many meeting in storefronts, old theaters, former synagogues, and assorted commercial buildings, "one finds enthusiastic communities of faith, bearing vibrant witness for Jesus Christ and nurturing those who come to faith."[30]

And dominating this picture, even more than in the African-American world, is the family of Pentecostal fellowships. One estimate suggests that nationally, 15 to 20 percent of all Hispanic evangelicals consider themselves Pentecostals.[31] Fed strongly by "the airborne migration" of Puerto Ricans in the late 1940s and 1950s, New York City has exploded from 25 Hispanic Pentecostal churches in 1937 to 560 by 1983. Latin America Mission found that 58 percent of all Latino Protestants in Florida's Miami/Dade County were Pentecostals.

A Holistic Ministry?

Unlike the black church of the 1960s and early 1970s, the Hispanic evangelical community has occupied no center stage in Anglo society that might underline its needs and galvanize an outward-oriented agenda of concerns. Looked on by the white community as even more marginal, made even more invisible by a language barrier the black does not share, it seems more narrow in its focus. It looks more comfortable with revival meetings and mass evangelism than with some larger call to transform the city for good.

And within the church itself there are other obstacles to holistic self-expression. Theological commitments for some restrict the vitality of the gospel to a life of discipleship lived only within the doors of the church. The call to warfare against "the world, the flesh, and the devil" minimizes the role of the church in society as an agent of justice, freedom, and peace. Negative eschatological views are reinforced by the church's experience in its home-base cultures of Central and South America where the evangelical church has been forced

---

29. *Language Mission Facts: 1988 Update* (Atlanta: Home Mission Board, Southern Baptist Convention, 1988), 16.

30. Orlando Costas, "Evangelizing an Awakening Giant: Hispanics in the U.S.," *Signs of the Kingdom in the Secular City*, Helen J. Ujvarosy, ed. (Chicago: Covenant Press, 1984), 63.

31. Tapia, "¡Viva Los Evangelicos!" 20.

into a withdrawn minority role. And the church sees "the world" as a dying place and social expression outside the church, therefore, as a fruitless waste of time. The church takes on the look of a "haven for the masses."

Reinforcing these concerns may be Hispanic evangelicals' past experiences with what they perceived as "secularizing" efforts by mainline U.S. churches to aid the influx of the growing community in their adjustments to a new culture. One sample is provided by the "Houses of Neighborliness" and community centers erected by sponsoring interdenominational agencies in the 1930s.

They had "become so important in some communities that the people began to regard them as 'theirs' and to 'secularize' them. Neighborhood priorities displaced the evangelistic emphases and strained the relationships with the churches that conceived the centers as places where evangelization, if not proselytism, might occur."[32] Underlining this evangelical concern, often strongly anti-Catholic in its temperament, was the involvement of Roman Catholics in forming policy for the centers.

In the end, "Anglo sponsors as well as many 'pietistic' Hispanic congregations, offended by the social activism of the centers, resisted the success of these ministries."[33] And that ambivalent resistance has continued.

The Sanctuary movement of the early 1980s repeats the pattern. From 1982 to 1985 approximately 200 churches nationwide defied U.S. law and provided refuge for illegal Salvadoran and Guatemalan aliens who were unwilling to apply for political asylum. It would appear from news reports that the large majority of official sanctuary churches were Anglo, not Hispanic. And though many Hispanic congregations offered help to the Central American refugees on a more informal level, how many with clearcut evangelical credentials is difficult to evaluate based on the literature.[34]

32. Moises Sandoval, *On the Move: A History of the Hispanic Church in the United States* (Maryknoll: Orbis, 1990), 123. I am grateful to Michael Kelly for drawing my attention to this history.

33. Ibid.

34. Donovan J. Cook, "'Public Sanctuary' for Central American Refugees: Its Meaning and Implications," *American Baptist Quarterly* 3, no. 4 (December 1984): 315–20; Eldonna Fisher, "Help for the Homeless," *Presbyterian Survey* (May 1984): 24–27; Michael McConnell, "Sanctuary: No Stopping It Now," *The Other Side* 21, no. 2 (March 1985): 32–35; Daniel Ritchie, "Sanctuary," *Eternity* 36, no. 6 (June 1985): 24–28, 35.

And if Tom Sine is correct, there is still another barrier that many of the Hispanic evangelical churches must cross to a fuller urban ministry. Most of the Pentecostal and Baptist churches in its fold are essentially rural churches planted in urban areas.[35]

Yet the potential is here. And more than potential. The Hispanic evangelical cannot simply be dismissed as irrelevant and escapist in relation to the urban struggle. Financial pressures, language barriers, theological worldviews, and Anglo social perceptions may limit the scope of their holistic ministry to their own community. But it is real nonetheless.

In the small church homes are visited and the ill and disturbed find a caring community. Emergency financial aid is provided as possible newcomers to the country are met at the airport and oriented to the city. Pentecostal and non-Pentecostal alike locate housing and employment for members through their congregational grapevine. There is an open door of welcome and help for drug addicts, prostitutes, and other social outcasts.[36]

And in the larger churches there is elbow room for a larger ministry. The mission field of Love Gospel Assembly is the Fordham section of the Bronx, New York. The population there has dropped by 20 percent in the last twenty years. Forty percent of those who remain were on public assistance in the 1980s (14 percent for New York City as a whole). In Fordham, 44.3 percent of the population live below the poverty line; 42.9 percent are unemployed. All the figures seem to say, "Nothing can grow here."

Love Gospel Assembly, now a thirteen-year-old multiethnic congregation of about 300 members with a strong Hispanic base, has adopted that community. And in the words of one of its members, "The church has a good reputation in the community, because the vision has enabled us to institute people-oriented ministries instead of a 'fortress mentality.'"[37]

Door-to-door evangelism and street preaching take place on a weekly basis. A Love Kitchen lunch program feeds 600 people a day. Care services are staffed by trained counselors and a full-time lawyer,

35. Tom Sine, *Wild Hope* (Dallas: Word, 1991), 192.

36. Melvin Delgado and Denise Humn-Delgado, "Natural Support Systems: Source of Strength in Hispanic Communities," *Social Work* (January 1982): 83–89.

37. Luis Carlo, "Love Gospel Assembly: A Current Urban Ministry," unpublished paper, Alliance Theological Seminary, Nyack, N.Y., 8.

providing crisis counseling, referral services, and contacts with professional agencies and parachurch organizations. A coffeehouse ministry the last Saturday of each month is designed to evangelize the community on a more social level.

And their vision for the city? "Listen, the Lord is calling to the city . . . Hear, O tribe and assembly of the city" (Mic. 6:9).

In the South Bronx one finds another Pentecostal assembly, Iglesia Cristiana Juan 3:16, the largest Hispanic church in the U.S. by 1977. By the same year, this "Citadel of the City" had planted seventeen new churches throughout the Northeast, Puerto Rico, and the Dominican Republic. Fifty-four ministers had been nurtured there and sent out all over the Spanish-speaking world. Its Sunday school averaged over 1,500; over 1,000 attended every Sunday night service.

"It had several evangelistic teams and prison ministry teams, several standing Benevolent Programs, and provided the inspiration and leadership for a social service agency in the church's premises serving the church and community at large."[38] Its commitment to the poor stands firm. As the church grew in numbers and economic strength, many have wanted to move out of the ghetto. Its pastor for thirty-four years, the Rev. Ricardo Tañon, has resisted that temptation. Lighthouses are needed at the point of danger. And all the lights must be burning brightly.

New Insider/Outsiders: The Asian Churches

Where do we place the Asian-American churches? On the periphery or at the urban center? We focus for our answer on China and Korea. But their journey is a much more complex and diverse history than the African-American or the Hispanic.

Late Arrivals

For one thing, Asians come in large numbers more recently in American history. As we have noted in an earlier chapter, the Chinese Exclusionary Act of 1882 made the Chinese, for example, "the only foreign race formally excluded from immigration to the U.S."[39]

In those early years of anti-Chinese sentiment, the community sought refuge in the emerging Chinatowns of cities like San Fran-

---

38. Villafañe, *The Liberating Spirit*, 98.
39. Samuel Ling, "The Metamorphosis of Chinese Church Growth in North America, 1943–1983," *Chinese Around the World* (October 1983): 1.

cisco, Los Angeles, and New York. Self-insulation and segregation provided the poverty-stricken Chinese with a common cultural "identity and security where they could adjust to a new social, economic, political, and physical setting."[40] More severely isolated by language than even the Hispanic population, they planted their churches here also.

That exclusionary act was not repealed until 1943.[41] And until it was, the number of Chinese churches remained small. By 1931, there was a total of 64 churches in the United States and Canada. By 1952, there were 65 in the United States (43 connected to denominations, 14 independent, and 5 interdenominational). After a full century in the United States, "there were only 7,500 believers, roughly four percent of the total Chinese population, unevenly distributed among 62 Protestant churches."[42]

In the decades that followed, new waves of immigrants came and church growth began its expansion. By 1979, spread across a Chinese-American population of 705,600, there were 366 churches in the United States. In 27 years the Chinese Christian community had grown from an estimated 7,500 to approximately 50,000.[43] By 1985 that figure had reached 526 organized congregations, with an additional 159 designated as "Bible study groups or fellowships."[44] Congregations, by and large, have remained small, averaging 135 (according to a 1982 study).[45]

The rate of church growth, however, seems discouraging when compared with larger population estimates. One observer commented in 1977 that "during the past decade . . . the yearly increase of Christians is less than 2,000; only four percent of the population

40. Moses Chow, *Reconciling Our Kinsmen in the Gold Mountain* (Washington, D.C.: Ambassadors for Christ, Inc., 1972), 9.

41. For a full study of the effect of immigration policies on Asian-American church growth, consult Wi-jo Kang, "The Background of the U.S. Immigration Policy Toward Asians: Implications for the Urban Church Today," in *Signs of the Kingdom in the Secular City*, ed. Helen J. Ujvarosy (Chicago: Covenant, 1984), 75–80.

42. John Peter Chow, "Evangelism Among American Chinese," *Interlit* 14, no. 4 (December 1971): 11.

43. Felix Liu, "A Comparative Study of Selected Growing Chinese Churches in Los Angeles County" (Unpublished D.Miss. dissertation, Fuller Theological Seminary, Pasadena, 1981), 54.

44. Edward K. Knittler, "Development of a Manual for a Culturally Related Evangelism Program for Chinese Churches in North America," unpublished D.Min. dissertation, Eastern Baptist Theological Seminary, Philadelphia, 1988, 12–13.

45. Gail Law, *Chinese Churches Handbook* (Hong Kong: Chinese Coordination Centre of World Evangelism, 1982), 243.

growth. Actually, the increase is mainly due to migration of Christian families rather than by conversions."[46]

The growth of the Korean-American population and its churches follows a similar pattern in some ways—a small trickle at first, then a tidal wave of growth in the last half of the century. But several things mark it as unique.

Whereas the Chinese community's presence in the United States has spanned over a century and a half, the Korean history is briefer. Not until the first decade of the twentieth century did the first immigrants arrive on the U.S. mainland.

Further, "unlike the Chinese and Japanese immigrants, a majority of the early Korean immigrants had had some exposure to Christian missionaries, and many of them were already baptized Christians prior to their emigration from Korea . . . The number of Buddhists among the early Korean immigrants was negligible, and most were converted to Christianity later."[47]

This Christian legacy of Korean immigrants persists today in the massive population change since the 1960s. Never more than a community of 10,000 until the end of World War II, rapid demographic changes followed the U.S. Immigration Act of 1965. By 1980, sixteen years after the abandonment of the old quota system, the Korean population numbered 357,393. By the time of the 1990 census, it was closer to 814,000, a growth of 125.3 percent in ten years.

More remarkable yet has been the growth of the church during this time. "The number of Korean immigrant churches has grown even faster than the population from about 75 churches in 1970 to about 2,000 today—an unprecedented increase of about 27 times. This would mean that there is one Korean ethnic church for every 350 Koreans in the United States."[48]

A new proverb current among Korean-Americans summarizes well the picture: "When two Japanese meet, they set up a business firm; when two Chinese meet, they open a Chinese restaurant; and when two Koreans meet, they establish a church."[49] The comparison

46. Chow, "Evangelism Among American Chinese," 2.
47. Won-moo Hurh and Kwang-chung Kim, "Religious Participation of Korean Immigrants in the United States," *Journal for the Scientific Study of Religion* 29, no. 1 (1990): 21.
48. Ibid., 19.
49. Il-soo Kim, "Organizational Patterns of Korean American Methodist Churches: Denominationalism and Personal Community," unpublished paper read at the Bicentennial Consultation on Methodism and Ministry, Drew University, Madison, N.J., 13 April 1983, 2.

with the church in Korea is even more startling. Estimates place the church in the homeland between 30 and 35 percent of the population. By contrast, that proportion in the U.S. Korean community by 1984 had reached 70 percent, and 77 percent by 1988. Approximately half, 51.3 percent, are said to have been Christians prior to their emigration from Korea.[50]

Middle-Class/Suburban Orientation

Also unlike the African-American and Hispanic church communities, the Asian-American evangelical community of recent years has a larger constituency among the middle class. A greater degree of wealth represented by a larger number of university-trained professionals is present in the Chinese and Korean congregations today.

In fact, Asian-American households are more affluent than any other racial or ethnic group, including whites. "The median household income of Asians was $31,578 in 1988, compared with $28,661 for non-Hispanic whites, $20,000 for Hispanics, and $16,004 for blacks. Fully 32 percent of Asian-American households have incomes of $50,000 or more, compared with only 29 percent of non-Hispanic white households."[51]

Like the whites, this has turned the Asian-American communities and their churches to the suburbs recently in increasing numbers. By 1990, about half lived in central cities and half in suburbs. This contrasts with whites, who are twice as likely to live in suburbs as in central cities.[52]

As a result, "the Chinese community in major North American cities is rapidly polarized into two ecologies: affluence among Chinese dispersed or clustered in suburban neighborhoods and poverty among Chinese concentrated in the traditional inner-city Chinatowns."[53]

What effect has this had on the churches? In the suburban areas, there are more and more new churches or branch churches planted

---

50. Yong-soo Hyun, "The Relationship Between Cultural Assimilation Models, Religiosity, and Spiritual Well-Being Among Korean-American College Students and Young Adults in Korean Churches in Southern California," unpublished Ed.D. dissertation, Biola University, LaMirada, Calif., 1990, 1.

51. William O'Hare, "A New Look at Asian Americans," *American Demographics* 12, no. 10 (October 1990): 30.

52. Ibid.

53. Wing-ning Pang, "The Chinese Protestant Church in North America," *Chinese World Pulse* 6, no. 1 (March 1982): 4.

in emerging "Chinatowns" like Monterey Park or Alhambra in Los Angeles County. They represent a high degree of wealth and the new Chinese professional community. And their presence indicates that the suburban church has had some degree of success in evangelizing the Chinese in this socioeconomic group.

On the other hand, many of the churches remaining in the local Chinatown or its vicinity appear to be struggling in other ways. Like the suburban churches, they have yet to make a strong impact on subgroups in the community—the poor hidden behind the facade of the "gilded ghetto," the working class and elderly people, the Indo-Chinese refugees who find their homes in the Chinatowns of Houston and Philadelphia. And, like the white churches of recent history, they can be in danger of moving into the commuter church model, fed by suburbanites who come to church only on Sundays.

The recent history of the Korean-American community follows a somewhat similar pattern. "It was mainly the middle-class who had access to and resources for immigration, and who were in a position to take advantage of the U.S. Immigration Act of 1965, which favored family reunion and migration of professional and technical workers."[54]

And it is that urban middle class that continues to be highly represented among Korea's immigrant population. Between 1974 and 1977, 40 percent of the arrivals had previously engaged in professional and technical occupations in the homeland.[55] By 1975, 65 percent of the 560 Korean householders living in the New York metropolitan area had finished university studies in the homeland.[56] Their adjustment to urban life must have been a relatively easy one. Out of 622 Korean immigrants interviewed for a 1990 study, 97.4 percent came from the major cities of Korea, predominantly Seoul (74 percent).[57]

By and large, like the Chinese, recent church planting remains suburban in orientation. Small businesses proliferate in black neighborhoods. But Koreans, and their churches, remain in the suburbs,

54. Won-moo Huhr and Kwang-chung Kim, "Religious Participation of Korean Immigrants in the United States," 29.

55. Eui-young Yu, *Migug eui Hanin Sahoe* (Seoul: Bak Young Sa, 1983), 475.

56. Won-moo Huhr and Kwang-chung Kim, *Korean Immigrants in America* (Rutherford, N.J.: Fairleigh Dickenson University Press, 1984), 58.

57. Won-moo Huhr and Kwang-chung Kim, "Religious Participation of Korean Immigrants in the United States," 29.

avoiding living in the communities from where they draw their income. In 1991, for example, there were probably fewer than fifteen Korean congregations in Philadelphia proper but twenty-eight in the neighboring suburb of Montgomery County.[58] And in the larger metropolitan area covering several surrounding suburban counties that total figure reaches over one hundred.

Language and Assimilation

As we have pointed out in an earlier chapter, the Asian community has not escaped the racist stigma of being a peripheral "outsider" in the American city's history. Can its church escape that label now? Especially in view of its growing move, not to the city, but to the suburbs? Will it join the white church there and become a different model, a kind of "new insider/outsider"?

Both churches retain a strong sense of ethnic self-identity that makes any movement in this area difficult to plot. Both continue to struggle with the overwhelming barriers of communication in a language other than English. With the African-American and the Hispanic, both feel a growing sense of alienation from the majority white culture in which they have sought a home. Even their place in the suburbs with the whites does not always eliminate the sense of isolation or break the siren call to withdrawal.

The Chinese evangelical church, by virtue of its longer history in the U.S., shows signs of deep struggle in this whole area. And in this community the conflict often revolves around the issue of American-born Chinese (ABCs) and Overseas-born Chinese (OBCs).

Between these two groups the difference is much larger than place of birth. There are cultural and social differences that have left the church with a basic, unresolved tension over assimilation.[59] And these differences also have effected those churches located both in the city and in the suburbs.

Unlike the white urban churches of the post-1950s, creating transitional churches that would move from an OBC orientation to an ABC one, from a Chinese-dialect church to an English-speaking one, will not work easily at all. The ABC community obviously continues

58. James H. Chun, "Korean Communities in Montgomery County, Pa.," unpublished paper, Westminster Seminary, Philadelphia, 1991, 1, 14.

59. Cecilia Yau, ed., *A Winning Combination: ABC-OBC. Understanding the Cultural Tensions in Chinese Churches* (Petaluma, Calif.: Chinese Christian Mission, 1986), 1–15, 37–58.

Figure 12
Urban America 1990

U.S. counties with over 100 people per square mile.

Source: U.S. Census, 1990

to grow (40 percent of the entire U.S. Chinese population by 1980). But so does the OBC!

In this situation, assimilation is not a once-for-all battle the community can win and then move beyond. After all, is it ever once-for-all anyway? It is an ongoing struggle with which the church wrestles.

Can it be transcended by planting more Chinese evangelical churches in the suburbs where the ABC locate in larger numbers? Assuredly that will be needed and, in fact, appears to be the major trend already. Such churches also may have a stronger chance of integrating ABCs more deeply into the fellowship and leadership of the Chinese church where they have long felt a "housing shortage."[60] The potential for reaching ABCs for Christ in such fellowships seems high.

At the same time, there will be newcomers in the suburbs too who will need ministering in their own linguistic and cultural idiom—fam-

60. Hoover Wong, "The ABC Housing Problem," *Chinese Around the World* (October 1990): 1–6.

ily and friends uncomfortable still with either American monoculturalism or ABC biculturalism; young people just arrived who are neither first generation nor second generation. Language and ethnic issues will not disappear in the suburban setting.

By comparison, will the churches of Chinatown fade away? As long as OBC population continues to grow, as long as first-generation immigrants continue to seek a place where they may "feel at home" with family or friends in their own languages and cultures, as long as the Chinatowns of America's cities continue to welcome these newcomers and to be reception centers for the poor and the blue-collar workers, they will not. With the Chinese church there appears to be a blurring of the city/suburban distinction. Assimilation does much of the blurring.

The Korean Christian community now begins to face these same issues of assimilation, and probably on a more intense scale than even the Chinese. Their history in the U.S. is much briefer than the Chinese, and pressed therefore into a narrower assimilation timespan. Ninety percent of the Koreans residing in the U.S. by 1986 had come since 1965. To cite one local sample, the 1980 census notes that 94 percent of the Korean-born population in the New York metropolitan area arrived since 1965.[61]

Compounding the combined difficulties of this narrow time band and rapid growth of the Christian community are the large amount of first-generation Korean pastors serving these immigrant churches. Trained in Korea with the bulk of their church experience there, they come with an orientation and theological focus still directed by the needs of the homeland. The assimilation issues of the immigrant church are not always faced adequately by these pastors. Their orientation, by and large, remains monocultural, not bicultural.

The effect of all this on the Korean churches is a general preoccupation with their internal needs and their own survival. The focal point of social interaction and the center of community life, they often display what one author calls a "conservativeness and introvertedness" that tends "to reinforce Korean values and traditions."[62]

61. Nancy Fonder, *New Immigrants in New York* (New York: Columbia University Press, 1987), 221.
62. Dae-gee Kim, "Major Factors Conditioning the Acculturation of Korean-Americans with Respect to the Presbyterian Church in America and Its Missionary Obedience," unpublished D.Miss. dissertation, Fuller Theological Seminary, Pasadena, Calif., 1985, 102.

Until future generations change this picture of Chinese and Korean evangelicals and look for new models of ministry structured around the needs of an assimilating people of God, we are faced with churches characterized by great ambiguity in their philosophy of ministry. They will find serious difficulty in breaking through their "outsider" mentality to become full "insiders" in either city or suburb.

10

Into the Future

As the United States moves into the twenty-first century, it moves toward the future of what *Time* magazine calls "the world's first multicultural society." Sometime during the second half of that coming century, the white community, "the arbiters of the core national culture for most of its existence, are likely to slip into minority status."[1]

In fact, the picture we have drawn clearly suggests that process has begun. And not only in the place where America began, the city. Changes are touching the suburbs as well. More than one sign says that assimilation, traditionally seen as the responsibility of the non-white, non-Western part of America's population, is now also becoming the calling of the dwindling white majority.

And behind this new shape to assimilation in a multicultural society is a new direction for the city. Its boundary widens its impact on culture, politics, and society. It extends its impact past suburb, county, state, and even nation. Television imprints "Los Angelization" on the world through its images. Stock exchanges cross international boundaries bearing the names not of countries but of cities—London, Paris, New York. Instant electronic contact links Seattle to Pittsburgh, Austin to Louisville, bypassing county and state sovereignty zones. America's rural areas exhibit more city traits.[2]

---

1. "America's Immigrant Challenge," *Time*, special issue (Fall 1993), 5.
2. Walter F. Naedele, "Adieu to Country Bumpkins," *Philadelphia Inquirer*, 1 November 1993, B1–B2.

Neal Peirce suggests we are returning to something resembling the old age of the city-state. "Great metropolitan regions—not cities, not states, not even the nation states—are starting to emerge as the world's most influential players."[3]

How will the evangelical churches confront America's part in this new 'citistate' face on the future?

New White Commitments

There are indications that some white evangelical denominations may be beginning to come to grips with an urban minority future. At the 1986 General Conference of the Evangelical Free Church, a mandate was given to the Church Ministries Department—2,000 new congregations in the U.S. by 2000.

Included in the developing master plan are the following objectives: the targeting of 10 world-class cities in the country through the recruiting and deployment of 40 church planting teams; the creation of a network of community centers and mercy ministries providing a holistic Christian approach to the poor and helpless; the cultivation and planting of 600 ethnic churches. The target? To have 20 percent of the denomination's congregations ethnic by the end of this century.

Other bodies begin to stir. In May 1993, the Division of Home Missions of the Assemblies of God convened a prayer and strategy conference, *Cities '93,* to focus on urban needs. Their concern? Only 25 percent of their churches are in cities of 50,000 or more. The Presbyterian Church of America joins them in that same concern. Excited by the rapid growth of a newly planted congregation in New York in the late 1980s,[4] they now make plans for a network of similar "flagship churches" in major centers like Boston, San Francisco, and Toronto. Undeterred by denominational inability to plant or attract black and Hispanic churches, their desire is to see created around these flagships multicultural presbyteries reaching into minority communities.

And leading all these white denominations is the crosscultural vision of the Southern Baptist Convention (SBC). A conservative

3. Neal Peirce, "The 'Citistates' Are on the Rise, and the Competition Is Fierce," *Philadelphia Inquirer,* 26 July 1993, A11.

4. Timothy Keller, "An Evangelical Mission in a Secular City," *Center City Churches,* ed. Lyle Schaller (Nashville: Abingdon, 1993), 31–41.

membership estimate based on 1993 data "indicates that there are at least 4,000 units or congregations among 101 ethnic groups and 97 American Indian tribes utilizing 98 different languages. The ethnic groups and the number of congregations are: Hispanic (1578), American Indian (478), Deaf (477), Korean (400), Chinese (159), French (150), Vietnamese (89), Filipino (58), and Haitian (48). During 1991, 466 new units were established and during the decade from 1980 to 1990 all the ethnic congregation in cooperation with the SBC experienced a growth rate of 147 percent."[5]

Another shift in direction comes from some evangelical relief and development agencies traditionally oriented to overseas ministries. "Though none of the groups plans to diminish its overseas emphasis, many are exploring new ways to meet the needs of urban America."[6] Oceans need no crossing to minister to the world's needy.

Organizations like Compassion International change their U.S. budget commitments from less than 1 percent in 1993 to 20 percent during the next five years. World Relief, the international assistance arm of the National Association of Evangelicals, by 1992 had nearly doubled its U.S. budget program to 43 percent from 1987. World Vision spent 1.78 percent of its total monies in America in 1988; by 1992, that figure was up to 2.6 percent.

Rising Concerns

How far will these interests take the white evangelical churches and institutions? Is it the initiative of an integrating breakthrough for a new day? Only the future will tell. But the past speaks too loudly of disappointment to be too optimistic.

Minority churches, especially those of the African-American and Hispanic communities, have watched these overtures before. "They know that white churches opted out of the city years ago, thus forfeiting the right to define anything for them."[7] And with the deepening roots of the white church in a suburban mentality, few signs appear

5. David D'Amico, "Evangelization Across Cultures in the United States: What to Do with the World Come to Us?" *Review and Expositor* 90, no. 1 (Winter 1993): 88.

6. Thomas S. Giles, "Overseas Ministries Step Up Fight Against U.S. Ills," *Christianity Today* 37, no. 7 (21 June 1993): 57.

7. William Pannell, *The Coming Race Wars? A Cry for Reconciliation* (Grand Rapids: Zondervan, 1993), 110.

to indicate the white church has any radical comprehension of the hopelessness of a mission field only miles away.

Speaking in a 1989 consultation, the Reverend H. O. Espinoza, president of the evangelical Hispanic organization *Promesa,* reflects this frustration. "There exists," he remarks, "no interaction, fellowship, communion, consultation, or even conversation between Hispanic and Anglo churches even within the same denomination."[8]

At the 1993 convention of the National Association of Evangelicals, to cite another example, one workshop leader spoke with frustration of his feeling like a "token minority." He continued, "I'm not sure NAE understands what racial reconciliation means. A lot has been communicated to us by never speaking a word." Some who heard his comments nodded in agreement.[9] One NAE board member, by contrast, said he considered the organization was integrated. On what basis? The NAE, he responded, had "at least four African Americans, one Asian, and several Hispanics leading workshops" at the convention!

New Minority Challenges

In the meantime, black and Hispanic churches especially look to a future with new questions. And one of the largest concerns a new social change in their communities.

The Rise of the Middle Class

In both societies a growing class division is sending a middle-income working class and middle class to the suburbs. And left behind is the hard-core urban poor. Blacks and Hispanics each are becoming two societies.

Paralleling the experience of the African-American community (see chap. 7), almost 43 percent of U.S. Hispanics were living in metropolitan-area suburbs by the time of the 1990 census (an increase of 3 percent since 1980). The suburbs gained 15.3 million people during the 1980s, and Hispanics accounted for 23 percent of that total gain.

8. H. O. Espinoza, "Response to William H. and Ruth Lewis Bentley," in *Evangelical Affirmations,* ed. Kenneth Kantzer and Carl F. H. Henry (Grand Rapids: Zondervan, 1990), 340.

9. Jo Kadlecek, "The Coloring of the American Church," *National and International Religion Report* 7, no. 9 (19 April 1993): 4.

In these suburbs the median income grows. For Hispanic house-holds it was $26,811 in 1991, 33 percent higher than that of Hispanic households in central cities ($20,387). "This gap is even wider in metropolitan areas with populations of 1 million or more. In the largest metros, suburban Hispanic incomes are 40 percent higher than in central cities."[10]

How does all this effect the church? As the black and Hispanic middle class evacuates the inner city, following their white counterparts before them, the churches lose valuable resources for leadership, economic support, and incarnational ministry in those inner-city neighborhoods.

In some cases, new black suburban churches appear in areas like Fort Washington, just outside of Washington, D.C. And they grow rapidly. A very small percentage of believers find their way into predominantly white suburban churches.[11] And still others wend their way back to the inner city on Sundays, now more pilgrims than full participants in the churches that nurtured them in the past.

The challenge for the future is twofold. One is oriented to the inner-city churches. Will African-American and Hispanic churches, denuded of a now disappearing middle class, be able to continue transcending class boundaries and reach out to the hard-core urban poor? Can they encourage a missiological commitment on the part of that middle class to continue to reach out in that ministry with them?

William Bentley and Ruth Bentley, speaking of these questions in the black church, could easily be speaking also for the Hispanic evangelical. They note, "Intentional or not, along with the new independence of such middle-classes, went the simultaneous loss of much of the historical Black leadership. This loss of leadership, along with the loss of physical presence in many cases, is a major factor in the collapse of the Black communities. In far too many cases, Black professionals and other members of the Black nouveau riche no longer find it necessary to live among their people; and many of them admit to finding it unnecessary to feel responsible to fill leadership roles."[12]

10. William H. Frey and William P. O'Hare, "¡Vivan los Suburbios!" *American Demographics* 15, no. 4 (April 1993): 32.

11. Thomas A. Van Eck, "Racial Diversity in Suburban Congregations," *Christ and Community Forum* 11, no. 2 (Spring 1992): 1, 6.

12. William F. Bentley and Ruth Lewis Bentley, "Reflections on the Scope and Function of a Black Evangelical Black Theology," in *Evangelical Affirmations,* ed. Kenneth Kantzer and Carl F. H. Henry, 318.

A second challenge also faces these minority churches as they wrestle with the suburbanization of their middle class. These congregations will also have to turn their eyes to a new kind of neighborhood, to the growing suburbs where African-Americans and Hispanics are moving in a new migration. The new reality is a call to these fellowships to begin again a church planting movement, this time to the suburbs to meet the minority newcomers; the church cannot ignore them either. The suburbs also need black and Hispanic churches.[13]

The Rise of the Separatist Movement

A new issue is also rising on the minority agenda. There is an emerging separatist movement among some in those ethnic groups that have particularly suffered from socioeconomic exclusion. Blacks and Hispanics who have been ethnocultural outsiders for so long are now the demographical insiders in the city. White patterns of segregation have drawn social, economic, and geographical walls around them for centuries. Now blacks and Hispanics, more disillusioned than ever by unkept promises, are themselves turning to separate development as a positive response to those exclusionary practices.

The plea is coming not only from radical voices within the communities. It is not reverse segregationism nor is it new; the earlier pleas of Marcus Garvey and Malcolm X echoed it.[14] But now, with a growing economic power base and a black constituency that is fast becoming demographically mainline and sociologically more representative, it is closer to possibility.

"The train of thought runs the whole gamut, from all-black private schools, universities, churches and neighborhoods to a separate black state federally funded as restitution for slavery. 'If we can do it for Israel, why not for blacks?' is the rationale."[15]

Although these suggestions are not receiving too much popular support, there is growing enthusiasm for less radical programs. On campuses like Duke University, black middle-class students are withdrawing into black enclaves to build their own cultural self-awareness. In the area of schooling, Molefe Asante, black crusader for

---

13. Harvie M. Conn, "The Suburban Black Movement," *Metro-Voice* (Fall 1993): 3–4.

14. Wilson O. O. Mututua, "Garveyism and the Rise of the American Muslim Mission (AMM)," Unpublished M.A. thesis, Drew University, Madison, N.J., 1981; James Cone, *Martin and Malcolm and America: A Dream or a Nightmare* (Maryknoll: Orbis, 1991), 105–10.

15. Spencer Perkins and Chris Rice, *More Than Equals: Racial Healing for the Sake of the Gospel* (Downers Grove: InterVarsity, 1993), 27.

Afrocentrism, pleads for curricular changes that will highlight African roots for black youth. If African-Americans are to become whole again, he contends, they must reclaim their culture and history and stop becoming imitation whites.[16]

Now the church is wrestling with these same ideas on a scaled-down dimension. In December 1990, for example, the Pew Foundation brought together Hispanic church leaders from across the nation to look at the future of that church. "One of the major outcomes of the gathering was the discussion of the possibility of creating their own seminaries and support institutions instead of being chronically dependent on the Anglo church."[17]

African-American church leaders, with a long history of such institutions, are finding new cultural support for these early commitments. As the torch is passed from one black generation of scholars and preachers to another, the rocky relationship between the black church and white mainline evangelicalism is prompting a new look at an old pattern.

At a June 1993, symposium sponsored by Philadelphia's Center for Urban Theological Studies, Clarence Hilliard echoed some of these themes. "White folks are unwilling to empower black people," said the chairman of the Commission of Social Action for the National Black Evangelical Association. Continued Hilliard, "Look at the top. We ain't there. We need to learn to do for ourselves."[18] The senior bishop of the AME Church in Atlanta, John Hurst Adams, repeats the refrain. "We are not buying the integration route. We never have and never will. We seek an inclusive society that need not be integrated but values diversity and respects it."[19]

New/Old Remaining Questions

Are things changing? Demographically, they are. In 1990, the U.S. population had the following breakdown: Anglo 76 percent, Afro-American 12 percent, Latino 9 percent, Asian 3 percent. By 2050, if

16. Molefi Kete Asante, *The Afrocentric Idea* (Philadelphia: Temple University Press, 1987). See also Tanya Barrientos, "In Camden, Afrocentrism is Bringing Academic Gains," *Philadelphia Inquirer,* 4 March 1991, 1B, 4B.

17. Tom Sine, *Wild Hope* (Dallas: Word, 1991), 194.

18. Rebekah Schreffler, "Blacks Passing Leadership Torch," *Christianity Today* 37, no. 9 (16 August 1993): 41.

19. Richard Ostling, "Strains on the Heart," *Time,* 19 November 1990, 90.

the Lord tarries, the breakdown is projected to be: Anglo 52 percent, Afro-American 16 percent, Latino 22 percent, and Asian 10 percent.[20]

Geographically, things are changing as well. By 1990, cities have become metropolitan areas, suburbs have become "edge cities." By 2050, metropolitan areas will absorb the emerging "edge cities" and be "citistates." Communities fleeing from the "citistate" will be looking for a new word to describe suburb.

Racism and Ethnic Conflict

Ethnic tensions have taken new turns as ethnic complexity grows. Added to continuing conflicts between whites and blacks have also come conflicts between blacks and Koreans. Barriers cultural and geographic grow between the hard-core urban black and Hispanic poor and the emerging black and Hispanic middle class. Asian communities struggle with the antagonism between first generation and second generation, while the growth of both generations continues, unhindered now by restrictive immigration laws or residential segregation to the city.

Rodney King's question, "Can we get along?" becomes one created more out of hopelessness and despair than out of anger. Race fatigue exhausts both white and black.

And yet, the race question remains, expanding past the city to the suburbs and past white/black relations to white/black/Korean/Hispanic. "Koreans and Latinos have well-documented racist attitudes toward African Americans. Blacks carry negative stereotypes of Koreans (as witnessed in last year's L.A. riots) and are participating in black flight from communities turning increasingly brown or yellow in cities like L.A. and Chicago."[21] Korean and Chinese responses parallel that of whites who fled neighborhoods when blacks began to move in. Racial progress in the evangelical circle remains a myth still waiting to be challenged.

Evangelism and Church Planting

The importance of evangelism and church planting in the metropolitan areas will not go away. After World War II, suburbia was seen as the new frontier for church planting. But, in retrospect, says Lyle

20. "The Numbers Game," *Time,* special issue (Fall 1993), 15.
21. Andrés Tapia, "The Myth of Racial Progress," *Christianity Today* 37, no. 11 (4 October 1993): 18.

Schaller, "it can be argued the most creative new frontier was back in the central cities."[22] More than one-half of the forty largest Protestant congregations in the United States, he notes, are to be found in large central cities. And in those cities one finds more than one-half of the forty fastest growing churches.

With the continued shifting of urban populations in and out of the inner city and the growth of ethnic communities, there is wisdom to the adage: "new churches for new generations." Church planting, we fear, has not kept up with the massive urban growth of America's minorities nor sometimes remembered the diversity within them. The continued concentration of the U.S. churches on white population that has been documented in these pages will miss one of the most potentially fruitful fields for evangelization and church planting.

Minority churches have long known that not all ethnics are the same. A significant number of African-Americans and Hispanics have moved into a middle class that is not always at home in its former churches. This number will grow as the middle class grows in these communities. ABC Chinese often feel like displaced persons in churches where leadership and style is oriented to the OBC Christian.

Cubans are not at home in predominantly Puerto Rican churches. Central Americans are not always comfortable in Dallas and Los Angeles churches whose constituency is largely Mexican. Vietnamese do not stay long in Cambodian-American congregations.

Peter Wagner calls on us to see these differences as we plot our evangelistic strategies. Some he calls nuclear ethnics; these will require language churches. Some are fellow-traveler or marginal ethnics and will need bilingual churches, even English-speaking Korean or Latino churches. A few are alienated ethnics, happy in Anglo churches.[23] And, we add, there are crosscultural ethnics, finding their place best in multiethnic churches. If we are to reach America's ethnic communities in the future that is already here, the path of church planting will follow these groups on their own contextual terms, struggling as we do with the church's obligation to demonstrate its unity and catholicity.

22. Schaller, ed., *Center City Churches,* 13.
23. C. Peter Wagner, "Evangelizing the Real America," *Evangelical Newsletter,* 24 May 1985, 4; C. Peter Wagner, "A Vision for Evangelizing the Real America," *International Bulletin of Missionary Research* 10, no. 2 (April 1986): 59–64. Compare also Manuel Ortiz, *The Hispanic Challenge: Opportunities Confronting the Church* (Downers Grove: InterVarsity, 1993), 118–22.

The Megachurch Movement

How will the "megachurch" phenomenon play a part in all this? Schaller heralds it as "one of the four or five most significant developments in contemporary American church history."[24] With membership running above a minimum of 1,000 (and some definitions begin at 2,000), as many as 1,000 of these may have appeared during the last 25 years. John N. Vaughan, director of the International Megachurch Research Center, suggests that about thirty Protestant churches move into the megachurch ranks every year.[25]

Willow Creek Community Church in a Chicago suburb is one of the more well known. Begun in 1975, it had a weekly attendance of over 14,000 by 1990.[26] One of its teacher-pastors predicts that by 2001 "many major U.S. cities will support evangelical metachurches with 100,000 to 300,000 members!"[27]

Drawing a careful picture of the phenomenon is still difficult. Popularizing research like that of Schaller and Towns tend to focus their case studies on white churches while admitting also that many of the megachurches are African-American or multiethnic congregations. No distinctions are clearly drawn between center city (another euphemism for downtown), inner city, and suburb. This makes it difficult to analyze carefully the movement in terms of its context and the interests of this study.

There also appear to be some differences in defining and evaluating the megachurch. At what membership level do we begin to speak of them? Definitions seem heavily oriented to size; is that the real key to understanding it?

How are these megachurches growing? What is the proportion between those who join through conversion or the transfer of those already Christians who want what a larger church can offer? Some megachurches like Willow Creek Community Church and the 2,000-member Calvary Church in Grand Rapids, Michigan, have developed "seeker-sensitive" styles of worship and a mission strategy ori-

24. Lyle Schaller, "Megachurch!" *Christianity Today* 34, no. 4 (5 March 1990): 20.

25. Quoted in Russell Chandler, *Racing Toward 2001: The Forces Shaping America's Religious Future* (Grand Rapids: Zondervan, 1992), 163. See also John Vaughan, *Megachurches and American Cities* (Grand Rapids: Baker, 1993).

26. Elmer Towns, *Ten of Today's Most Innovative Churches* (Ventura, Calif.: Regal, 1990), 44.

27. Quoted in Chandler, *Racing Toward 2001*, 164.

ented to the unchurched.[28] Is this focus on the unchurched characteristic of megachurches as a whole?

When did these churches begin to appear? If, as Schaller admits, "a few can trace their origins back into the nineteenth century,"[29] what makes the contemporary movement so new?

We see the growth of the movement linked strongly to the shift of the church's center of ministry from a local neighborhood to a larger and more regional one. Two-thirds of the congregations cited in Schaller's study of center city churches are regional bodies. The community church has become a regional church. And in becoming a regional church it becomes a megachurch.

Older black megachurches have long displayed this characteristic, drawing membership united by race but not necessarily by proximity. And among more recently planted Korean and Chinese megachurches one can see this pattern repeated. A commonly shared ethnicity overcomes long distances and draws members from a wide geographical area for fellowship and nurture.

The recent changes in suburban life to "edge cities" have now opened the door for white congregations to move in this same direction. "Edge cities," their history chronicled in chapter 7, are based on time, not space. And they breed churches oriented to the same change in the understanding of "neighborhood."

People, we have argued, are now creating their own urban centers out of the destination they can reach by car in a reasonable length of time. The supermarket is ten minutes away in one direction. The shopping mall is thirty minutes in another direction and one's job an hour away by still another route.

In this decentralized world the church loses its grip on local geographical neighborhood and is transformed into a megachurch, twenty-five minutes away by car. The size of the megachurch becomes limited only by the size of its parking lot. And the lost community created by this change finds its replacement in the small cell groups and house meetings also characteristic of the successful megachurch.

28. Ed Dobson, *Starting a Seeker Sensitive Service* (Grand Rapids: Zondervan, 1993); *An Inside Look at the Willow Creek Worship Service: "Values Vital to Our Future,"* videocassette available from Grand Rapids: Zondervan, 1992.
29. Schaller, "Megachurch!" 20.

It may be too early to expect careful evaluations of the model. Too little is still known about its central structure and development. Is the megachurch, for example, a dangerous sample of modernity in which the evangelical syncretistically adopts patterns for the church that will eventually destroy it? An enthusiastic critic of modernity like Os Guinness argues for this conclusion.

Seeing it as tied to the roots of the Church Growth movement led by Donald McGavran, Guinness warns against the dangers of both.[30] Cautions like these are always needed. But his argument leaves unanswered questions.

Is it really modernity that shapes the megachurch model? Is Guinness's understanding of the Church Growth movement fully supported by his rather scanty treatment of the scanty evidence presented? Is the megachurch as intimately linked to the heart of the movement as he claims? Does his rather simplistic analysis of the megachurch provide enough data to link it, in all its variations, with modernity? Modernity in the end seems more the issue for him than the megachurch.

Our questions move in another direction, dictated by the concerns of this book and the place where the megachurch appears to function best as a church model. Does it represent at its heart another shift of the church from a neighborhood community to a regional orientation? Will such a shift move it closer to the new "edge city" change in suburbanization? Is it so controlled by a desire to satisfy the felt needs of individual concerns that it is in danger of moving its members again to yet another outer limit of choices and ecclesiastical options? Will it leave behind once more the poor as part of its monosocial constituency? Will the high priority given by some megachurch congregations to "reaching people where they are" minimize a costly discipleship?

Among the black and Hispanic megachurches located in the city, these dangers seem minimal. Like Deliverance Evangelistic Church of Philadelphia and 8,000-member First AME Church of Los Angeles, the black megachurch is too tied to the historic needs of its besieged constituency to lose its roots even to its regional character. But the predominantly white megachurch may succumb more easily.

---

30. Os Guinness, *Dining with the Devil: The Megachurch Movement Flirts with Modernity* (Grand Rapids: Baker, 1993), 13–15, 20–30.

The Church and Urban Transformation

The evangelical church, even in the city, remains divided over its understanding of the role of the church in urban renewal and social transformation. Will the twenty-first century see changes here also?

A large block of churches, we suggest, will continue to see the urban mission of the church as evangelism alone. The individualism that has been characteristic of American culture from its beginnings will continue to impact the evangelical message for and about the city. Bible-believing pulpits will continue to understand persons, sin, the gospel, and redemption in individualistic terms.

Greed will continue to be condemned as personal avarice; missing will be the social theme of economic oppression or the quest for ethnic power. The kingdom continuity of a shalom of wholeness and justice fulfilled in Christ will be reduced to the individual assurance of peace in some inward, spiritual sense.

Among suburban white and Asian "model minority" churches, this syncretized message will be especially strong. It is harder to see and hear and feel the pain of the city from the edge of the suburbs.

But even in such churches there may be indications of the Spirit's stirrings. National opinion polls would seem to suggest that even congregations reluctant to participate directly in urban renewal may, as a matter of fact, be doing more than they suspect. The power of an intimate, personal faith in Christ is a transforming one. Conversion by its very nature calls on us to love our neighbors in ways that transcend even the limitations set by a conservative pulpit.

"A Gallup Poll discovered that church members in general (37%) are more likely to help the poor, sick, and elderly than people who are not members of churches (22%). Furthermore, evangelical Christians who regularly pray and study the Bible are more likely (42%) than other Christians (30%) to do social ministry. A more recent Gallup Poll discovered that the 'highly spiritually committed' are twice as likely to work among the poor, sick, and elderly as the 'highly uncommitted.'"[31]

And rising to concretize these sentiments into ministry will be congregations like True Vine Missionary Baptist Church in West Oakland, California. A black storefront church in 1962 when it began, it

---

31. Ronald J. Sider, *One-Sided Christianity? Uniting the Church to Heal a Lost and Broken World* (Grand Rapids: Zondervan; San Francisco: HarperSanFrancisco, 1993), 117.

added 300 new members in 1990 to reach a total membership of 1,200. Its commitment to witnessing and evangelism sends teams out on the street the fourth Saturday of every month, and into nearby housing projects. And that same commitment has plans for a "trade center" where job training could help break the poverty cycle. Its most innovative program, say some, is its fourteen-week "God, Help Me Stop!" class on addictions and compulsions.

In Chicago's inner city Jesus People USA moves along the same path. Operating now out of a ten-story apartment building, its members live in community, numbering around 450 by 1991. Twenty years old, its original goal remains the same—"to reach the radical and often ragged fringes of society with a conservative, straight Bible message."[32]

In fleshing out that purpose, it supports itself and a wide variety of outreach ministries through an income pool earned through a half-dozen or more community-run businesses. No dichotomy between evangelism and urban transformation appears in its programs—a touring, recording, hard-rock band, REZ (short for Resurrection); a shelter for fifty-five homeless women and children; a crisis pregnancy center; a neighborhood food pantry and daily feeding program; ministries to young mothers, AIDS patients, jail inmates, juvenile delinquents, and elderly shut-ins. Its Cornerstone Festival draws an annual crowd of 10,000 to a celebration that features Christian "rock 'n roll with a conscience" and issue-oriented lecturers.

May we expect to see more of these integrated models in the future? Hope utters a qualified yes.

Anti-Urbanism

The history of the evangelical church in the American city has been liberally sprinkled with a cultural pessimism toward things urban. Syncretistically borrowed from a predominantly middle-class white mentality, anti-urban sentiments have continually surfaced throughout the history recorded in this book. Recently arrived Asian immigrants have "voted with their feet" in favor of this same urban perception.

These images of the city are not unique to the evangelical. The history of academic disciplines like urban anthropology and urban soci-

---

32. Chandler, *Racing Toward 2001*, 298.

ology are embedded in similar perceptions.[33] But, as we have pointed out elsewhere, the generalizations and stereotypes have often been repeated in church circles.[34] May we expect to see some changes in these perceptions?

If it does happen, it will not happen easily. Demographic realities have isolated the bulk of white churches in pilgrimage to the suburbs from the problems of their minority counterparts in the inner city. And absence does not make the suburban heart fonder. Evangelical white perceptions are still shaped more by the urban horror stories of fires and violence featured on the late news of TV; a sense of menace, not mission, is cultivated.

The polarity of city and suburb still dominates the white evangelical self-image. And, as tensions between blacks and Koreans rise, the Korean church community increasingly turns to these same images. Its wealth and relative freedom from the stigma of white racism offer it an open door to the suburbs also.

Multiculturalism still seems a long way off in spite of the realities we have sketched in this chapter. The white evangelical has become a demographic "outsider" to the city and the black, Hispanic, and Asian have become demographic "insiders." But the issue is still power. For America, still a "pigmentocracy" at its core, "the fundamental issue in all this talk about multiculturalism is power, specifically white male power."[35] Demographics alone does not make "outsiders" or "insiders." Wealth and social control is a dominating part of the picture.

Theological histories also continue to inhibit a more positive impression of the city as a gift of God. To cite only one example, the white evangelical church still looks over its shoulder at the Social Gospel controversies of the past and traces its continued presence in any congregation that speaks too loudly of holistic urban mission or "social action."

But, as William Pannell has said, "the term is as redundant as 'Social Gospel.' What other kind of Gospel is there? What kind of action is there that is not social, that does not at some level involve peo-

33. David Karp, Gregory Stone, and William Yoels, *Being Urban: A Sociology of City Life* (New York: Praeger, 1991), 3–44; John Gulick, *The Humanity of Cities: An Introduction to Urban Societies* (Granby, Mass.: Bergin and Garvey Publishers, 1989), 5–10.

34. Harvie M. Conn, *A Clarified Vision for Urban Mission: Dispelling the Urban Stereotypes* (Grand Rapids: Zondervan, 1987), 18–34.

35. Pannell, *The Coming Race Wars?* 81.

ple?"[36] What other ways exist to show a sceptical city tired of talk and "one more hustle" that believing in Jesus does make a difference?

And behind the history we must overcome are the profound theological styles of urban mission whose roots must be explored, discussed, and reconstructed.[37] This volume has focused strongly on the demographic and sociological side to the city and the church. But what of the theological paradigms created by the evangelical church in the history of its dialogue with the American city?[38]

"How do these paradigms affect our image of the city and model our ministries to it? In what way can our anti-urban and pro-urban biases be traced to them? The still strong evangelical differences over the relationship of evangelism to social transformation would indicate they play a prominent role in shaping our pre-understanding of urbanism."[39]

What does all this add up to? As we began, we end with a reminder again of the evangelical church's ambiguity, past, present, and future, toward the city. And perhaps it can be best illustrated in current literature flowing out of the Pentecostal and charismatic churches. As we have seen, their achievements in the American cities has been a sterling one in the twentieth century. The city is seen by some as the key to winning the country for Christ. "To turn our backs on the city," argues one author, "is to turn away from God's eternal purposes of salvation and justice for His whole creation. To accept this challenge is to embrace God's call to seek the *shalom* of the city. Blessed are the peacemakers . . . "[40]

And yet, there is a bleak side to this new call. Cities are perceived strongly as Satanic strongholds, the grip of whose demonizing power and territorial spirits may be broken only by "strategic-level intercession."[41]

36. Ibid., 142.

37. Donald Dayton, "Pentecostal/Charismatic Renewal and Social Change: A Western Perspective," *Transformation* 5, no. 4 (October/December 1988): 13.

38. A preliminary effort at sketching these paradigms historically will be found in Harvie M. Conn, "The Kingdom of God and the City of Man: a History of the City/Church Dialogue," *Discipling the City*, 2d ed., ed. Roger Greenway (Grand Rapids: Baker, 1992), 247–77.

39. Harvie M. Conn, "A Contextual Theology of Mission for the City," *The Good News of the Kingdom: Mission Theology for the Third Millennium*, ed. Charles Van Engen, Dean Gilliland, and Paul Pierson (Maryknoll: Orbis, 1993), 102–3.

40. Floyd McClung, *Seeing the City with the Eyes of God: How Christians Can Rise to the Urban Challenge* (Tarrytown, N.Y.: Chosen Books/Revell, 1991), 10.

41. C. Peter Wagner, *Warfare Prayer* (Ventura, Calif.: Regal, 1992), 12; C. Peter Wagner, ed., *Breaking Strongholds in Your City* (Ventura, Calif.: Regal, 1993).

No evangelical dares to deny much of what is said. The impact of the evil one's power on the city is too clear to escape, the call to prayer too plain, the need for "spiritual warfare" too unavoidable. A theology of the city needs to deal with the problem of the demonic.

But is this image of the city too dark to miss the victory of Christ at Calvary over principalities and powers? Why does one recent book oriented to this perspective pepper its picture of the city with adjectives like "dark," "impersonal, looming"? Why does he characterize the city as disoriented and provide a twelve-point list to prove it, speaking only of modern urban dwellers as feeling powerless, alone, vulnerable, lost, rejected, bewildered, insecure, used, void of meaning?[42]

Where is also the image of the city as the display case of God's common grace to his creation (Matt. 5:45)? However misshapen by pride, the place of community and security (Gen. 4:17; 11:6–8), the center of cultural innovation (Gen. 4:20–22)?

Christian ambiguity misses this dual perspective of the city. And when it does, the history of the church in the city will repeat itself. And the path we have traced through that history will take us "back to the future."

---

42. John Dawson, *Taking Our Cities for God: How to Break Spiritual Strongholds* (Lake Mary, Fla.: Creation House, 1989), 34, 36, 49–50.

Bibliography

Abbott, Carl. "To Boldly Go Where No Data Have Gone Before." *Journal of Urban History* 19, no. 3 (May 1993): 139–45.

Abell, Aaron I. *The Urban Impact on American Protestantism, 1865–1900.* Hamden, Conn.: Archon, 1962.

Addams, Jane. "Hull House, Chicago: An Effort Toward Social Democracy." *The Forum* 14 (October 1892): 226–41.

Ahlstrom, Sydney. *A Religious History of the American People.* New Haven: Yale University Press, 1972.

Allen, David, and James Jekel. *Crack: the Broken Promise.* New York: St. Martin's, 1991.

Allen, James, and Eugene Turner. "Where Diversity Reigns." *American Demographics* 12, no. 5 (August 1990): 34–38.

Allen, Jere. "Stages of Transition." *Urban Review* 1, no. 3 (October 1985): 4–12.

"America's Immigrant Challenge." *Time,* special issue (Fall 1993), 3–9.

Anderson, Elijah. *Street Wise: Race, Class, and Change in an Urban Neighborhood.* Chicago: University of Chicago Press, 1990.

Appleby, Jerry. *The Church Is in a Stew: Developing Multicongregational Churches.* Kansas City: Beacon Hill, 1990.

Asante, Molefi Kete. *The Afrocentric Idea.* Philadelphia: Temple University Press, 1987.

Bahr, Howard, Bruce Chadwick, and Joseph Strauss. *American Ethnicity.* Lexington, Mass.: D.C. Heath, 1979.

Bakke, Ray, with Jim Hart. *The Urban Christian: Effective Ministries in Today's Urban World.* Downers Grove: InterVarsity, 1987.

Bakke, Ray, and Samuel Roberts. *The Expanded Mission of 'Old First' Churches.* Valley Forge: Judson, 1986.

Barrientos, Tanya. "In Camden, Afrocentrism is Bringing Academic Gains." *Philadelphia Inquirer,* 4 March 1991, 1B, 4B.

Barringer, Felicity. "A Shift for Urban Renewal: Nurture the Grass Roots." *New York Times,* 29 November 1992, 1, 30.

Bartlett, Richard. *The New Country: A Social History of the American Frontier, 1776–1890.* London: Oxford University Press, 1974.

Bauman, John, Norman Hummon, and Edward Muller. "Public Housing, Isolation, and the Urban Underclass: Philadelphia's Richard Allen Homes, 1941–1965." *Journal of Urban History* 17, no. 3 (May 1991): 264–92.

Beck, Carolyn. "Entrepreneurs in God's Economy: Christian Stronghold Baptist Church." *Urban Mission* 7, no. 5 (May 1990): 7–19.

Bedell, Kenneth, ed. *Yearbook of American and Canadian Churches, 1993.* Nashville: Abingdon, 1993.

Beidel, Tim. "The Lord's Work Cannot Wait for the Bureaucrats." *West Chester Sunday Local News,* 16 November 1986, A15.

Bennett, G. Willis. *Effective Urban Church Ministry.* Nashville: Broadman, 1983.

Bennett, Lerone, Jr. *Before the Mayflower: A History of the Negro in America, 1619–1954.* Baltimore: Penguin, 1966.

Bentley, William, and Ruth Lewis Bentley. "Reflections on the Scope and Function of a Black Evangelical Black Theology." In *Evangelical Affirmations,* edited by Kenneth Kantzer and Carl F. H. Henry, 299–333. Grand Rapids: Zondervan, 1990.

"Beyond the Melting Pot," *Time,* 9 April 1990, 28–31.

Bibby, Reginald. *Mosaic Madness.* Toronto: Stoddard, 1990.

Bilhartz, Terry. *Urban Religion and the Second Great Awakening.* Cranbury, N.J.: Associated Universities Presses, 1986.

Boles, John. *The Great Revival, 1787–1895.* Lexington: University of Kentucky Press, 1972.

Borowski, Neill. "Joblessness Persisting, Especially for Minorities." *Philadelphia Inquirer,* 9 August 1993, C1, C8.

——— "Minorities Accounted for Area Population Gain." *Philadelphia Inquirer,* 20 February 1991, 1A, 13A, 15A.

Borowski, Neill, and Murray Dubin. "Black Segregation Up in Philadelphia, Census Shows." *Philadelphia Inquirer,* 11 April 1991, 1B.

Bowden, Henry. *American Indians and Christian Missions.* Chicago: University of Chicago Press, 1981.

Boyer, Paul. *Urban Masses and Moral Order in America, 1820–1920.* Cambridge: Harvard University Press, 1978.

Brace, Charles. *The Best Method of Disposing of Our Pauper and Vagrant Children.* New York: Wynkoop, Hallenbeck and Thomas, 1859.

Brownell, Blaine, and David Goldfield, eds. *The City in Southern History: The Growth of Urban Civilization in the South.* Port Washington, N.Y.: Kennikat, 1977.

Burger, Steve. "A Night in the Life of Rescue." *Rescue* 4, no. 4 (Winter 1989): 4.

Burgess, Stanley, and Gary McGee, eds. *Dictionary of Pentecostal and Charismatic Movements.* Grand Rapids: Zondervan, 1988.

Callow, A. B., Jr., ed. *American Urban History.* New York: Oxford University Press, 1969.

Carlo, Luis. "Love Gospel Assembly: A Current Urban Ministry." Unpublished paper, Alliance Theological Seminary, Nyack, N.Y., 1989.

Carpenter, Joel. "Fundamentalist Institutions and the Rise of Evangelical Protestantism, 1929–1942." *Church History* 49 (1980): 62–75.

Cayton, Horace, and Anne Lively. *The Chinese in the United States and the Chinese Christian Church.* New York: National Council of the Churches of Christ in the U.S.A., 1955.

"The Census Bureau's Report on Cities." *New York Times*, 27 January 1991, A20.

Chandler, Russell. *Racing Toward 2001: The Forces Shaping America's Religious Future*. Grand Rapids: Zondervan, 1992.

Chow, John Peter. "Evangelism Among American Chinese." *Interlit* 14, no. 4 (December 1971): 10–11.

Chow, Moses. *Reconciling Our Kinsmen in the Gold Mountain*. Washington, D.C: Ambassadors for Christ, 1972.

Christian Community Development Association: 1990–1991 Membership Directory. Chicago: CCDA, 1991.

Christensen, Michael. *City Streets City People: A Call for Compassion*. Nashville: Abingdon, 1988.

Chudacoff, Howard. *The Evolution of American Urban Society*. 2d ed. Englewood Cliff, N.J.: Prentice-Hall, 1981.

Chun, James. "Korean Communities in Montgomery County, PA." Unpublished paper, Westminster Seminary, Philadelphia, 1991.

Church, George. "The Boom Towns." *Time*, 15 June 1987, 15–17.

Claerbaut, David. *The Reluctant Defender*. Wheaton: Tyndale House, 1978.

Cone, James. *For My People: Black Theology and the Black Church*. Maryknoll: Orbis, 1984.

———. *Martin and Malcolm and America: A Dream or a Nightmare*. Maryknoll: Orbis, 1992.

Conn, Harvie M. *A Clarified Vision for Urban Mission: Dispelling the Urban Stereotypes*. Grand Rapids: Zondervan, 1987.

———. "A Contextual Theology of Mission for the City." In *The Good News of the Kingdom: Theology for the Third Millennium*, edited by Charles Van Engen, Dean Gilliland, and Paul Pierson, 96–104. Maryknoll: Orbis, 1993.

———. *Evangelism: Doing Justice and Preaching Grace*. Grand Rapids: Zondervan, 1982; reprint, Phillipsburg, N.J.: Presbyterian and Reformed, 1992.

———. "The Kingdom of God and the City of Man: A History of the City/Church Dialogue." In *Discipling the City*, 2d ed., edited by Roger Greenway, 247–77. Grand Rapids: Baker, 1992.

———. "The Suburban Black Movement." *Metro-Voice* (Fall 1993): 3–4.

Cook, Donovan. "'Public Sanctuary' for Central American Refugees: Its Meaning and Implications." *American Baptist Quarterly* 3, no. 4 (December 1984): 315–20.

Cosby, Gordon. *Handbook for Mission Groups*. Waco: Word, 1975.

Costas, Orlando. "Evangelizing an Awakening Giant: Hispanics in the U.S." In *Signs of the Kingdom in the Secular City*, edited by Helen Ujvarosy, 55–64. Chicago: Covenant, 1984.

———. "Proclaiming Christ in the Two Thirds World." In *Sharing Jesus in the Two Thirds World*, edited by Vinay Samuel and Chris Sugden, 1–11. Grand Rapids: Eerdmans, 1983.

Cox, Harvey. *Religion in the Secular City: Toward a Postmodern Theology*. New York: Simon and Schuster, 1984.

———. "*The Secular City* 25 Years Later." *The Christian Century* 107, no. 32 (7 November 1990): 1025–29.

Cully, Kendig Brubaker, and F. Nile Harper, eds. *Will the Church Lose the City?* New York: World, 1969.

Curtis, Susan. *A Consuming Faith: The Social Gospel and Modern American Culture.* Baltimore: Johns Hopkins University Press, 1991.

Dahms, John. "The Social Interest and Concern of A.B. Simpson." In *The Birth of a Vision*, edited by David Hartzfeld and Charles Nienkirchen, 49–74. Regina: *His Dominion* Supplement No. 1, 1986.

D'Amico, David. "Evangelization Across Cultures in the United States: What to Do with the World Come to Us?" *Review and Expositor* 90, no. 1 (Winter 1993): 83–98.

Davis, J. H. *Dilemmas of Racial Transition: Proceedings of the National Leadership Conference.* Atlanta: Black Church Relations Dept., Home Mission Board, Southern Baptist Convention, 1981.

Davis, William, ed. *Bradford's History of Plymouth Plantation.* New York: Scribners, 1908.

Dawson, John. *Taking Our Cities for God.* Lake Mary, Fla.: Creation House, 1989.

Dayton, Donald. "Pentecostal/Charismatic Renewal and Social Change: A Western Perspective," *Transformation* 5, no. 4 (October/December 1988): 7–13.

———. *Rediscovering an Evangelical Heritage.* New York: Harper and Row, 1976.

Dayton, Donald, and Robert K. Johnston, eds. *The Variety of American Evangelicalism.* Knoxville: University of Tennessee Press, 1991.

DeForest, Robert, and Lawrence Veiller, eds. *The Tenement House Problem, Vol. 1.* New York: Macmillan, 1903.

Delgado, Melvin, and Denise Humn-Delgado. "Natural Support Systems: Source of Strength in Hispanic Communities." *Social Work* (January 1982): 83–89.

Dobson, Ed. *Starting a Seeker Sensitive Service.* Grand Rapids: Zondervan, 1993.

Dorsett, Lyle. "Billy Sunday: Evangelist to Urban America." *Urban Mission* 8, no. 1 (September 1990): 6–13.

———. *Billy Sunday and the Redemption of Urban America.* Grand Rapids: Eerdmans, 1991.

Douglass, H. Paul. *The Suburban Trend.* New York: The Century Company, 1925.

Driggers, B. Carlisle, comp. *Models of Metropolitan Ministry.* Nashville: Broadman, 1979.

DuBose, Francis. *How Churches Grow in an Urban World.* Nashville: Broadman, 1978.

Dudley, Carl. "Churches in Changing Communities." In *Metro-Ministry: Ways and Means for the Urban Church*, edited by David Frenchak and Sharrel Keyes, 78–91. Elgin, Ill.: David C. Cook, 1979.

———. *Where Have All Our People Gone? New Choices for Old Churches.* New York: Pilgrim, 1979.

Dyrness, William. *How Does America Hear the Gospel?* Grand Rapids: Eerdmans, 1989.

Edelman, Peter. "Urban Poverty: Where Do We Go From Here?" In *The Future of National Urban Policy*, edited by Marshall Kaplan and Franklin James, 89–100. Durham: Duke University Press, 1990.

Ellis, Carl. *Beyond Liberation.* Downers Grove: InterVarsity, 1983.

Ellison, Craig, ed. *The Urban Mission.* Grand Rapids: Eerdmans, 1974.

Escobar, Samuel. "From Lausanne 1974 to Manila 1989: The Pilgrimage of Urban Mission." *Urban Mission* 7, no. 4 (March 1990): 21–29.

Espinoza, H. O. "Response to William H. and Ruth Lewis Bentley." In *Evangelical Affirmations*, edited by Kenneth Kantzer and Carl F. H. Henry, 335–42. Grand Rapids: Zondervan, 1990.

Evangelism and Social Responsibility: An Evangelical Commitment. Wheaton: Lausanne Committee for World Evangelization, 1982.

Finke, Roger, and Rodney Stark. *The Churching of America, 1776–1990.* New Brunswick: Rutgers University Press, 1992.

Fisher, Eldonna. "Help for the Homeless." *Presbyterian Survey* (May 1984): 24–27.

Fishman, Robert. *Bourgeois Utopias.* New York: Basic, 1987.

———. "Metropolis Unbound." *Wilson Quarterly* 14, no. 1 (Winter 1990): 25–48.

Flynt, Wayne. "One in the Spirit, Many in the Flesh: Southern Evangelicals." In *Varieties of Southern Evangelicalism*, edited by David Harrell Jr., 23–44. Macon, Ga.: Mercer University Press, 1981.

Fonder, Nancy. *New Immigrants in New York.* New York: Columbia University Press, 1987.

Fondersmith, John. "Downtown 2040: Making Cities Fun!" *The Futurist* 22, no. 2 (March–April, 1988): 9–15.

Fong, Kenneth. *Insights for Growing Asian-American Ministries.* Rosemead, Calif.: Ever Growing Publications, 1990.

Ford, Leighton. *One Way to Change the World.* New York: Harper and Row, 1970.

———. "Social Action Through Evangelism." *Christianity Today* 2, no. 15 (23 June 1967): 970.

Forstall, Richard. "Going to Town." *American Demographics* 15, no. 5 (May 1993): 42–47.

Fost, Dan. "California's Asian Market." *American Demographics* 12, no. 10 (October 1990): 34–37.

Fowler, R. Booth. *A New Engagement: Evangelical Political Thought, 1966–1976.* Grand Rapids: Eerdmans, 1983.

Frazier, E. Franklin. *The Negro Church in America.* New York: Schocken, 1964.

Frey, William, and William O'Hare. "¡Vivan los Suburbios!" *American Demographics* 15, no. 4 (April 1993): 30–37.

Fries, Sylvia Doughty. *The Urban Idea in Colonial America.* Philadelphia: Temple University Press, 1977.

Fritz, Christian. "Due Process, Treaty Rights, and Chinese Exclusion, 1882–1891." In *Entry Denied: Exclusion and the Chinese Community in America, 1882–1941*, edited by Sucheng Chan, 25–56. Philadelphia: Temple University Press, 1991.

Fuller, Millard, with Diane Scott. *No More Shacks!* Waco: Word, 1986.

Gallup, George, Jr., and David Poling. *The Search for America's Faith.* Nashville: Abingdon, 1980.

Gans, Herbert. *The Levittowners: Ways of Life and Politics in a New Suburban Community.* New York: Random House, 1967.

Gariepy, Henry. *Christianity in Action: The Salvation Army in the USA Today.* Wheaton: Victor, 1990.

Garraty, John. *The New Commonwealth, 1877–1890.* New York: Harper and Row, 1968.

Garreau, Joel. *Edge City: Life on the New Frontier.* New York: Doubleday/Anchor Books, 1991.

Gasper, Louis. *The Fundamentalist Movement.* the Hague: Mouton, 1963.

Gaustad, Edwin. *The Great Awakening in New England.* New York: Harper and Brothers, 1957.

Gaxiola-Gaxiola, Manuel. "Latin American Pentecostalism: A Mosaic within a Mosaic." *Pneuma: the Journal of the Society for Pentecostal Studies* 13, no. 2 (Fall 1991): 107–29.

Gelfand, Mark. *A Nation of Cities: The Federal Government and Urban America, 1933–1965.* New York: Oxford University Press, 1975.

Giles, Thomas. "Overseas Ministries Step Up Fight Against U.S. Ills." *Christianity Today* 37, no. 7 (21 June 1993): 57–58.

Gill, Athol. "Christian Social Responsibility." In *The New Face of Evangelicalism,* edited by René Padilla, 87–102. Downers Grove: InterVarsity, 1975.

Glaab, Charles, ed. *The American City: A Documentary History.* Homewood, Ill.: Dorsey, 1963.

Glaab, Charles, and Theodore Brown. *A History of Urban America.* 3d ed. New York: Macmillan, 1983.

Goldberg, Steve. "It Wasn't Supposed to Be Like This: Mentally Ill on Streets Signs of a Failed Policy." *Richmond Times-Dispatch,* 29 December 1991, D-5.

Goldfield, David, and Blaine Brownell. *Urban America: A History.* 2d ed. Boston: Houghton-Mifflin, 1990.

Gompers, Samuel. "The Church and Labor." *American Federationist* 2 (August 1896): 119–20.

Greenway, Roger. "Reflections on Lausanne II." *Urban Mission* 7, no. 3 (January 1990): 3–7.

———, ed. *Discipling the City.* 2d ed. Grand Rapids: Baker, 1992.

Greenway, Roger, and Timothy Monsma. *Cities: Mission's New Frontier.* Grand Rapids: Baker, 1989.

Guinness, Os. *Dining with the Devil: The Metachurch Movement Flirts with Modernity.* Grand Rapids: Baker, 1993.

Gulick, John. *The Humanity of Cities: An Introduction to Urban Societies.* Granby, Mass.: Bergin and Garvey, 1989.

Hadaway, C. Kirk. "Types of Growing Churches in Transition." *Urban Review* 1, no. 3 (October 1985): 13–22.

Handy, Robert. "The American Religious Depression, 1925–1935." *Church History* 29 (1960): 3–16.

———. *A Christian America: Protestant Hopes and Historical Realities.* New York: Oxford University Press, 1984.

Harrell, David, Jr., ed. *Varieties of Southern Evangelicalism.* Macon, Ga.: Mercer University Press, 1981.

Harrington, Michael. *The New American Poverty.* New York: Holt, Rinehart and Winston, 1984.

Hartshorn, Truman. *Interpreting the City: An Urban Geography.* 2d ed. New York: John Wiley and Sons, 1992.

Hartley, Loyde. *Cities and Churches: An International Bibliography: Volumes I–III, 1800–1991.* Metuchen, N.J.: American Theological Library Association and the Scarecrow Press, 1992.

Hassey, Janette. *No Time for Silence.* Grand Rapids: Zondervan, 1986.

Hefley, James, and Marti Hefley. *The Church That Takes On Trouble.* Elgin, Ill.: David C. Cook, 1976.

Henry, Carl F. H. *The Uneasy Conscience of Modern Fundamentalism.* Grand Rapids: Eerdmans, 1947.

Hesselgrave, David. "Holes in 'Holistic Mission.'" *Trinity World Forum* 15, no. 3 (Spring 1990): 1–5.

Hill, Samuel, Jr. *Southern Churches in Crisis.* Boston: Beacon, 1968.

Hoge, Dean, and David Roozen, eds. *Understanding Church Growth and Decline, 1950–1978.* New York: Pilgrim, 1979.

Hoke, Donald, ed. *Evangelicals Face the Future.* South Pasadena: William Carey Library, 1978.

Hood, J. W. *One Hundred Years of the African Methodist Episcopal Zion Church.* New York: AME Zion Book Concern, 1895.

Hudson, Winthrop. *Religion in America.* 2d ed. New York: Charles Scribner's Sons, 1973.

Huhr, Won-moo, and Kwang-chung Kim. "Religious Participation of Korean Immigrants in the United States." *Journal for the Scientific Study of Religion* 29, no. 1 (1990): 19–34.

Hunter, James. *American Evangelicalism: Conservative Religion and the Quandary of Modernity.* New Brunswick: Rutgers University Press, 1983.

———. *Evangelicalism: The Coming Generation.* Chicago: University of Chicago Press, 1987.

Hutchison, William. *Errand to the World: American Protestant Thought and Foreign Missions.* Chicago: University of Chicago Press, 1987.

Hyun, Yong-soo. "The Relationship Between Cultural Assimilation Models, Religiosity, and Spiritual Well-Being Among Korean-American College Students and Young Adults in Korean Churches in Southern California." Unpublished Ed.D. dissertation, Biola University, LaMirada, Calif., 1990.

An Inside Look at the Willow Creek Worship Service: "Value Vital to Our Future." Videocassette. Grand Rapids: Zondervan, 1992.

Jackson, Alexander. "The Relation of the Classes to the Church." *Independent*, 1 March 1888, 258–59.

Jackson, Kenneth. *Crabgrass Frontier: The Suburbanization of the United States.* New York: Oxford University Press, 1985.

Jekel, James, and David Allen. "Trends in Drug Abuse in the Mid-1980s." *The Yale Journal of Biology and Medicine* 60 (1987): 45–52.

Johnson, Charles. *Frontier Camp Meeting.* Dallas: Southern Methodist University Press, 1955.

Jorstad, Erling. *The Politics of Moralism: The New Christian Right in American Life.* Minneapolis: Augsburg, 1981.

Kadlecek, Jo. "The Coloring of the American Church." *National and International Religion Report* 7, no. 9 (19 April 1993): 1–4.

Kang, Wi-jo. "The Background of the U.S. Immigration Policy Toward Asians: Implications for the Urban Church Today." In *Signs of the Kingdom in the Secular City*, edited by Helen Ujvarosy, 75–80. Chicago: Covenant, 1984.

Kantzer, Kenneth. "Reflections: Five Years of Change." *Christianity Today* 26, no. 19 (26 November 1982), 14–20.

Karp, David, Gregory Stone, and William Yoels. *Being Urban: A Sociology of City Life.* New York: Praeger, 1991.

Keats, John. *The Crack in the Picture Window.* Boston: Houghton Mifflin, 1957.

Keller, Timothy. "An Evangelical Mission in a Secular City." In *Center City Churches,* edited by Lyle Schaller, 31–41. Nashville: Abingdon, 1993.

Kelley, Dean. *Why Conservative Churches Are Growing.* New York: Harper and Row, 1972.

Kenrick, Bruce. *Come Out the Wilderness.* London: Fontana Books/William Collins and Sons, 1962.

Kim, Dae-gee. "Major Factors Conditioning the Acculturation of Korean-Americans with Respect to the Presbyterian Church in America and Its Missionary Obedience." Unpublished D.Miss. dissertation, Fuller Theological Seminary, Pasadena, 1985.

Kim, Il-soo. "Organizational Patterns of Korean-American Methodist Churches: Denominationalism and Personal Community." Paper read at the Bicentennial Consultation on Methodism and Ministry, Drew University, Madison, N.J., 1983.

Kirk, Andrew. *Good News of the Kingdom Coming: The Marriage of Evangelism and Social Responsibility.* Downers Grove: InterVarsity, 1983.

Knittler, Edward. "Development of a Manual for a Culturally Related Evangelism Program for Chinese Churches in North America." Unpublished D.Min. dissertation, Eastern Baptist Theological Seminary, Philadelphia, 1988.

Language Mission Facts: 1988 Update. Atlanta: Home Mission Board, Southern Baptist Convention, 1988.

Larsen, Lawrence. *The Rise of the Urban South.* Lexington: University Press of Kentucky, 1985.

Law, Gail. *Chinese Churches Handbook.* Hong Kong: Chinese Coordination Centre of World Evangelism, 1982.

Lee, Robert, ed. *The Church and the Exploding Metropolis.* Richmond: John Knox, 1965.

Lees, Andrew. *Cities Perceived.* New York: Columbia University Press, 1985.

Lehman, Kevin. "Homelessness: A Growing National Disgrace." *Washington Memo, Mennonite Central Committee* (July–August 1991): 6–7.

Leinberger, Christopher, and Charles Lockwood. "How Business is Reshaping America." *The Atlantic* 258, no. 4 (October 1986): 43–52.

Leslie, William. "The Ministering Church." In *Metro-Ministry: Ways and Means for the Urban Church,* edited by David Frenchak and Sharrel Keyes, 126–34. Elgin, Ill.: David C. Cook, 1979.

Lincoln, C. Eric, and Lawrence Mamiya. *The Black Church in the African American Experience.* Durham: Duke University Press, 1990.

Linder, Robert. "The Resurgence of Evangelical Social Concerns (1925–1975)." In *The Evangelicals: What They Believe, Who They Are, Where They Are Changing,* rev. ed., edited by David Wells and John Woodbridge, 209–30. Grand Rapids: Baker, 1977.

Ling, Samuel. "The Metamorphosis of Chinese Church Growth in North America. 1943–1983." *Chinese Around the World* (October 1983): 1–4.

Linthicum, Robert. *City of God, City of Satan: A Biblical Theology of the Urban Church.* Grand Rapids: Zondervan, 1991.

———. *Empowering the Poor.* Monrovia, Calif.: MARC, 1991.

———. "The Urban World and World Vision." *Urban Mission* 5, no. 1 (September 1987): 5–12.

Liu, Felix. "A Comparative Study of Selected Growing Chinese Churches in Los Angeles County." Unpublished D.Miss. dissertation, Fuller Theological Seminary, Pasadena, 1981.

Lockard, David. *The Unheard Billy Graham.* Waco: Word, 1971.

Loomis, Samuel. *Modern Cities and Their Religious Problems.* New York: Baker and Taylor, 1887.

Lovelace, Richard. *Dynamics of Spiritual Life.* Downers Grove: InterVarsity, 1979.

Lupton, Robert. *Theirs Is the Kingdom: Celebrating the Gospel in Urban America.* San Francisco: Harper and Row, 1989.

Lynd, Robert, and Helen Lynd. *Middletown in Transition: A Study in Cultural Conflicts.* New York: Harcourt, Brace, 1937.

Magnuson, Norris. *Salvation in the Slums: Evangelical Social Work, 1865–1920.* Grand Rapids: Baker, 1990 reprint.

Mains, David. *Full Circle.* Waco: Word, 1971.

Marsden, George. *Fundamentalism and American Culture: the Shaping of Twentieth-Century Evangelicalism, 1870–1925.* New York: Oxford University Press, 1980.

———. *Understanding Fundamentalism and Evangelicalism.* Grand Rapids: Eerdmans, 1991.

Marty, Martin E. *Pilgrims in Their Own Land: 500 Years of Religion in America.* Boston: Little, Brown, 1984.

———. *Protestantism in the United States.* New York: Charles Scribner's Sons, 1986.

———. *Righteous Empire.* New York: Dial, 1970.

Mather, Cotton. *The Boston Ebenezer.* Boston: n.p., 1698.

———. *Some Seasonable Advice unto the Poor: to be Annexed unto the Kindnesses of God, that are Dispensed unto Them.* Boston: n.p., 1712.

Matos, Alderi. "Boston's Ethnic Churches." In *The Boston Church Directory, 1989–1990*, edited by Rudy Mitchell, 255–56. Boston: Emmanuel Gospel Center, 1990.

Mays, Benjamin, and Joseph Nicholson. *The Negro's Church.* New York: Russell and Russell, 1969 reprint.

Maxson, Charles. *The Great Awakening in the Middle Colonies.* Gloucester, Mass.: Peter Smith, 1958.

McClung, Floyd. *Seeing the City with the Eyes of God: How Christians Can Rise to the Urban Challenge.* Tarrytown, N.Y.: Chosen Books/Revell, 1991.

McConnell, Michael. "Sanctuary: No Stopping It Now." *The Other Side* 21, no. 2 (March 1985): 32–35.

McKenna, David, ed. *The Urban Crisis.* Grand Rapids: Zondervan, 1969.

McLoughlin, William. *Revivals, Awakenings, and Reform.* Chicago: University of Chicago Press, 1978.

McSwain, Larry. "Practical Approaches to Ethnic Ministry: Integrating What Is with What Should Be." *Urban Review* 1, no. 4 (January 1986): 6–14.

Meehan, Brenda. "A. C. Dixon: An Early Fundamentalist." *Foundations* 10 no. 1 (January–March 1967): 50–63.

Miller, Randall, and George Pozzetta, eds. *Shades of the Sunbelt.* New York: Greenwood, 1988.

Miller, Robert. *American Protestantism and Social Issues, 1919–1939.* Chapel Hill: University of North Carolina, 1958.

Miller, Zane. *The Urbanization of Modern America: A Brief History.* New York: Harcourt Brace Jovanovich, 1973.

Moberg, David. *The Great Reversal.* Philadelphia: J. B. Lippincott, 1972.

Mohl, Raymond, ed. *The Making of Urban America.* Wilmington, Del.: SR Books, 1988.

Monkkonen, Eric. *America Becomes Urban: The Development of U.S. Cities and Towns, 1780–1980.* Berkeley: University of California Press, 1988.

Moody, Dwight. *New Sermons.* New York: Henry S. Goodspeed, 1880.

Moore, Paul. *Shepherd of Times Square.* Nashville: Nelson, 1978.

Morse, Verranus. *An Analytical Sketch of the Young Men's Christian Association in North America From 1851 to 1876.* New York: International Committee of Young Men's Christian Associations, 1901.

Mukenge, Ida. *The Black Church in Urban America.* New York: University Press of America, 1983.

Muller, Dorothea. "The Social Philosophy of Josiah Strong: Social Christianity and American Progressivism." *Church History* 28 (1959): 183–201.

Murch, James. *Cooperation Without Compromise.* Grand Rapids: Eerdmans, 1956.

Mussina, Malcolm. "The Background and Origin of the American Religious Tract Movement." Unpublished Ph.D. dissertation, Drew University, Madison, N.J., 1936.

Mututua, Wilson. "Garveyism and the Rise of the American Muslim Mission (AMM)." Unpublished M.A. thesis, Drew University, Madison, N.J., 1981.

Naedele, Walter. "Adieu to Country Bumpkins." *Philadelphia Inquirer,* 1 November 1993, B1–B2.

Nash, Dennison. "And A Little Child Shall Lead Them: A Test of an Hypothesis That Children were the Source of the American 'Religious Revival.'" *Journal for the Scientific Study of Religion* 7 (Fall 1968): 238–40.

Nash, Gary. *Forging Freedom: The Formation of Philadelphia's Black Community, 1720–1840.* Cambridge : Harvard University Press, 1988.

———. *Red, White, and Black.* Englewood Cliffs, N.J.: Prentice-Hall, 1974.

———. "The Social Evolution of Preindustrial American Cities, 1700–1820: Reflections and New Directions." *Journal of Urban History* 13, no. 2 (February 1987): 115–45.

Nelsen, Hart. "Unchurched Black Americans: Patterns of Religiosity and Affiliation." *Review of Religious Research* 29, no. 4 (June 1988): 408–9.

"New Women's and Children's Residence Opens." *Ministries in Progress* (Spring 1990): 1, 3.

Newman, William. "Religion in Suburban America." In *The Changing Face of the Suburbs,* edited by Barry Schwartz, 265–78. Chicago: University of Chicago Press, 1976.

Noll, Mark. *Christians in the American Revolution.* Washington, D.C.: Christian University Press, 1977.

Noyce, Gaylord. *Survival and Mission for the City Church.* Philadelphia: Westminster, 1975.

"The Numbers Game." *Time,* special issue (Fall 1993): 14–15.

O'Connor, Elisabeth. *Journey Inward, Journey Outward.* New York: Harper and Row, 1968.

O'Hare, William. "A New Look at Asian Americans." *American Demographics* 12, no. 10 (October 1990): 26–31.

O'Hare, William, and William Frey. "Booming, Suburban, Black." *American Demographics* 14, no. 9 (September 1992): 30–38.

Ortiz, Manuel. "Circle Church: A Case Study in Contextualization." *Urban Mission* 8, no. 3 (January 1991): 6–18.

———. *The Hispanic Challenge: Opportunities Confronting the Church.* Downers Grove: InterVarsity, 1993.

Ostling, Richard. "Strains on the Heart." *Time,* 19 November 1990, 90.

"Our Big Cities Go Ethnic." *U.S. News and World Report,* 21 March 1983, 49–53.

"Outreach Among Hispanics Increasing in NAE Denominations." *Action* (July–August 1988): 10.

Palen, J. John. *The Urban World.* 3d ed. New York: McGraw-Hill, 1987.

Pang, Wing-ning. "The Chinese Protestant Church in North America." *Chinese World Pulse* 6, no. 1 (March 1982): 2–6.

Pannell, William. *The Coming Race Wars? A Cry for Reconciliation.* Grand Rapids: Zondervan, 1993.

Pasquariello, Ronald, Donald Shriver, Jr., and Alan Geyer. *Redeeming the City: Theology, Politics, and Urban Policy.* New York: Pilgrim, 1982.

Pear, Robert. "Rich Got Richer in '80s, Others Held Even." *New York Times,* 10 January 1991, A1.

Perkins, John. *Let Justice Roll Down: John Perkins Tells His Own Story.* Ventura, Calif.: Regal, 1976.

———. *A Quiet Revolution.* Waco: Word, 1976.

———. *With Justice For All.* Ventura, Calif.: Regal, 1982.

Perkins, Spencer, and Chris Rice. *More Than Equals: Racial Healing for the Sake of the Gospel.* Downers Grove: InterVarsity, 1993.

Peirce, Neal. "The 'Citistates' Are on the Rise, and the Competition Is Fierce." *Philadelphia Inquirer,* 26 July 1993, A11.

Peters, Harvey, Jr. "The Lutheran Church and Urban Ministry in North America: An Overview." In *The Experience of Hope,* edited by Wayne Stumme, 23–32. Minneapolis: Augsburg Fortress, 1991.

Peterson, Janice. "The Feminization of Poverty." *Journal of Economic Issues* 21 (1987): 329–37.

Pierce, Benjamin. "Harambee Christian Family Center." *Urban Mission* 7, no. 5 (May 1990): 45–53.

Pope, Liston. *Millhands and Preachers.* New Haven: Yale University Press, 1965.

Quebedeaux, Richard. *The Young Evangelicals.* New York: Harper and Row, 1974.

Raboteau, Albert. "The Black Church: Continuity Within Change." In *Altered Landscapes: Christianity in America, 1935–1985,* edited by David Lotz, Donald Shriver, Jr., and John Wilson, 77–91. Grand Rapids: Eerdmans, 1989.

Ramsing, Nick. "The Greater Boston Development Coalition." *Urban Mission* 2, no. 2 (December 1993): 50–56.

Rauschenbusch, Walter. *Christianity and the Social Crisis*. New York: Macmillan, 1907.

Recinos, Harold. *Jesus Weeps: Global Encounters on Our Doorstep*. Nashville: Abingdon, 1992.

Reitz, George. "A. B. Simpson, Urban Evangelist." *Urban Mission* 8, no. 3 (January 1991): 19–26.

Reps, John. *The Making of Urban America: A History of City Planning in the United States*. Princeton: Princeton University Press, 1965.

Richardson, James. "The Evolving Dynamics of America's Urban Development." In *Cities in the 21st Century*, edited by Gary Gappert and Richard Knight, 37–46. Beverly Hills: Sage, 1982.

Riis, Jacob. *How the Other Half Lives: Studies Among the Tenements of New York*. New York: Charles Scribner's Sons, 1890.

Ringheim, Karin. "Investigating the Structural Determinants of Homelessness: The Case of Houston." *Urban Affairs Quarterly* 28, no. 4 (June 1993): 617–40.

Ritchie, Daniel. "Sanctuary." *Eternity* 36, no. 6 (June 1985): 24–28, 35.

Robert, Dana. "The Legacy of Adoniram Judson Gordon." *International Bulletin of Missionary Research* 2, no. 4 (October 1987): 176–81.

Roberts, J. Deotis. *Black Theology in Dialogue*. Philadelphia: Westminster, 1987.

Roof, Wade Clark, and Wiliam McKinney. *American Mainline Religion: Its Changing Shape and Future*. New Brunswick: Rutgers University Press, 1987.

Rose, Larry, and Kirk Hadaway, eds. *The Urban Challenge: Reaching America's Cities with the Gospel*. Nashville: Broadman, 1982.

Rothchild, John. "Florida: Sunset in the Sunshine State." *Rolling Stone*, 1 October 1981, 20–23.

Sample, Tex. *U. S. Lifestyles and Mainline Churches*. Louisville: Westminster/John Knox, 1990.

Sandoval, Moises. *On the Move: A History of the Hispanic Church in the United States*. Maryknoll: Orbis, 1990.

Sanson, Jean. "Young Life: A Model for Urban Ministry." *Urban Mission* 9, no. 4 (March 1992): 50–53.

Schaller, Lyle. "Megachurch!" *Christianity Today* 34, no. 4 (5 March 1990), 20–24.

———. *Planning for Protestantism in Urban America*. Nashville: Abingdon, 1965.

———. *Survival Tactics in the Parish*. Nashville: Abingdon, 1977.

———. *Understanding Tomorrow*. Nashville: Abingdon, 1977.

———, ed. *Center City Churches*. Nashville: Abingdon, 1993.

Schreffler, Rebekah. "Blacks Passing Leadership Torch." *Christianity Today* 37, no. 9 (16 August 1993): 41.

Shippey, Frederick. *Protestantism in Suburban Life*. Nashville: Abingdon, 1964.

Shriver, Donald, Jr., and Karl Ostram. *Is There Hope for the City?* Philadelphia: Westminster, 1977.

Shupe, Anson, and William Stacey. "The Moral Majority Constituency." In *The New Christian Right: Mobilization and Legitimation*, edited by Robert Liebman and Robert Wuthnow, 103–16. New York: Aldine, 1983.

Sider, Ronald. *One-Sided Christianity? Uniting the Church to Heal a Lost and Broken World.* Grand Rapids: Zondervan; San Francisco: HarperSanFrancisco, 1993.

———, ed. *The Chicago Declaration.* Carol Stream, Ill.: Creation House, 1974.

Simpson, John. "Moral Issues and Status Politics." In *The New Christian Right: Mobilization and Legitimation,* edited by Robert Liebman and Robert Wuthnow, 187–205. New York: Aldine, 1983.

Sine, Tom. *The Mustard Seed Conspiracy.* Waco: Word, 1982.

———. *Wild Hope.* Dallas: Word, 1991.

Singleton, Gregory. "Fundamentalism and Urbanization: A Quantitative Critique of Impressionistic Interpretations." In *The New Urban History,* edited by Leo Schnore, 205–27. Princeton: Princeton University Press, 1975.

Sizer, Sandra. *Gospel Hymns and Social Religion.* Philadelphia: Temple University Press, 1978.

Skinner, Tom. *How Black Is the Gospel.* Philadelphia and New York: J. B. Lippincott, 1970.

——— "The U.S. Racial Crisis and World Evangelism." In *Christ the Liberator,* 189–209. Downers Grove: InterVarsity, 1971.

———. *Words of Revolution.* Grand Rapids: Zondervan, 1970.

Smith, Timothy. *Revivalism and Social Reform.* Nashville: Abingdon, 1967.

Snyder, Howard, with Daniel Runyon. *Foresight.* Nashville: Nelson, 1986.

Sowell, Thomas. *Ethnic America.* New York: Basic, 1981.

Spalding, John. "The Country" and "the City, 1880." In *The Church and the City, 1865–1910,* edited by Robert D. Cross, 3–28. New York: Bobbs-Merrill, 1967.

Spike, Robert. "The Metropolis: Crucible for Theological Reconstruction." In *The Church and the Exploding Metropolis,* edited by Robert Lee, 27–43. Richmond: John Knox, 1965.

Stewart, Edward. *American Cultural Patterns: A Cross-Cultural Perspective.* Washington, D.C.: Society for Intercultural Education, Training, and Research, 1972.

Still, Bayrd., ed. *Urban America: A History with Documents.* Boston: Little, Brown, 1974.

Stockwell, Clinton. "The New Urban Reality: Hope for a Remnant." In *Envisioning the New City,* edited by Eleanor Scott Meyers, 80–89. Louisville: Westminster/John Knox, 1992.

Stott, John. "An Open Letter to David Hesselgrave." *Trinity World Forum* 16, no. 3 (Spring 1991): 1–2.

Strong, Josiah. *Our Country: Its Possible Future and Its Present Crisis.* Cambridge: Harvard University Press, 1963 reprint of 1885 edition.

Suro, Roberto. "Switch by Hispanic Catholics Changes Face of U.S. Religion." *New York Times,* 14 May 1989, 1, 22.

Suzuki, Bob. "Asian Americans as the 'Model Minority.'" *Change* (November/December 1989): 12–19.

Sweet, Leonard. "The Modernization of Protestant Religion in America." In *Altered Landscapes: Christianity in America, 1935–1985,* edited by David Lotz, Donald Shriver, Jr., and John Wilson, 19–41. Grand Rapids: Eerdmans, 1989.

Sweet, William. *Religion in the Development of American Culture, 1765–1840.* New York: Charles Scribner's Sons, 1952.

Synan, Vinson. *The Holiness–Pentecostal Movement in the United States*. Grand Rapids: Eerdmans, 1971.

Tapia, Andrés. "The Myth of Racial Progress." *Christianity Today* 37, no. 11 (4 October 1993): 16–18.

———. "¡Viva Los Evangelicos!" *Christianity Today* 35, no. 12 (25 October 1991): 16–21.

Teaford, Jon C. *The Rough Road to Renaissance: Urban Revitalization in America, 1940–1985*. Baltimore: Johns Hopkins University Press, 1990.

———. *The Twentieth-Century American City: Problem, Promise, and Reality*. Baltimore: Johns Hopkins University Press, 1986.

Thurber, Francis. "Lay Criticism on the Ministry and Methods of Church Work." *Homiletic Review* 8 (April 1884): 412–14.

Tillapaugh, Frank. *Unleashing the Church*. Ventura, Calif.: Regal, 1982.

Tink, Fletcher. "The Strand Hotel: A Case Study in Faith or Failure." *Urban Mission* 7, no. 5 (May 1990): 28–35.

de Tocqueville, Alexis. *Democracy in America, Vol. 2*. New Rochelle, N.Y.: Arlington House, n.d.

Todd, John. *The Sabbath School Teacher*. Northampton, Mass., 1837.

Torney, George, ed. *Toward Creative Urban Strategy*. Waco: Word, 1970.

Toulouse, Mark. "*Christianity Today* and American Public Life: A Case Study." *Journal of Church and State* 35, no. 2 (Spring 1993): 241–84.

Towns, Elmer. *Ten of Today's Most Innovative Churches*. Ventura, Calif.: Regal, 1990.

Travis, William. "His Word to His World: First Baptist Church, Flushing, New York." *Urban Mission* 6, no. 3 (January 1989): 37–41.

Van Eck, Thomas. "Racial Diversity in Suburban Congregations." *Church and Community Forum* 2, no. 2 (Spring 1992): 1, 6–7.

Van Houten, Mark. *God's Inner-City Address: Crossing the Boundaries*. Grand Rapids: Zondervan, 1988.

Vaughan, John. *Megachurches and America's Cities*. Grand Rapids: Baker, 1993.

Villafañe, Eldin. *The Liberating Spirit: Toward an Hispanic-American Pentecostal Social Ethic*. Grand Rapids: Eerdmans, 1993.

Wade, Richard. "The Enduring Ghetto: Urbanization and the Color Line in American History." *Journal of Urban History* 17, no. 1 (November 1990): 4–13.

Wagner, C. Peter. *Church Planting for a Greater Harvest*. Ventura, Calif.: Regal, 1990.

———. "Evangelizing the Real America." *Evangelical Newsletter*, 24 May 1985, 4.

———. "A Vision for Evangelizing the Real America." *International Bulletin of Missionary Research* 10, no. 2 (April 1986): 59–64.

———. *Warfare Prayer*. Ventura, Calif.: Regal, 1992.

———, ed. *Breaking Strongholds in Your City*. Ventura, Calif.: Regal, 1993.

Waldrup, Judith. "You'll Know It's the 21st Century When . . ." *American Demographics* 12, no. 12 (December 1990): 22–27.

Wallis, Jim. "Post-American Christianity." *The Post American* 1, no. 1 (Fall 1971): 2–3.

Wallock, Leonard. "The Myth of the Master Builder: Robert Moses, New York, and the Dynamics of Metropolitan Development Since World War II." *Journal of Urban History* 17, no. 4 (August 1991): 339–62.

Ward, David. *Poverty, Ethnicity, and the American City, 1840–1925.* Cambridge and New York: Cambridge University Press, 1989.

Warner, Sam Bass. *The Private City: Philadelphia in Three Periods of Its Growth.* Philadelphia: University of Pennsylvania Press, 1968.

———. *Streetcar Suburbs.* 2d ed. Cambridge: Harvard University Press, 1978.

———. *The Urban Wilderness: A History of the American City.* New York: Harper and Row, 1972.

Weber, H. C. *Evangelism: A Graphic Survey.* New York: Macmillan, 1929.

Weber, Timothy P. *Living in the Shadow of the Second Coming: American Premillennialism, 1875–1920.* Grand Rapids: Zondervan, 1983.

Webber, George. *God's Colony in Man's World.* Nashville: Abingdon, 1960.

Whacker, Grant. "Searching for Norman Rockwell Popular Evangelicalism in Contemporary America." In *The Evangelical Tradition in America,* edited by Leonard Sweet, 289–315. Macon, Ga.: Mercer University Press, 1984.

———. "Uneasy in Zion: Evangelicals in Postmodern Society." In *Evangelicalism and Modern America,* edited by George Marsden, 17–28. Grand Rapids: Eerdmans, 1984.

Wheeler, Kenneth. *To Wear a City's Crown: The Beginnings of Urban Growth in Texas, 1836–1865.* Cambridge and New York: Cambridge University Press, 1968.

White, Andrew. "Reaching the Lost at Any Cost." In *Center City Churches,* edited by Lyle Schaller, 63–71. Nashville: Abingdon, 1993.

White, Morton, and Lucia White. *The Intellectual Versus the City.* New York: Oxford University Press, 1977.

White, Ronald, Jr. *Liberty and Justice For All: Racial Reform and the Social Gospel (1877–1925).* San Francisco: Harper and Row, 1990.

White, Ronald, Jr., and C. Howard Hopkins. *The Social Gospel: Religion and Reform in Changing America.* Philadelphia: Temple University Press, 1976.

Wiese, Andrew. "Places of Our Own: Suburban Black Towns Before 1960." *Journal of Urban History* 19, no. 3 (May 1993): 30–54.

Wiley, Chris. "Toward a New Vision for Urban Youth Ministry." *Urban Mission* 9, no. 4 (March 1992): 6–16.

Williams, Colin. *Where in the World?* New York: National Council of the Churches of Christ in the U.S.A., 1963.

Williams, Melvin. *Community in a Black Pentecostal Church: An Anthropological Study.* Prospect Heights, Ill.: Waveland, 1974.

Williams, Vanessa. "Blacks, Too, Are Becoming Two Societies." *Philadelphia Inquirer,* 4 April 1993, C1, C3.

Wilmore, Gayraud. *Black Religion and Black Radicalism.* 2d ed. Maryknoll: Orbis, 1983.

Wilmore, Gayraud, and James Cone, eds. *Black Theology: A Documentary History, 1966–1979.* Maryknoll: Orbis, 1979.

Winch, Julie. *Philadelphia's Black Elite.* Philadelphia: Temple University Press, 1988.

Winter, Gibson. *The Suburban Captivity of the Churches.* Garden City, N.Y.: Doubleday, 1961.

Wong, Hoover. "The ABC Housing Problem." *Chinese Around the World* (October 1990): 1–6.

Wuthnow, Robert. *The Restructuring of American Religion*. Princeton: Princeton University Press, 1988.

Yau, Cecilia, ed. *A Winning Combination: ABC–OBC. Understanding the Cultural Tensions in Chinese Churches*. Petaluma, Calif.: Chinese Christian Mission, 1986.

Younger, George. *From New Creation to Urban Crisis: A History of Action Training Ministries, 1962–1975*. Chicago: Center for the Scientific Study of Religion, 1987.

Yu, Eui-young. *Migug eui Hanin Sahoe*. Seoul: Bak Young Sa, 1984.

Ziegenhals, Walter. *Urban Churches in Transition*. New York: Pilgrim, 1976.

Zwier, Robert. *Born-Again Politics: The New Christian Right in America*. Downers Grove: InterVarsity, 1982.

Index of Names

Index of Subjects

Golden Gate Ministries, 155
holistic models in minority churches, 164
homelessness, 126
minorities, 27, 162
Oak Street House, 158
Presbyterian Church of America, 182
race riots, 83
rescue missions, 65
services replacing industry, 122, 134
street children in, 40, 43
suburbanization, 134
westward migration, 23
urban growth, 23, 59
World War II and economic expansion, 83
San Jose, California, 156
Sanctuary movement, 170
Seattle, Washington
automobile, impact of, 77
rescue missions, 65
urban training programs, 101
World War II and economic expansion, 83
Second Great Awakening, 40–41
Secular City, The (Cox), 101
Selma, Alabama, civil rights movement, 86
Seminary Consortium for Urban Pastoral Education (SCUPE), 112
Settlement houses
Hull House, Chicago, 56
University Settlement, New York, 56
Shaker Heights, Ohio, suburban growth, 77
Shreveport, Louisiana, 117
Slavery
in colonial life, 21–22
Great Awakening and abolition, 34–35
opposition by Clapham Sect, 47–48
Social concerns, 10–12, 89–91, 182
black leadership, 111–13, 163–66
and evangelicals, 103, 144, 150–51, 157, 160
holistic ministry, 106–8, 150–60, 163–66, 169–72, 195
job training and placement, 153, 155, 156, 171, 194
medical and health services, 62, 63, 69, 153, 156, 164, 165
National Association of Evangelicals, 105–6, 160

sanctuary movement, 170
and urban retreat, 93
urban training centers, 100–101, 102
Young Evangelicals, 106–8, 111–12, 113
Social Gospel movement, 65–70, 91–93
demise of, 101
and fundamentalism, 93, 95, 102
evangelical reactions to, 70–73, 102, 104–8, 150–51, 155, 195
"Social sins" and revival movement, 91
Society for the Propagation of the Gospel in Foreign Parts, 35
Sojourners, 107
Sons of Liberty, 20
Souls of Black Folks, The (DuBois), 95
Soup kitchens, 12
South, the, 23–24
black migration to the North, 78
black population, 39, 120
and civil rights, 109
evangelicalism, its role in, 108, 143
federal intervention, reaction to, 82
Great Awakening, reaction to, 33
Great Depression and public welfare, 80
and individualism, 71
and institutional church movement, 69
New Christian Right and, 143
population growth, 116
pro-rural mentality, 69–70, 143
Second Great Awakening, 39
slavery, 46
suburban growth, 84, 117–18
World War II and Southern expansion, 82–83
Southern Baptist Convention, 168
crosscultural ministries, 182–83
growth of, 140–41, 168–69
Springfield, Massachusetts, 68
Steamboats, accelerating riverside urban growth, 24–25
Streetcars
automobile age, effect on mass transit, 77
development of upper- and middle-class suburbia, 26, 56–58
Suburban Captivity of the Church, The (Winter), 99
Suburbanization
Asian-Americans, 175–77
automobile, effect of, 76–80